NEVILLE GODDARD

LECTURE SERIES

VOLUME XII

Audio Enlightenment Press

Giving Voice to the Wisdom of the Ages

Printed in the United States of America

First Printing 2014

1 2 3 4 5 6 7 8 9 10

ISBN 978-1-941489-11-6

www.TheNevilleGoddardProject.org

www.AudioEnlightenmentPress.com

A Gnostic Audio Selection

Neville Goddard Lecture Series: Volume XII

First Audio Enlightenment Press Printing

March 2014

Editor's Introduction

I can think of no greater privilege than to bring to light the incredible works of a great American mystic, Neville Goddard, a prolific author, teacher and a true man of God. Over his forty years of teaching he left behind a legacy of printed material that rivals most metaphysical authors.

It would be impossible to over-estimate the spiritual value of the teachings he left behind. He not only published ten books, which are now available in one complete volume, "Neville Goddard: The Complete Reader", but he left us over three hundred and fifty printed lectures during his lifetime.

It is the purpose of "The Neville Goddard Project" to bring to print all the works of this incredible American mystic, of whom another metaphysical giant, Dr. Joseph Murphy, wrote, "Neville Goddard may come to be known as the greatest American mystic of our generation."

A great portion of these lectures are not dated, so we have chosen to begin by alphabetical order based on the documents that we currently have in our archive. When complete, this series of lectures, in addition to The Complete Reader, will comprise the largest and most complete collection of Neville Goddard works available in print.

We will be assembling and editing twenty-five lectures per volume and when complete, the set will include twelve to fifteen volumes, which will be appended as new lectures are located and edited.

I would like to thank Rachel Claxton for her meticulous manuscript preparation which helped make this series possible.

Barry J. Peterson

The Neville Goddard Project

Neville Goddard Lecture Series

Lecture Index: Volume XII

Neville (02-03-1969)

WONDER WORKING POWER

You have within you a wonder working power! To understand this power, let us turn to the Book of Joshua, where we are told: "Wherever the sole of your foot shall tread, I have given you." The Hebrew form of the word "Joshua" is Yad He Vav [corr. Yod Hey Vav Shin Hey, pron. Ye-ho-SHOO-ah] and means, "Jehovah saves". So you see, Joshua is not promising another, but himself!

Jehovah leads the dance of life. We are his dancers, yet his very self; for God and his eternal name is one I AM. There is no place you can go and not know that you are! You may suffer from amnesia and not know who you are or where you are, but you know that you are; so without voicing it you are saying I AM! That's God. There is no place where God is not and there is nothing that God is not; for if there is something, it has to be God!

Now, all things by a law divine in one another's being mingle. If you will take the idea of inner penetration seriously, you will find its possibilities are staggering. Everything in this world penetrates your brain. You penetrate my brain just as I penetrate yours. My apartment is several miles from here. New York City is three thousand miles, and the place where I was born is five thousand miles away. I know they are there, but if I accept the thought of inner penetration then I believe they are also in my brain.

If I desire to visit my island home in Barbados, but do not have the means or the time to go there, I can enter its image in my imagination by approaching it on the fiery chariot of my contemplative thought. I have done it. I do not use this wonder working power lightly anymore, because I know that after

1

imagining, my desire fulfilled (although I may forget it) I will be compelled to experience it in this world of shadows.

This wonder working power is to be used for anything you desire. It now penetrates your brain, and it is wherever you are. I know that Barbados is in the outer world, but I also know that I am all imagination. I know that God is Man and exists in us and we in Him; that the eternal body of Man is the Imagination, and that is God Himself. So if I - imagination - enter into an image I desire to occupy, no earthly power can stop that image from becoming an objective fact.

What is the secret that makes this wonder working power operate? Feeling! Reality is controlled by feeling, as told us in the 27th chapter of Genesis. The central character in this chapter is the state called Isaac, who has two sons - Esau and Jacob. Esau is clothed in objective reality, while Jacob wears subjective reality as longings, wishes, and desires. When Jacob disguised himself as an objective fact, Isaac said: "Come near that I may feel you to determine whether you are Esau or not." And when he asked: "Are you really Esau?" Jacob answered, "I am."

Put yourself into a subjective state. Then feel the objectivity of the state by giving it sensory vividness and tones of reality. Then deceive yourself into believing that the image into which you have entered is now objectively real. Do that, and you have entered the state called Isaac. And we are told that when Isaac once more saw his objective world, Esau returned and Jacob disappeared. Then he realized that he had been self-deceived, but could not take back the blessing given to the subjective state.

Although your objective world denies the reality of what you have done in your imagination, that which you have subjectively assumed is on its way to supplant your objective world and become your Esau. You see, in life you are playing the part of Isaac with your two sons: Esau - your objective world, and Jacob - your subjective one. Your subjective world may seem to be clothed in unreality; but when you enter into its image in your imagination and clothe that image with feeling, your subjective desire takes on the tones of reality.

This is how I do it: When I close my eyes this world is shut out and I, like Isaac, am blind to the outer world. Then I feel myself into the state of my desire. With my inner eye I see it all around me. I sense its solidity, and when my five senses are awakened I have the feeling of relief, knowing it is accomplished. When I open my physical eyes, Esau - my physical world - returns and tries to persuade me that what I did was unreal. But having done it time and time again, I know that my desire is moving towards its objective fulfillment.

This is what I mean by wonder working power. It is all within your own wonderful human imagination, for that is God. The promise to Joshua is God's promise to himself, for there was no one to play the part that is so uniquely you, but God. Having conceived a play which existed only for him, God, the director and author, became the actor. His name is I am! Before I am known as John, Peter, man, or woman - I simply am! Clothing myself in what I would like to be, I am rich, poor, known, or unknown. Although my objective world denies the reality of what I have done, when I have felt the reality of my desired state, I have given it my blessing and cannot take it back.

The moment that which was subjective becomes objectively real to you, you have given it your blessing and cannot take it back. Clothed in the feeling of insecurity, your outer world (Esau) reflects that feeling. But when you clothe yourself in the feeling of being rich, even though it is subjective, watch - for as insecurity will no longer have your blessing to remain alive, riches will supplant it.

Every state of consciousness is within you, for everything is God made visible! And all things by a law divine in one another's being mingle. The moon is remote in space, yet it penetrates your brain; therefore it is in your brain. I can't take you with me to view the earth from the moon, but you can go there yourself. You can go to any point in space that you can conceive of, by just imagining you are already there.

When I was in the army, my commanding officer denied my request for discharge. His word was final in the world of Caesar - but not in the world of God, for that very day I assumed I was honorably discharged and living in my apartment in New York City, 2000 miles away.

Sleeping on a little cot in the barracks, I assumed I was in my own comfortable bed. I made it quite clear to myself that I was not on furlough, but was honorably discharged and once more a civilian. In my imagination, my wife was in her bed and my little girl in hers.

Then I got off the bed, walked over to the window, and looked out upon a familiar scene that could only be seen from there. I saw the Holly Apartments across the way, as well as Washington Square. I walked through every room in the apartment, touching familiar objects, and then returned to my bed to sleep in New York City as though it were a fact.

Early the next morning, I saw a sheet of paper which resembled the application I had made. Then a hand holding a pen scratched out the word "Disapproved," and boldly wrote the word "Approved"! And I heard a voice say: "That which I have done, I have done! Do nothing!" Knowing exactly what I had done, I knew I was moving towards its objective confirmation and no power on earth could stop it. Nine days later, the man who disapproved my application gave me an honorable discharge!

I tell you: everything is possible to the individual when he knows who he is. You are the Joshua of the Old Testament and the Jesus of the New. And Jesus, your own wonderful human imagination, is Jehovah. He is your awareness, but as long as you see Jehovah as someone other than yourself you will not apply this principle. You must be willing to give up all foreign gods, all idols, and return to the one and only God, whose name is in you as your very being!

If you were trained in the Christian faith, you were taught to believe that Jesus was on the outside. But how can you put him to the test if he is another? There never was another Joshua or Jehovah. There is only God, the director of the great dance of life whose dancers are himself. God plays the part of the bum and dances the dance of poverty. He also plays the part of a millionaire and dances to the tune of millions, as every part is being played by God.

Now, everyone must act from where he is! Ask yourself: where am I? If I am God, where can I go and God is not? If I make my bed in hell, God is there. If I make it in heaven, God is there, for everything penetrates me! I do not have to physically move. Simply by adjusting my thinking I can move from one state to another.

I remember one cold winter night in New York City. I was lecturing in a church off Times Square where the usual crowd was in excess of a thousand, but because of the cold and snow there were only about 200 in attendance. My first book had just been released, and that night maybe 50 copies were sold, and since I had run the presses on 5000 I was eager to get the book in distribution.

Because of the storm outside, that night I spoke of the warmth of Barbados: the palm trees and the odors of the tropics. And when I retired, I felt myself in my mother's home in Barbados. I listened to the movement of the leaves and smelled the tropical atmosphere. Then a cable came saying that mother was dying and I should return home. Within 24 hours my wife and I set sail for Barbados. I had put myself there and had to fulfill my imaginal act, even though it was an inconvenient time for me to go; so I do not treat my wonder working power lightly!

When I ask you to adjust yourself to a certain state, I mean for you to feel it is real, for reality is controlled by feeling. The day will come when feeling will modify, or even void, that which you think are the laws of nature and science, and you will discover they are not so at all.

This wonder working power is all within you, and can be operated consciously when you know who you are. If you get down on your knees and pray to an external God, you do not know this power. Whether you are in a church or a bar, God is there; and wherever God is, that place is holy. A bar is just as holy as a church, when you are there knowing who you are!

It does not matter where you are or what time it is; you can adjust your mind and make anything real through feeling. Although your objective world will deny its reality, the state you entered subjectively is moving towards fulfillment. We are always imagining, although totally unaware of what we are doing.

Yeats once said: "I will never be certain it was not some woman treading in the winepress who started a subtle change in men's mind, or that a passion, because of which so many countries have given to the sword, did not begin in the mind of some poor shepherd boy, lighting up his day for a moment before it ran upon its way."

Someone in prison feeling abused by society can cause the combustion of the world by imagining getting even with those who placed him there, while those who did it think they are safe, not realizing that - although the man is in prison - he is God, using his wonder working power.

If you know there is only God, who would you want to hurt? You would realize that no man could ever shoot another, for there is no other. There is nothing but God, the one and only reality. This is the Sh'ma, the great confession of faith: "Hear O Israel, the LORD our God, the LORD is one." Keep this in mind and you will never go wrong.

If God is one, there cannot be another. I am the one body fragmented in order for the poem to become alive. As I gather myself together to rebuild the temple which was destroyed when I deliberately shattered myself, the dead stones are made alive once more. One by one each fragmentation returns to the same body, making it more luminous, more transparent, and more creative, for God is an ever-expanding creative being.

This wonder working power is in your own wonderful human imagination. That is God. Man is all imagination, and God is Man and exists in us and we in Him. The Eternal body of Man is the imagination, and that is God Himself. A Christian calls the imagination Jesus. A Jew calls it Jehovah. Tradition claims Jesus and Jehovah are idols - but God's true name is I am!

Believe in the human imagination, the only true God, by consciously using your wonder working power. Where can you go that you are not imagining? No matter where you are, you are imagining (aware of) being there. A newborn child does not know who he is, where he is, or what he is; but he knows he is. That is God. He is your wonder working awareness, the wonder working power of Imagination!

I hope you take me seriously and learn to consciously believe in your inner penetration. Everything penetrates your brain, or you could not be aware of it - be it good, bad or indifferent. You don't have to take a train, a boat, or a car to go anywhere. All you need do is adjust your thinking. Affirm: "I am possessing it now" and persist until you feel the relief of possession. Then go about your business, knowing that in a way you know not of, you will be led to the fulfillment of what you did within yourself!

You do not have to consciously determine the series of events you will encounter; they will simply unfold in your world. You may meet a seeming stranger. Others may appear, and - upon reflection - you may even give them credit for your success; but they were only playing a part, as all things by a law divine in one another's being mingle.

Others penetrate you and you penetrate them, for we are all one. If someone can play the part necessary for you to climb on that rung of the ladder, then he will do it without his knowledge of consent. Do not think of individuals, but of what you want as an end!

Shape your life wisely by becoming aware of the desire you are shaping in your mind, for without desire there is no power in life. Your power line is I am, while your desire is the light bulb. Just as it is impossible for a light bulb to give off light when it is not attached to the power line, so it is with you. You must attach your desire to your I am for it to illuminate and become objective to you.

Give lovely gifts to all you meet, for everyone is yourself pushed out. Take a noble concept you would like to experience, and adjust your thinking to it, by feeling you have moved into its fulfillment. Give it reality through feeling. Look at your world from this point, then open your eyes knowing that although your objective world denies it, you have given your desire its right of birth, and nothing can stop its fulfillment.

Read the 27th chapter of Genesis carefully, remembering that all of the characters spoken of there are personifications of states within you. As Isaac, you always have two sons: your present objective world and your present subjective world. The story tells you how to clothe yourself with the subjective desire, through feeling, until it supplants its objective brother.

That is how you move from one state to another until you reach the state called Jesus. Then the story recorded in the gospels will fulfill itself in you, casting you in the central role. Only this experience can save you from this world of Caesar, for you are redeemed, from within yourself, by recreating the story of Jesus Christ.

Now let us go into the silence.

Neville (05-02-1969)

YOU ARE A COSMIC BEING

Tonight I want you to think of Christ as a cosmic being who contains everyone within him. Having died for all, this one being is in all, and will rise in all. Only one being can rise, for only one being fell. Having deliberately destroyed his temple in the fall, God, (this one being) is rebuilding his temple out of the redeemed, in order for it to become something far greater than it was prior to its destruction. One being, containing all within him, fell into this world of death to become individualized as you, as me. That same being will rise in us all, individually: and when he does the divine name "Lord" will be conferred upon the individual in whom he rose.

In Paul's wonderful letter to the Corinthians, he tells us: "From now on I regard no one from the human point of view; even though I once regarded Christ from a human point of view, I regard him thus no longer." Why? Because Paul was led from tradition to self-discovery. While determined to destroy those who believed in a savior other than the one he was taught to believe in, Paul discovered that the Christ of whom they spoke was a pattern of salvation contained within every child born of woman. It was Paul who said: "When it pleased God to reveal himself in me, I conferred not with flesh and blood." The pattern unfolds in only one way, and Paul tried to describe how it unfolded in him. I cannot find the true detail by his description of it, but Paul does tell us to imitate God as dear children.

Now, in order to imitate anyone or anything, it must be seen or heard first. How can you imitate something you cannot see or hear? It is my purpose to tell you how to imitate God as a dear child, for imitation can only be accomplished by hearing what took place and believing it. Now, the question is asked: "How can men imitate him

11

whom they have never heard, and how can men hear unless there is a preacher? And how can there be a preacher unless he is sent." Faith comes from what is heard, and what is heard comes by preaching Christ. If, when I tell you I came out from the Father, you will accept my words and believe I am telling you the truth, then you will set your hope fully upon this promise and its unfoldment in you.

I tell you: one being fell to become all, and one being is going to rise in all, as each is called according to His purpose. I was called in 1959. He may call you tonight, but each one of us will be called individually by the same being who is rising in all.

I cannot conceive of anything comparable to this, for unless we are born from above we remain in the world of death, turning the wheel of recurrence over and over again. I can assure you from what I know from my inner vision, that everyone will escape. God will not leave one section of himself in the world of death. He is one being who - containing all -fell into the world of death. That same being, rising in each, individually according to his purpose, rebuilds his temple out of the redeemed.

If you would imitate God as a dear child you must first have a pattern from which you may follow. This is true in all walks of life. There must be a mold into which molten metal is poured in order to form a casting. Jesus Christ is the mold which "Must be perfect as your heavenly Father is perfect." Perfection is a molten state into which you must be reduced. Your physical body, when it is burned, it is reduced to dust; so it cannot be this body that is reduced to a molten state. No. It is not your physical body, but your Spiritual body.

Christianity is based upon the claim that a certain series of events happened in which God revealed himself in action for the salvation of man. It hasn't a thing to do with any individual man on the outside. Paul's story, which preceded the gospels by twenty or twenty-five years, is not concerned with what happens to the individual between the cradle and the grave.

If the one called Jesus was a carpenter, a mason, a bricklayer, or a pimp, it would not concern Paul. He was only interested in what happened in an individual. Paul knew he had awakened from the dream of life, but could not share his experiences with others except in words. We are told that he spent his last days from morning to night discussing the kingdom of God and trying to persuade others concerning Jesus, and some believed while others disbelieved.

This is true in this world in which we live. When I tell of what happened to me, individually, my experiences are so unusual the average person will not accept them. They - still in the world of Caesar - are more concerned with how to make that extra dollar then they are in the eternal world of life.

Although this world of death is temporal, it will continue as though it is forever, until the individual hears the Word of God and responds with faith by setting his hope fully upon the grace that is coming to him at the revelation of Jesus Christ within him. That is where the one being, containing all of us, fell. It was a deliberate act, and necessary in order to expand beyond what He was prior to the fall. We did nothing wrong to warrant our fall; rather we desired to enter this world of death. We agreed to take upon ourselves these dead garments; to be enslaved by them and to overcome them. We did it in perfect confidence that He who contained us all, would redeem us all.

In the 32nd chapter of the Book of Deuteronomy we are told that: "He has set bounds to the people according to the number of the sons of God;" therefore, every child is a garment worn by a son of God, and God will not leave one of his sons in this world of death. Rather, every son will rise, individually, to the realization that he is God the Father, as it takes all of us to form that one being who is God and Father of all.

When I speak of Jesus Christ I do not mean a man, but a pattern. Like Paul, I no longer regard Christ from the human point of view. I once regarded him as such, but not any more. Now I see him as a pattern of salvation which began to unfold in me back in 1959 when I awoke in my skull. Until that moment in time I - like you - had no idea I was buried there; but, because it happened to me, I will now prophecy for you. A storm wind will possess you, and you will awaken within yourself to discover you are entombed in your skull, from which you will emerge. That will be your birth from above, of which John speaks, saying: "Unless you are born from above you cannot enter the kingdom of God." This kingdom is the new age spoken of as that age - as opposed to this age.

This is the age of death where everything begins and ends, while that age is eternal life. Having overcome the world of death, Jesus Christ (the pattern) unfolds as you rise, victorious, into the world of eternal life; for you are the gods who came down, individualized yourselves in order to rise as the Lord, as there is no other being.

The world may condemn you if you are a thief by profession, but Paul doesn't. It matters little what happens to you individually between the cradle and the grave. But it matters much if, when you hear my story of salvation you believe it; for then you will break the shell and rise above all this worldly nonsense. Salvation's story was told to us as it was to them; but it did not benefit them because - believing this world of death was real - they were more interested in achieving greater intellect and more wealth here; therefore, the story was not received with faith.

I read a story concerning Lord Russell who, although loving to be called "Lord," said: "I regard religion as a disease, born of fear. A source of untold misery to the human race." Well, I tell you it is not a disease, although I know there are numberless forms of interpretation of the great mystery.

Like Paul, I was taught that Christ was a man who came into the world and claimed he was the Messiah to save the world. But I tell you, Christianity is based upon the claim that a certain series of supernatural events happened, in which God revealed himself in action for the salvation of man. When I realized that these events spelled out the pattern man who was Christ, I knew there was no other.

It takes the many blows of the world to reduce us to that liquid, cosmic being who awakens in the grave. That grave is not in some cemetery, but in the skull from which a storm wind will awaken you. In the Jerusalem Talmud, there is a tradition that the Messiah was born in Bethlehem the night of the destruction of Jerusalem, and he was carried off by a storm wind. I tell you this is true.

When the storm wind possessed me I reverberated from head to foot. I felt as though my body was being shattered as I awoke. Expecting to see the same room I had retired in, I awoke to find myself in a tomb which I intuitively knew to be my skull. It was sealed, and when I rolled a stone away, I discovered that I could force my head into the opening found there. This I did and I came out of that skull as a child comes out of the womb of a woman; but this was the womb from above rather than the womb from below, for you must be born from above in order to inherit the kingdom of God. Then the entire imagery as told us in scripture surrounded me, witnessing the event.

It is written that the angel of the Lord said to those who were going to be witnesses: "Go and you will find him, for God is born this day in Bethlehem. Look for this sign, which is a babe wrapped in swaddling clothes, lying on the floor." The witnesses then went hastily and found the sign; but they could not see he who was having the experience because he was Spirit, and since God is Spirit, it was God who was born.

Although I could not be seen by mortal eye, my witnesses could not see me; but I could see them and their every thought was objective to me. Then the sign of my birth was carried away by a storm wind.

Now, knowing myself to be God, who is a father, I must have a son to bear witness to my fatherhood. Five months later God's son David stood before me and called me father and I fulfilled his promise. Then I returned to the limitation of my cross in order to share my experiences with you, my brothers, to encourage you to believe. I saw my only son who is God's only son.

That son is the personification of all the generations of men and their experiences, proving that the race is finished and the crown of righteousness is mine. I have played every lovely and unlovely part in this world. I had to in order to see my son, whose beauty is beyond measure, and whose name is David.

Now, the third mighty act reveals your true identity as that of molten gold. In the Book of Zechariah, we read: "He stood upon the Mount of Olives when it was split from east to west as one half moved northward and the other half moved southward." You will discover, as I did, that the Mount of Olives spoken of here is your body; for the Old Testament is an adumbration, a forecasting in a not altogether conclusive and immediately evident way.

It is a shadow, but not the substance. Zechariah refers to a mountain, but when it happens to you, you will realize that the mountain is yourself. It is your body which is split from top to bottom, from east to west, as one side moves northward as the other side moves southward, revealing liquid, molten gold at its base. As I looked at this living, liquid gold I knew it to be myself; and I fused with it and up I went into my skull - into the kingdom of heaven, for the kingdom is within, At that moment I departed the world of generation and returned to the world of regeneration, as the heavens reverberated like thunder. Having returned to the molten state, I cast myself into the mold which was prepared for me before that the world was, to become the living image that radiates and reflects God's glory. I am now the express image of God Himself. God's primal wish was, "Let us make man in our image."

I tell you, He has wrought it! As one of the gods, I have completed the journey; but because we are all brothers, I am compelled to remain in the world to tell you in the hope that you who are still asleep will believe me. I say the Christ of scripture is a pattern of salvation and not a man separate from yourself.

The four mighty acts which form that redemption begin with your awakening within yourself and end with the descent of the dove. Two years and nine months after my ascent into the kingdom of heaven, the Holy Spirit descended upon me in bodily form as a dove and smothered me with love. Then I knew I had filled the entire role and was now a glorious, living stone in the living body of the Risen Christ.

Christ is the one being who fell containing all within himself. He chose us in him before the foundation of the world. Because he could not fall without all of us, we agreed to fall with him. That was an agreement for expansion, for truth is an ever expanding illumination. God, having reached the limit of contraction and

17

opacity, died in order to rise into limitless expansion and translucency.

Opacity (which is doubt) is personified as a thing and called the devil; and this being called "man," is the limit of contraction. It may be hard to believe, but - as Paul said after his revelation: "The wisdom of this world is foolish in the eyes of God, and the foolishness of God is wiser than men and the weakness of God is stronger then men." Man believes he is getting wiser and wiser, yet it is only wiser and wiser nonsense. But God allows the nonsense to go on as men give each other medals, knowing that after the revelation man will know that the Bible is not speaking of a messiah to come from without, but from within.

One man fell, saying: "I say, 'You are gods, Sons of the Most High, all of you. Nevertheless you will fall like men and die as one man, O princes.'" Can you imagine that? Falling as one man we are princes; and if that is true, then our father is a king. I tell you, our Father is the King of kings and the Lord of lords, for he is the Lord God Jehovah who is raising us to himself that each one of us may become fully aware of being the Father. Regardless of your present sex, you are a son of Sod destined to awaken as the Father.

This wonderful story of scripture is completely misunderstood. Today's preachers are not sent, for they have not yet been awakened; therefore they will give you all kinds of stories concerning the interpretation of scripture. Prior to 1959 I was not sent, but in 1959 I was called, incorporated into the body of God and sent. This incorporation is like an impression made by a seal on wax or clay, for I came out bearing the image of God. The mortal eye cannot see that image, and when I die here, my physical body will disintegrate like all bodies do. My friends will say I am dead, for to them I am a mortal being with weaknesses and limitations of the flesh.

Those who see me as Neville are misled, as they cannot hear what I am saying; for they are seeing a body disintegrating before their eyes. They are judging by appearances and cannot understand that God does not see as man sees. Man sees the outward man, while God sees the inner man; and I, the inner man, have been impressed upon God like a great seal upon wax. I wear this little body that continues to decay; yet I, unseen by mortal eye, am radiating and reflecting the glory of God. I am the express image of the person that is God, but only those whose eyes are open will see me.

I promise you who hear me tonight, that it won't be long before you will depart this world. Don't be afraid. You will be restored to life, in a world just like this, to continue your journey. If you believe what you have heard from me, although I will not be there, wherever you go they will talk of the work I did here. Individually, I have left the world of death. I am only waiting for the moment when this little garment is taken off for the last time. I will not be restored to a world of mortality like this any more, for I have finished the race; I have fought the good fight; I have kept the faith. Now there is laid up for me the crown of righteousness where I go to wait for all my brothers to come into that union and be the one being that came down bearing all.

Mark my words, I am not fooling you. It isn't long to wait before you will take off this garment and find yourself restored to life. You will meet many of your friends there who went before you. It will be a world just like this, where you will do all of the things we do here. And you will remember who taught you. You will not see me there, but eventually you will see me. Now I am going to where you cannot come; but you will, for everyone will awaken as God the Father.

I am not trying to persuade you to change your attitude towards the speaker. I am only telling you what I know from experience.

Like Paul, I did not receive this knowledge from a man; it came through revelation of the true nature of salvation. It's something entirely different. Salvation is not a man, but a pattern man buried in all, who will awaken in all in a first-person, singular, present-tense experience. When the experience is yours, you, too, will know who you are. I was taught to believe God was another; but when the pattern awakened in me, I knew I was He. Now I remain in the world only to share this wisdom with my brothers.

The unknown author of the Book of Hebrews said: "Holy brethren, look to Jesus, the apostle and high priest of our confession." We are all sharers in this great gift, so let us now look to Jesus, the apostle who is called and sent. It is Jesus who is called. That's who you really are. As the apostle, you are called and sent to tell the story of salvation from experience. You will tell your good news, knowing that not everyone who hears it will respond. In fact many, being more interested in the honors of men, will discount it.

Those who have $50 million are only interested in increasing their wealth to $100 million; and, although they may be eighty when they hear your story, it will not interest them, as they will still want more of what they must leave behind when they depart this world - as they won't be able to take it with them, as you know. They will make a world like this, only devoid of what they had built up here, and cast themselves in a role best suited for the work yet to be done in them by the son of God who is wearing that garment. He may zap him from the role of a millionaire and place him in the role of a shoe-shine boy or one who cleans latrines, if that is necessary for the work yet to be done in him.

The world into which they go is just as real as this. I know this is true from experience. I have sat in a chair and felt something happen within me and I see a world that is solidly real. As my consciousness follows vision, I step into that world and it closes upon me as this world is shut out. While in that world my body is real. It is seen and heard by others. If, in that world I have a body like this, yet those who are here see my body asleep in a chair, how did I get that body? It was just as real to me and to those who saw and heard me there as this body you now see here. You could destroy this body, but you would not have destroyed that body in that world.

William Blake once said: "The oak is cut down with the ax and the lamb is slain by the knife, but their forms eternal remain forever and are reproduced by the seed of contemplative thought." When I stepped into that world I knew myself to be a man called Neville. I was so aware of being Neville I clothed myself in the body that was Neville; yet I knew there was a body that was Neville, sound asleep on a chair.

How did it happen? By the seed of contemplative thought. When you die here, you remold yourself in the likeness that you know - only you reduce it in age to a time that pleases you. An eighty-year-old man, knowing what he knows now, will wear a twenty year old body, produced by the seed of contemplative thought. Who does it? The God in him. He will not go through the womb of a woman, but will create a new body by the seed of contemplative thought. He goes on in that world, just as he does here, to die there and begin all over again until he hears the story of salvation and believes.

Now let us go into the silence.

Neville (03-29-1963)

YOU CAN FORGIVE SIN

"You Can Forgive Sin." That, to most people, will be blasphemy as you will hear later on, quoting from scripture. It is so common among all of us to ascribe our ills and troubles to outward things – like the present conditions of the world, to our environment, or simply to things. And these things may be things that are absent from our world, or things we have in our world, but still things, while all along the real cause of our ills is sin. So we are told he was called Jesus because he came to save men from their sins; his only concern was the saving of men from sin.

Now what is sin? Sin means "missing the mark," missing the road, "missing the goal" in life. If you haven't a mark you can't sin. If you have a goal in this world and do not realize it and miss it, then you have sinned. So his purpose is to show man how not to sin in this world. No condemnation. Tell me you sin – tell me your goal, and I will tell you God's word. That is what he said. He has come only to show man how not to miss his objective in this world.

Now we turn to Mark 2:3 – or the same thing with a different twist in Matthew 9:2. It is the story of the paralytic. We are told he was preaching the word, that is, the story of salvation, and they brought in a paralytic carried by four men; and seeing their faith, he said to the paralytic: "My son, your sins are forgiven." (2:5) And scribes sitting around thought in their heart, "Why does this man speak thus? It is blasphemy! Who can forgive sins but God alone?" And discerning in their hearts what they contemplated, he said, "Why do you question thus in your hearts? Which is easier, to say to the paralytic, 'Your sins are forgiven,' or to say 'Rise, take up your pallet and walk?'" So he said to him, "Take up your bed and walk and go home" and he rose and went on his way. Then we are told, ".

. . they were all amazed and glorified God . . ." who had given such authority to men, for it was a man who did it. We are that man. It is to us that this authority to forgive sin has been given. And the world thought they were simply the exclusive power of some being outside of man. Read it in Mark 2 and Matthew 9.

Now what is this ability to forgive sin? We know that "sin" means missing the mark. The one that forgave it called himself, "The Truth." He said: "I am the Truth. If you know my word and abide in my word, then you will know the Truth and the Truth will set you free." (John 8:31, 32) For the whole story begins he was teaching the truth – the word. Now, he calls himself "the truth." If I said to you tonight, what would you like to be in this world? And you name it – I would like to be__ (no matter what it is) and I turned to you and said: You are that, you are it; right now you are it - you would say: I am it? I can't believe it! Then you are denying the truth. He said: "I am the Truth" – I AM everything in this world; everything man can ever imagine, I AM. So, you imagine what you would like to be. If you cannot remain faithful and loyal to that vision of yourself, then you are sinning. Not to sin is to have a goal. What would it be like? If I remain faithful to that vision as though it were true, no power in this world could stop me from realizing it – but no power. I could realize it. How? Don't ask me. But if it took the entire world of three billion to play parts to aid me in the fulfillment of my vision, they would play it without knowing they had played it. It would make no difference if they knew or did not know. They would have to contribute to the fulfillment of my vision, if I remain loyal to that vision.

So, what would it be like if I were the man I would like to be? If I said to you tonight: is there a man in this room who is rich? And no one said, I am rich – that is not your goal, and if it is, you are missing the mark. If there is a man in this room – general man – who is known, who is contributing to the world's good, and no one replies, I am he, then either it is not your goal - or if it is your goal, you are missing it. So the name is "I AM he", as told in John 8:24: "I told you that you would die in your sins, for you will die in your sins unless you believe that I am he." This is not a man talking to me. This is taking place in the depths of the soul of man. If you don't believe now that I AM the one that I would be, then you are missing your goal and you are sinning. So it does not come from without; it is not caused by anything on the outside at all. My health problems are not caused by conditions and by environment, or anything else; it is caused only by sin – and sin is missing the mark. There is only one being – one person in the world – who can hit that mark, and it is God. God forgives sin, as told us in Isaiah: "I am the Lord, I am thy Savior, and there is no other savior." "I, I am the Lord, and besides me there is no savior. No one has formed before me or no one will be formed after me. I am the Savior." (Isaiah 43:3; 43:11)

You will be saved from what you are. There is only one being in the world that can save you, and that Being is "I AM." So, you save yourself. What would it be like were it true – if I were now the man or woman I would like to be? Assume it and dare to believe it and walk as though it were true, and no power in this world can stop it – but no power! There is no one greater than God. Say, "I am" – that is God. You stand in the presence of a being and because he has a little tag – or because he is the Premier of a certain country, or Queen, or President of a certain land, you think he is greater than you are? You are missing the mark. You can't stand in the presence of anyone who is greater than you, if you know who you are. You are not going to lord it over them, knowing, but no one will be smaller, either – all are God. Then you are told to go and tell them. (Ezekiel 3:18, 33:8) – "go and tell them. If you do not tell them, and they sin and you do not tell them - they will die in their sin, but their blood will be upon your head. If you tell them and they do not repent, they will die in their sin, but the blood will not be upon your head. So tell them." So Jesus is made to confess that he told them, that the blood might not be upon his head.

I Acts 20:26, 27 Paul makes the confession: ". . . for I did not shrink from declaring to you the whole counsel of God. Therefore I testify to you this day that I am innocent of the blood of all of you, for I did not shrink from declaring to you the whole counsel of God." He told them that, that he may not carry that secret to the grave and not share it with the world. So I have told them all, that this is a principle that cannot fail.

Now let us come back to the paralytic. You came here tonight on your own steam, as it were. If I tell you we are the paralytic of scripture, you will be surprised. They were brought into the place by four men. Do you know who the four men are? The ancients always called us by the four senses – the four rivers that ran out of Eden. They did not speak of five, they spoke always of four. They joined taste and touch together because they depended upon contact. To taste something or touch something, it must be contacted. But they separated sight, sound, and scent. These three were separate in the great symbolism of scripture. But taste and touch were joined. They called them the four senses, and we came here tonight borne by these four men. I know my bank balance, and in two weeks Uncle Sam wants part of what I earned. I do not even know Uncle Sam. They tell me he exists somewhere, but I do not know where; so I am supposed to pay on the 15th of next month "x" number of dollars. Regardless of how I live, I must save something to pay him. It is the land of Caesar, I am fully aware of that. I can see my bank balance. I know what it is in my world. I can take my senses and bring it to play on what is taking place.

I was brought here tonight on the shoulders of these men. He tells me: your sins are forgiven, and, walk. How can I do it, knowing what I must pay on the 15th, knowing what I must do between now and the 15th? How will I do it? Your sins are forgiven, but who can forgive but God? Only God can forgive, and God is I AM. All right, I will now see the world as I would see it were it now May 1st and all things behind me, completely paid, paid in full.

Suppose I was unemployed. I was brought here tonight on the backs of these men. I know I have rent to pay and food to buy – all of these things – and he tells me my sins were forgiven, to rise and take up my bed and walk! How? I was brought in here on the backs of four men and called upon to rise – ignore these four and walk on my own steam now. Don't walk based on what the four allow me to see, to hear, and smell, and to be. Walk out of here unaided by these four. Walk on my own. How? I ignore the evidence of the senses. They brought me in here. I completely ignore what they tell me I really have in this world, and I see what I would like to see and assume things are what I would like them to be, and influence every being in the world to play their part to fulfill what I am assuming that I am in this world. I came in a paralytic, and walk out on my own steam. That is the story.

Every being in the world is called upon to rise and walk out, for he forgives your sin. He comes into the world only to free man of sin, no matter what you have ever done in this world. Don't look back on things as they are; look on things as they ought to be, the man or woman you would like to be, and assume that you are and see that only. And then you will know what it is to forgive sin. Who forgives? God forgives. He forgave you. I assumed. Who assumed? I assumed, that is – God. "I AM" is His name. I AM assuming I AM the man I would like to be. That is God. I begin to name it and walk in that state, and that is God. There is nothing but God. Forget what you have done or what you are seemingly doing, and dream of the man or woman you would like to be and dare to assume you are it.

Now we are told by the great Blake: "The spirit of Jesus is continual forgiveness of sin" – forgiveness of sin every moment of time. Tonight when we go into the silence we can sit here for a minute and forgive each other. Suppose I could hear everyone here rise and tell the most fantastic story in the world about themselves or a friend, or a relative – or someone. Suppose I, really wanting it to be told from this platform, sit in the silence and listen to that and that only – the most fantastic story in the world that you could tell me individually. If I walk out of here tonight convinced that I heard it and remain loyal to what I have imagined I heard, I must hear it – no power can stop it, if I remain loyal. If anyone says it has not worked, I am not asking any questions, but as far as I am concerned, it has worked. I am sure when I know the vision I am holding for you "has its own appointed hour, it will ripen and it will flower. If it seems long in coming, wait. It is sure, it will not be late." If I actually assume things are as I would like them to be of every being here, and I remain loyal, I either know the story is true or it is false. I know it is true. It can't fail. There is no power in the world to make it fail.

Another word for sin in the Bible is "trespass." In our wonderful Lord's Prayer, "Forgive us our trespasses as we forgive those who trespass against us." It is a minor infraction of this principle. "Trespassing" means an individual lapse, a temporary relapse. You and I begin to discuss a personality. What am I doing? He is only in a state. So, I must think he is unemployed when you and I get into the discussion. I discuss a man who is unemployed and we see him as unemployed and begin to say: Well, conditions are bad, or maybe he was not good enough for the job, and you and I are discussing a man that is unemployed and we see only the state. I am trespassing. He is in the state. But I may fall into this little trap. We all do it, every day, all day long.

28

We read the paper, and a man is called a great man because he happens to be President, or maybe some other person in this world. We read some columnist about him and you are carried away with what the columnist tells us, and suddenly we begin to think as he would have you think, and you are trespassing. "Lord, forgive us our trespasses as we forgive those who trespass against us." It is a slight departure from our goal. We are moved aside by what we read, or heard, or saw in this world. So, that is trespassing. So, I discuss someone who cannot find the job – well, will he qualify? I am asking all these things, and they are irrelevant to this principle. Not with this principle do they have any value whatsoever. What does he want? He wants a job. And how much does he want? He names a figure. Suppose that he had what he wanted – then let me assume it is true and I begin to see the world as I would see it for him were it true and feel the joy that would be mine were he now gainfully employed, earning that sort of money. This is either true, or it is false. I tell you: it is true.

If today you and I can say The Lord's Prayer – but really say it – and ask forgiveness for our trespasses and let him show mercy for having gotten off the mark as it were. Read the story. He is brought in on the backs of four men. He himself had no faith. But in spite of what they knew, there was still a certain faith, and they brought him into the presence of God, knowing God could forgive sin. And he said: "Because of your faith" – he speaks now to those who brought him; he did not speak to the man at first, then he addresses the paralytic: "My son, your sins are forgiven you." Here, a vicarious faith. So, I can have the faith for you if you do not have it for yourself. You can have it for me if I don't have it for myself. Quite often vicarious faith is easier than the direct faith. If I can turn to you, if you really believe an imaginal act is a fact, and you could actually believe I am now what I would like to be, and although at the moment I doubt and am not faithful, you can say - in spite of myself you can pull me out - for a minute I would know faith. Those who brought him on their backs showed faith in bringing him into the presence of God. God commended them for their faith. And he turned to the paralytic and said: "My son, your sins are forgiven." Those who heard thought it blasphemy. Who could forgive sin but God alone?

He did forgive sin, for he was the "I AM." "Unless you believe I AM he, you die in your sins." So, I ask you tonight, turn to your neighbor, and maybe you can hear what the other wants and rejoice in their good fortune, and they can rejoice in your good fortune Actually feel it is true, and see the world as it would be were they what they wanted to be – and they will become it.

So, this is the story of our ability to forgive sin. They were afraid when they saw what happened and then they crucified God because he had given such authority to men. We are told: "If you retain it, it is retained. If you release it, it is released." I see a man and judge him by my senses. I retain it. But I could release him by seeing him standing on his own feet and moving in this world in a glorious manner. So the material I formerly would discard as no good, I don't discard anymore. I take it and use it. I take the same man that formerly I would discard and see him as gainfully employed, loved, and loving, and believe that the thing I am seeing for him is true; and to the degree I am faithful to the concept for him, it becomes true in this world.

That is our power. We have power to forgive sin. If you don't have a mark in this world, you can't sin. If hasn't a thing to do with moral issues. No. Do you have a goal? Do you have some objective in this world? Then this is how you realize it. Suppose it were true. In Romans 8:4: ". . .walk not according to the flesh but according to the Spirit." Flesh would be my senses. My senses deny that I am what I would like to be. Let us not walk by flesh - let us walk by the

Spirit. Spirit is to see it in my imagination as though it were true. Tonight I may go home to find an empty cupboard or a notice at my door: "Tomorrow, or else." It is all right. If I believe what I am imagining, it would make no difference what threat was given me – if I really believed. "Now believe it," we are told. If you believe it, it will crystallize into fact. It does not really matter what threat at the moment my senses tell me -I have to ignore it. I have to ignore the four who brought me in this place. I will not now be borne anymore by these four. I will simply walk by spirit and not by flesh.

So, I ask you to try it. If you try it you can't fail and - realizing your objective, may I also ask you to share it with me so that I may tell it to you [the audience].

About three months ago a man sat in this audience, and he wrote me a sweet, wonderful letter which I received this morning. He expected a big bonus. He had worked hard with all the promise, and one who was never on the job, but by his estimate "one of the girl friends of the boss" - she got the big bonus. He, who had done all the work, got practically nothing. So, he and I agreed mentally that he would have the most wonderful job, with more money and everything. This is now going on April. It seemed a long while, but today he is on the job, with more money than he had – more than he expected – more responsibility and opportunity, and everything. I remained faithful to that letter I knew would come when he would write it. And all I did, I heard him tell me (mentally) what he would tell me were it true, and I never wavered.

So, I only ask you to be as faithful to any imaginal state in this world, no matter what it is. In everyone God resides. Everyone has to say, "I am." That is God. I am Einstein, I am Neville. I AM is God. Neville is a tiny thing resting on the foundation that is God. I am rich – that is a tiny thing on the foundation of God, and God is Infinity, God is Everything. Therefore, whatever you say, before you say it, you say, "I am" – and you listen and you notice the four men who brought him in, brought him in paralyzed. He isn't that at all. But they deny it – the four senses are bringing him in and the four senses deny it, the four senses ignore it.

When you call on the name of God, you don't say in the name of God, so-and-so; you ask with the name of God, and to ask with the name of God you say: "I AM wealthy, healthy, secure" - then you believe it. If you ask with the name of God and believe it mentally, you will see the world as you have never seen it before you made the claim, and remain faithful to that claim and it must crystallize in your world.

This is this principle and it goes with every being in the world, regardless of nationality or pigment of skin. It is all God. Everyone has to say, "I am" before he says, "I am – this . . ." "I am a man" - you say, "I am" before you said, "man." "I am American," "I am Indian," "I am Japanese," "I am Chinese." What kind of a being would you like to be? You name it. "I AM" is doing it. Take this fabulous world of ours and take all your dreams and put them on the only foundation – no other foundation than God – and God is I AM.

So, the paralytic came here tonight in all of us, and we were borne on the backs of four men, and the four are our four senses: sight, scent, [sound], taste, and touch. Taste and touch are joined into one because they depend on contact. These are the four streams – the four rivers of life that come from the Garden of Eden. Any moment of time we are in the presence of I AM! Let him forgive me my sin. I forgive myself by daring to assume I am what I would like to be and assuming that I walk in that assumption and it crystallizes into fact. No power in the world can stop it – but none!

When we speak of sin, don't let anyone scare you about sin. He comes to forgive the sinner. His only interest is in the sinner. The so-called moral violations – forget it! I do not ask you to violate them, but forget them. Everything will be ironed out. It is my duty. Through the consciousness of Paul, Ezekiel, Jesus – "If I don't tell you what I know of God's law, then your sin is upon my head; but if I tell you and you still will not believe me, you will die in your sin, but your blood will not be upon my head." So Paul said: "I will tell them. I have declared the entire counsel of God to them, so I am innocent of their blood." Infinite states. A man falls into a state and so he is in the state, but he is not the state. Take him out of the state by saying while he is in the state: "What would you like?" and he names the state that he would like to enter. And you put him into that state by asking what it would be like if he were now the thing he would like to be; and you remain faithful – leaving him where he is – but you remain faithful to this concept and he comes out of it. On reflection, he might say: "It would have happened anyway." It is all right – you know. Tell everyone the story, and tell them it is entirely up to them. If they believe it – as we are told: "If you do not believe I AM He you die in your sins." (John 8) When you read it, you might think a man is telling you: I am God, and you are not. The whole story is taking place in the soul of man. That is the story.

Now he tells us the truth: "You shall know the Truth and the Truth will set you free." And they complained: "we are free." Here they are enslaved, and we thought we were free. We are Americans, we are free. To what extent are we free? You can't pay the rent or buy the food, and we think we are free. I can only be free if I know the art of forgiving sin, and the only one that can forgive sin is God – and God's name is "I AM."

In this world today, in our wonderful land, there are hundred of thousands in prisons physically - but they are Americans. There are hundreds of thousands who are unemployed, who can't pay the rent. Free? They are Americans. I say go and tell every being in the world the story of God – as told us in both the Old and New Testament –

and set them free. They can be free if they know who they are. I must tell them the story. There is not one being in jail tonight, if you ask him who he is and how old he is, he will say: "I am John Smith, and I am . . ." and he will tell you his age. But before all these things, he tells you "I am." I have seen this, you see. It frightens people, as you are told in Matthew 9:8: "When the crowds saw it, they were afraid, and they glorified God, who had given such authority to men."

In San Francisco, when I told this story, a lady who sat in my audience had just received notice from the army that her brother had been tried, court marshaled, and sentenced to six months of hard labor. She went home and said: "If this man is telling the truth, I can set him free." She sat in her hotel apartment where she would see if anyone came in. She lost herself in the imaginal state that the bell was ringing and she ran down the stairs, threw the door open, and embraced a brother who was waiting there. She did it for one solid week. The next Sunday morning, before she came to my meeting, it happened. When she came to my meeting, she could not restrain the impulse to rise and she jumped up in the audience of 1,000 and said she must tell the story, and she told it. He was honorably discharged, though he had been court marshaled and sentenced to six months at hard labor.

Everyone can be forgiven. He is not the same being he was – whatever he did to warrant the court martial – why should he pay the last ounce, if she could redeem him by pulling him out of the state that caused him to do whatever he did. If I am pulled out of the state into another state – if I had someone tonight who was the most horrible beast in the world and I am determined to make him a loving, nice person, then he comes into my world and demonstrates his kindness by his act, by everything – he is not the same being he was when I disliked him – the same immortal soul, but he is in a different state. Always I was judging the state, but should I keep him in that state and make him pay a price that belongs only to that state? You see, there is such a thing in this world as God's mercy. No sins can be expiated unless God intervenes and is merciful – for you are God and you can intervene. He gave it to you. Only God can forgive sin, and you can forgive sin: therefore, are you not he? God is merciful. Can't you be merciful and completely transform any being in the world? And oh! What a thrill it is to transform a being and see them different in a little while!

So I ask you to try it, it cannot fail. But believe the statement in the Lord's Prayer: "Forgive us our trespasses." We have actually trespassed. We have heard a rumor and we got off the beam. We see the signs all over the place: "No Trespassing," but we step upon it. Don't. No matter what you hear of anyone, have no ears to hear it unless it is something lovely, for they are only discussing a state, and they are keeping that being in a state. Don't listen. Pull everyone out, but don't forget to pull yourself out. Put yourself into the most glorious state of being successful, being wanted, being happy. You try it. I promise you it will not fail you.

Now let us go in to the silence.

Neville (03-10-1969)

YOU CAN NEVER OUTGROW I AM

A man can never outgrow or lose the God he knows in a first person, present tense experience. And when he finds this God he tells his brothers, saying: "If I had not come and spoken to you, you would have no sin, but now you have no excuse for your sins." God reveals himself to man as his eternal contemporary, saying: "Unless you believe that I am he, you will die in your sins," but man finds it almost impossible to keep the tense. He thinks of God in the third person, addresses him in the second person, but can only know God in a first person, present tense experience. Just imagine - no one can sin until God reveals himself to the individual in a first person, present tense experience. Only then can man have no excuse for his sin. And when one who finds God tells his brothers, he receives no greater reception than the first one did, because they see him as a man of flesh and blood, and cannot see this invisible being who says: "I came down from heaven." Man is looking for Christ to come from without, but his revelation is whispered from within.

"I tell you: I have been crucified with Christ. It is not I who lives, but Christ who lives in me. And the life I now live in the flesh I live by faith in the Son of God, who loved me and gave himself for me." In that act he, whose name is I AM, became me. And if I do not believe that my I amness is he, I will die in my sin.

When asked to identify his Father, he said: "If you knew me, you would not ask, for no man can know me without knowing God, for he and I are one." This is not a physical man speaking to another, but self speaking to self. What child is not aware that he (or she) is? And to be aware is to say, "I am," the name God revealed to Moses on the mountaintop. All things are possible to God, but man has difficulty keeping the tense. He speaks of God in third person, prays

37

to God in the second person, but can only know God in first person, present tense, for "I am the Lord, thy God and besides me there is no other God." In the 50th Psalm these words are put into the mouth of David: "Against thee and against thee only have I sinned." Only I, who must know myself in a first person present tense experience, have sinned and I have only sinned against myself!

Do you believe that Jesus Christ is in you as your very self? Are you willing to test yourself? Let me tell you of one lady who did. Many years ago while living in a rooming house in Brooklyn, with very little money, this lady started each day with these words: "I am a very wealthy woman. I have $50,000 in cash." Every Sunday morning she would go to the corner and buy a Sunday Times for her neighbor, Miss Mead, who was a little old lady living frugally and rarely left the house. Within a year after this lady began starting her day claiming her wealth, Miss Mead died, leaving her $50,000 in cash, plus jewelry valued in excess of $30,000. She received an estate of over $100,000 by keeping God in the present tense.

My friend has now found him and I want all who hear me to find him, for when you find this God you will never outgrow - and therefore never lose - him, for you can never grow outside of self. You may believe in astrology, and outgrowing that belief you may then believe in tea leaves. Outgrowing that, you will find something else to believe in as you grow and outgrow, grow and outgrow; but you cannot outgrow the God you find in the first person, present tense, for when you find him to be your I amness, you have found the only God. One day everyone will find him and join their brothers who, already awakened, are in eternity contemplating this world of death, watching for the little stir of life.

I have been sent to tell you these things, for if I had not come and spoken to you, you would have no sin. You could not miss the mark because you did not have any, but now you have no excuse for missing it. I have revealed God to you in first person saying: "He who sees me sees him who sent me." I was sent by my Father, he whom you call God, only I know my Father and you know not your God, for I know that I and my Father are one.

In the 1st chapter of Colossians, Paul tells us: "The gospel which you have heard has been preached to every creature under heaven," and in the 3rd chapter of Galatians he states: "The scripture, foreseeing that all would be saved through faith, preached the gospel beforehand to Abraham, saying, "In you shall all the nations be blessed." In the state of faith called Abraham we heard the story and then went astray. Falling asleep, we forgot our true identity and worshiped idols. Speaking of God in the third person, and to him in the second person, we have forgotten the God who gave us birth. Yet I tell you: God is eternally contemporary for he is our awareness of being.

Now, without faith it is impossible to please God, and faith does work on this level. Everything you possess was brought into being through faith, and the glory of faith lies in its power to link us to the heavenly realm. Having heard salvation's story, can you have faith in this divine vision (which is the gospel) in the time of trouble? No matter what happens to you, can you center yourself upon the vision? Can you believe that, housed within you as your I amness, is the only creative power in the world? I hope so, because your faith in God is measured by your confidence in yourself.

When you imagine a state, do you believe that the scene has the power to externalize itself? Or do you feel you must pray to a being on the outside for help? I tell you: there is no being on the outside. The creative power of the world is housed within you now. Sit down and imagine a state of confidence that it must externalize itself. Believe that because all things are possible to imagine, the state you have imagined must become an external fact.

I have tried this time and time again, and it has always proved itself in performance. Now I share this knowledge with everyone who will listen. How many believe my words and put them into practice I do not know. I only know that man finds it hard to keep the tense. Religious leaders speak of God in the third person as if he were on the outside, yet I tell you he comes from within. When Moses heard the words: "I AM has sent me unto you," it seemed to come from without, yet it was whispered from within.

There is no evidence of an historical Jesus Christ. We have the essence of Christ, but not an historical one. The being within me that is speaking, is the Christ, but that which is talking to you is only a garment. Everyone knows its background. Its parents are known, its physical brothers and its limitations; yet the being wearing this garment of flesh came out from God who is my Father, for I am from above. The body I wear is from below. I am in the world but not of it, for the being who awoke within me is the one speaking to you now. It is not the same being who entertains guests in our home or enjoys dining in a good restaurant, for this being is not in any way a part of this world. This is the being in you that I am trying to reach tonight, trying to stir and awaken to return to the one grand I AM.

Believe me when I tell you the only purpose in life is to discover who you are. Against thee, O Lord, and thee only have I sinned. Addressing him in the second person as "against thee," he realizes the Lord is within him; that he is the "I" of man who inspired the prophets to write what they did. Having conceived the play and coming out from the Father to play it, "I" must fulfill what I foretold I would do, and I will.

Christianity is based upon the affirmation that a certain series of supernatural events happened in which God revealed himself in action for the salvation of man. I have experienced every one of these events. As each event took place I recorded the date in my bible, even to a simple little one like: "What you must do, do quickly." Against that statement I marked the date of October 10, 1966, for I had been preaching to a group of twelve men, all seated on the floor, when one man jumped up and departed quickly. Then a man dressed in costly robes entered, approached me and unveiled my arm revealing the arm of the Lord. But the one who revealed it moved quickly, as that simple statement dictated.

The words of the Lord recorded in the red letter edition of the Bible will be fulfilled by you. Whether he quotes the Old Testament or relates to it, you are predestined to fulfill the red letters recorded there.

The entire drama has unfolded in me, so I know the perfect pattern that God sent into the world. We are told the first shall be last, and the last first. In the story the last act is recorded as the crucifixion yet it is the first. I have been crucified with Christ. It is not I who live, but Christ who lives in me. And the life I now live in the flesh I live by faith in the Son of God, who loves me and gave himself for me by actually becoming me. His name is I AM. That's the Lord God Jehovah, who is Christ. He is God the Father who became you. His death - in the sense of complete forgetfulness as to his true identity and belief that he is actually you - is your life. It is this being who tells you: "Unless I die thou can'st not live, but if I die I shall rise again and thou with me." He rose in me. He proved that he could die and rise, for when he rose I rose knowing I AM He. He became me in the most intimate way by becoming my awareness. Then he talked to me and revealed himself to me from within my very self. In the beginning the words seemed to come from another, as though someone on the outside had spoken them; yet they were whispered from within as everything said of Jesus Christ unfolded in me.

Can you accept my words and keep the tense? It is so very important to do so, for if you turn to the second person, or the third, you have created a false God and a false Jesus Christ. Do you not realize that Jesus Christ is in you? For unless you believe that your I amness is He you will die in your sins. Put the little word 'is' in the sentence: "Unless you believe that I am is He, you die in your sins," to give it meaning, for without it you may think a being on the outside is speaking and keeping you from missing the mark. If you want to be rich and do not believe that you are the cause of wealth, then you will go on missing the mark by remaining poor. The true goal is to know God is your own wonderful human imagination. This God you will never lose, for when he reveals himself within you it is in a first person, present tense experience.

As God unfolds himself within you he doesn't call himself "God," but "I AM." It was "I" who awoke and rose in that tomb; no one else was there. I had no help getting out; "I" pushed the stone away myself. And when I looked back to see that out of which I came, I saw the three witnesses as recorded in Genesis. It is said that Abraham (the state of faith in which I started) was seated by the door of his tent in the heat of the day when the three men appeared. As one spoke concerning the child, Abraham knew he was the Lord. That child is Isaac, which means, "he laughs." I found that promised child. Like Simeon, I took that promised child in my arms and he laughed.

So who is Christ? And who is the Lord? Did scripture not fulfill itself in me? I have come only to fulfill scripture, and this I have done. I know I am the temple of the Living God, for my body was torn from top to bottom. I found my son, He who was set up in the beginning to reveal me as the Father. This is not what the priesthoods teach; but I am telling you what I have experienced, for I have found David. He cried unto me: "Thou art my Father."

I do not care what the priesthoods of the world may say; I am telling you what I know from experience. If they do not believe in me, they will continue to live in sin by worshipping a false God. All the priesthoods and rabbis worship an idol, for the true God cannot be worshipped in any tense other than the present. His name is I Am. No picture on a wall or stature in a garden is the Lord. "Make no graven image unto me." If you do not see him as yourself you will not find him, and when he comes he reveals himself through his son calling you Father. This you set up in the beginning and then you agreed to play all the parts. Not one part can you condemn, for all contribute to the end when you find God. The goal of life is to find him, not on the outside, but within yourself in the first person, present tense. The world thinks I am insane when I tell them who I am, for they see the garment of flesh I wear and know I am subject to all its weaknesses. But because the drama of the scripture has unfolded within me, I know how true scripture is.

I cannot describe the joy that is yours when you awaken. I can only say that the world into which I go night after night is entirely different, and earth does not contain anything which I can use as an image to describe that world. I return through darkness into this world every day to share my experiences with everyone who will listen, while some believe me and some do not. My most intimate friends may not believe me, for they know and judge me by my human weaknesses. My brothers, knowing we were sired by the same father and came out of the same mother's womb, cannot believe my experiences are related to scripture. But I am not asking you to believe in Neville, but to believe in God who is your own wonderful human awareness.

I have been sent to tell you who God is. He who sent me is one with me, for although he seemed to be another when I stood in his presence, when we embraced we fused and became one. The recording angel, the ledger, the being of love who embraced me, is within. In the beginning I foreknew myself. Through foreknowledge I was predestined to be called from the world of death, called from within myself by an infinite being of love, wearing the human form divine, to be embraced and sent. And the moment we embraced we fused, and I knew myself to be infinite love. There had been a seeming separation when I entered a world that was not mine, to experience all of its horrors until its end when I am called, acquitted, justified, and glorified. Now there is nothing left for me to do but tell it to everyone who will listen and urge them to set their entire hope upon this grace which is coming to all at the unveiling of Christ in each individual, in the first person, present tense.

While you are here you can become independently secure, certainly. All of these things are possible to you, but the real objective in your life is to find God, the cause of all life. To believe in God does not aid you. The question is: do you believe in yourself? Can you believe you are rich when you have no money? Can you continue to believe it throughout the day and fall asleep night after night as though you were? If you will, you will become rich. Then fulfill another desire and then another, and one day you will discover the one who made it possible. That one is God.

Millions of people claim to believe in God in the third person, but they do not know God. Only when God reveals himself in the first person, present tense can he be known. That God cannot be outgrown or lost, for you cannot outgrow I am. I am is the theme of the Book of John, which goes back to the 3rd chapter of the Book of Exodus, the 14th verse, as: "Go say, 'I am has sent me to you.'" As a man, I am revealing God's true name, but those who hear my words know the outer garment I wear and judge it. They know my weaknesses, but they do not know the Lord. I tell you: when you know the Lord (or rather are known by him) you will experience a thrill that is beyond description. Your shock will turn to joy, however, as the drama of one called Jesus Christ unfolds within you.

In the meantime you can test him in the world of Caesar. There is no limit to his power, so take that power which became you and attach it to your desire. Sleep every night so attached to your desire that you feel its reality, and in no time you will prove my words. Within a year the lady in New York City received her $50,000, pressed down and running over. She knew exactly what she did and would never have guessed that the little old lady she bought the paper for every Sunday morning would be used as the means to give her the wealth she claimed. This lady has found God, yet she is still inclined to speak of him in the third person.

Man is in the habit of thinking of God and not as God. It is so easy to forget to keep the tense. Every good, well-trained Jew is familiar with the first five books of the Old Testament. They have read the Book of Exodus many times and believe God is the great I AM; yet they still think of him in the third person. They would think that anyone who boldly stood up and proclaimed, "I Am He" was arrogant; yet I tell you that is the only way you will ever find God.

But when he comes, there is no need to brag about it. You know who you are, and when they call you by your earthly name you respond. Perhaps you will have dinner together, but they will continue to be totally unaware of the being within you, and you don't always throw pearls before swine, because they are not prepared to receive them. You will join their party and enjoy the evening as you let the outer man play his part, but you know the inner man, the one they know not of. That man is Jesus Christ.

There is only one Christ. Everyone has been crucified with that one Christ can make the statement: "It is not I who live, but Christ who lives in me. And the life I now live in this body of flesh and blood, I live by the faith of the Son of God, who loved me and gave himself for me." God actually became as you are, that you may rise to the one being called God the Father. As one power, we came down from God to become the gods. In order to descend in power and play these parts we had to enter complete forgetfulness. The actor cannot pretend. He must enter and become the part he has agreed to play. He cannot step upon the stage knowing he is a great actor who everyone recognizes. He must lose himself in the character by leaving his personality in the dressing room and entering the stage as the character he is to portray. So when God stepped upon the stage wearing this, he is Neville, one hundred per cent. He had to completely forget that he was God, yet knowing that he brought with him a pattern which would erupt and his memory would return. I agreed to play the part as Neville. He and I are one, but I am greater than he.

Look upon Jesus Christ as a pattern. I have told you how the pattern erupted in me in the hope that you will believe me. Although a few believe my words, the majority disbelieve fulfilling scripture. "He came unto his own and his own believed him not." What I tell you and what you are capable of conceiving may be entirely different. Can you receive what I tell you as my own personal experience? I can tell you that scripture is true from beginning to end, but can you believe me enough to set your hope fully upon the grace that is coming to you at the unveiling of God within you? I hope so, for God is in you as your I am. And when he awakes you go through a series of supernatural events called Jesus Christ. Then you will tell your experiences to those who will listen in the hope that they will accept them; but it does not matter if they do or do not, for in the end, you take off your garment of flesh and return to an intimacy that is indescribable.

Eyes have not seen or ears heard the things that are already prepared for you. In that world you are in control of everything and everything is alive. Every night I pass beyond the world of dream to enter the world of reality, and I return each morning through the world of dream to reenter this world of death. This I do night after night, and will continue to do until that moment in time when it pleases the depth of my own being (who is the Father) to take off this garment of flesh and call it a day.

Remember, you can only sin against that self of you who is God. And any time you think of God in any tense other than the first person, present, you are entertaining an idol, no matter what you call it. If you leave this auditorium tonight conscious of being God, you are walking in the knowledge of the true God and all things are possible to you. Walk in complete trust that things are as you want them to be. This is loyalty to unseen reality. This is faith. There are only two things that displease God: One is lack of faith in I AM He, and the other is eating of the tree of knowledge of good and evil.

Before descending into the land of forgetfulness you made yourself a promise that one day your memory would return and you would realize you were the creator of it all, for God gave you himself. He actually became you, as told in the story of Melchizedek. He had no father, no mother, no beginning, and no end. In the end you become a priest after the order of Melchizedek, knowing the whole vast infinite universe was created by and sustained by you. Now, this is really incredible. I recently read that the great Einstein said: "I rejoice in the discovery of the uniformity of the laws of nature and whoever is behind it that we call the Lord. But that man should survive the disintegration of the brain, to me is unthinkable." If a man as wonderful as Einstein feels that the story of the gospel is unthinkable, then condemn no one. You can't deny Einstein's greatness. He was tender, kind and sincere; but in spite of that gentility he was quite satisfied to dwell in the uniformity of the laws of nature and whoever is behind it.

I tell you there is one behind it all. He so loved you he became you and the day is coming when you will know that you are he. You will know you are not the creation of the city, but its creator. You are not the made, but the maker. Whether you are male or female, you are the emanation of the Lord yet his wife till the sleep of death is past. Then you will awake to know you never left your heavenly home, you were never born and never die, save in your dreams.

Now let us go into the silence.

Neville (06-19-1970)

YOU DARE TO ASSUME

Spiritual growth is a gradual transition from a God of tradition to a God of experience. In Blake's works – one of his letters, rather (23 August 1799) – he had this little difference of opinion with the Dr. Reverend Trusler; and Trusler said to him, "You need someone to elucidate your ideas."

Blake wrote him a letter saying, "You ought to know that what can be made explicit to the idiot is not worth my care. The wisest of the Ancients discovered that that which was not too explicit was fittest for instruction, because it rouses the faculties to act." Then he asked the Reverend, "Why is it that the Bible is the most instructive work in this world?" Then he answered the Reverend himself, "Is it not because it is addressed to the Imagination, and only mediately to the understanding or reason?"

Well, the Bible is addressed to the Reality of man, for the true identity of man is Jesus Christ; and Jesus Christ is the human imagination! That is the Lord Jesus Christ. "By him all things were made and without Him was not anything made that is made." [John 1:3] And that is the Creator of the world.

Now we will turn to the 17th chapter of the Book of Acts, and you will find a story that is not spelled out because, as Blake said, it is addressed to the imagination. Dig it out. So, Paul addresses the Athenians, and he said, "O men of Athens," – and then he compliments them on their religious devotions; but then he added, "But as I passed by, I observed over one of your altars this inscription: TO AN UNKNOWN GOD." Then said he to the Athenians, "What, therefore, you worship as unknown, this I proclaim to you: The God who created the world and everything within it is not far off from each one of us. It is in Him that we live, and move, and have our being." [Acts 17:22, 23, 27, 28]

Now you've got to dig it. Start asking questions. I live in Him. I move in Him, and I have my being in Him, and He created the world and everything within it. Blake said,

"I am not a God afar off. I am a brother and Friend;

Within your own bosoms I reside, and you reside in me,"

But the perturbed Man, away turned down the valleys dark,"

[from "Jerusalem"]

--- couldn't take it.

Well, I am going to go a little bit beyond that. I will say that God is not far off; in fact, He is never so far off as even to be near, because nearness implies separation. So, He's not even so far off as even to be near. He became – actually became – as we are. His name is I AM. Can you speak of yourself when you say, "I am," and point elsewhere?

In a dream, who is dreaming? I am.

In a vision, who is having the vision? I am.

In the prison, who is imprisoned? I am. And who is set free? I am.

You can't get away from it. So He can never be so far off as even to be near, for nearness implies separation.

This is the God of Whom Paul spoke when he addressed the Athenians, "O men of Athens," – he praised them, yes, for all their wonderful devotions – religious devotions. Then he brought up the

50

point, "But as I passed by, I observed this inscription over one of your altars, TO AN UNKNOWN GOD. What, therefore, you worship as unknown, this I proclaim to thee.... The God who created the world and everything within it is not so far off from each one of us, for in Him we live and move and have our being."

That God is your own wonderful human imagination. That's the God of the Universe. One day you will know it. But you are keyed low for Divine purposes, so you don't know it, and you are having this strange, strange, wonderful dream. And this is the dream, but who is dreaming? I am dreaming. One day you will awaken in that immortal head of yours, where the whole drama started and where it comes to an end; and you will discover that you really are the God who created the universe and all within it! But while you are on this level, you can test it and see if this thing is really true.

You mean, my own wonderful human imagination is God! And He, and He alone, creates everything in this world?

I answer, yes. I can't persuade you, I can only suggest that you try it. For, we are told that, "Do you not realize that Jesus Christ is in you? Test Him and see."

Well, how would I test him?

Well, tell me Who-He-Is.

He is your own wonderful human imagination.

So what? And He created everything in the world, and creates all that is being created, and will continue to create everything that will ever come into the world. And there is no other Creator! And He is in you – not near, He is your very Being, your own wonderful human imagination!

Well, how do I go about testing this? Well, I simply ignore all the facts of life – all that reason dictates all that my senses dictate, and I dare to assume that I am the man – or the woman – that I want to be. So, I no longer want to be it. I am it! And I walk in the assumption that I am it. Then I command, by that assumption, the whole vast world to obey my will.

"I have found –"What have you found? "I have found in David, the son of Jesse," – the word "Jesse" is "I AM" – "I have found in David, the son of Jesse, a man after my own heart, who will do all my will."

Now, who is this being? David is the symbol of humanity. Humanity must obey my will. I don't have to ask them anything. Ask no man, no woman, ask no one. You dare to assume that you are that which you want to be, and David, which is the symbol of humanity, will execute your will.

In the end, when you come to the very end of the drama – but not before, humanity is gathered together into a single being – one single unit, and he stands before you, and his name is David. And he calls you "Father."

"I will tell of the decree of the Lord. He said unto me, Thou art my son. Today I have begotten thee." Read that in the Second Psalm. This is David speaking.

Now David says, in the 40th Psalm, "I delight to do Thy will, my God."

If you know Who-You-Are, humanity delights to do your will. So, you dare to assume – I don't care what it is, it's your privilege to assume good, bad, or indifferent. For He said, "I kill, and I make alive, I wound and I heal. And there is none that can deliver out of my hands." [Deuteronomy 32:39]

52

If there is only one Creator, don't tell me that He does not also kill! Because who is it then killing? Well, that's a creative act! And who heals? Who wounds, that it may be healed? There is only one God.

"Hear, O Israel, the Lord our God, the Lord is one."

Find out Who-He-Is. I tell you Who-He-Is. He is your own wonderful human imagination. There is no other God. But God lowered Himself down to the limit of man – the limit of contraction, the limit of opacity – that he may, in this state of complete oblivion to Who he really is, burst it and start expanding beyond what He was prior to the decision to come down into this state. This is how God expands. He expands and expands and expands. So, He comes down into this state by assuming the limit that is man.

You are man. Well, He never left His name, for He and His name are one! And His name forever is I AM. "This is my name forever and forever, and by this name I shall be known throughout all generations. Go tell them this is my name. I AM hath sent you."

So I say, I AM has sent you. Well, does it make sense? You dwell upon it. It does make sense! And the day will come, you will find the one who has had the experience before you yourself have the experience and you will see him radiating the Glory of God. No questions about it – you will!

But he could never explain it to any one who does not have the eyes to see it. Many of you will see it. I have told you what I know from my own experience; and when my time is up and I depart this life, those who have eyes to see it will see and know the quality of the message that I am giving to the world.

I am telling you, there is no other God. Don't look at the speaker. Look at yourself! We are one. I dwell in you, and you dwell in me; and we are one.

I know Who-I-Am. For I have experienced it; but I am not greater than any being in this world. They are only now asleep to the Being that they really are. In the end, we are all one grand brotherhood. And the brotherhood of God forms God, for the God of the Scripture is a compound unity – one made up of others. We are the "gods," we are the brothers. All came down and assumed these limitations; and the day will come, these woven "garments" that we "wear" we will split from top to bottom; and we who are trapped within them will be set free.

So they said to him, "Is this not Jesus, the son of Joseph? And do we not know his father and mother? And how is it that he now says, I have come down from heaven?"

Here is the perfect example of what happens in every one when he follows the pattern as described in Scripture. He has everything and experiences everything within himself that is called the "events of the Lord Jesus Christ." And because there is only one Lord Jesus Christ, when he experiences that within himself, he is the Lord Jesus Christ!

But how can he tell it to any one? They will turn their backs upon him as arrogant, as insane, as mad. But he simply tells it, and he knows that every one who has the eyes to see it can see it now or when he departs this world; and soon after he departs the world, they will have eyes. Eyes will open, and they will see it. There is only one Being, there's only one God, there's only one Lord in the world! Nothing but God!

But here, in the world of Caesar, we can test it. So you want more money? You want a better job? You want an increase in position? Well, assume that you are it now. Don't wait for it. Don't read the papers and have them deny that these things are possible, for today everything is denied.

A little thing that just happened in England: They were so complacent, so sure, they didn't even go to the polls to vote; so Mr. Heath got in. I wondered who was pulling and "treading in the winepress." I wondered who was pulling and "treading in the winepress." I wondered who started the rumor in England that they were so "in" you didn't have to vote. It could be Mr. Heath himself! But it's all imagination.

You suggest, and they accept the suggestions; and then you, knowing they are going to act upon it, go out and then you do exactly what you have to do: work under compulsion to meet every one you can and get them out. And then he sits back with his pipe, and he is so stunned! He can't believe for one moment they would throw him out, any more than Churchill could believe they would throw him out after the victorious campaign in Europe. But they did!

Everything in this world is possible. Do not say "No" to anything if you want it to be "Yes." Don't give up. Everything is possible, because David does your will, and David is the symbol of humanity. Humanity does your will.

In the end, when you have played all the parts, then David stands before you, not as a group – as a single youth: this heavenly, heavenly, beautiful being; and you look at him, and he calls you "Father," and you know it. Your memory has returned!

It's all the returning of memory. It was your glory "before that the world" started. And you will say these words in the 17th chapter of the Book of John: "I have accomplished the work you sent me to do. Now return unto me the glory that was mine, the glory that I had with Thee before that the world was." [John 17:5]

He seems to be speaking of another, but the Being "sent" and the Sender are one. And the Being "sent" is not inferior in his Essential Being, but only as to the office of the One that is "sent." So, he is sent into the world. So while he is in the world as the one who is "sent," his office is inferior to the Sender who does not leave that stable state. But he, the "sent," and the Sender are one!

So "He who sees me sees Him who sent me."

So you will see me with your in-current eyes, and see me playing the part described in Scripture. I don't have to pretend. Neville – yes – a little, tiny man, meaning nothing in the world socially, financially, intellectually, or in any other manner – nothing, but it doesn't matter. I willed to play this part. Only through this part could I tell the story, and tell it so that unnumbered generations from now it will be told and retold, but magnified. For those now living will be eye witnesses to the event before the departure of the little garment. They will be eye witnesses to the story. For all you have to do is to go into the Bible, and there you will see the story. And if with in-current eyes you see him playing the parts recorded in Scripture two thousand years ago, then you know Who-He-Is. But I am not alone! Every one is going to play this part, for there is only God. He is not playing the part as one little being set aside -- no, He is not far off. He is not even near, for nearness implies separation.

"God actually became as we are, that we maybe as He is."

[Blake, from "There Is No Natural Religion"]

So when you imagine something, remember: It is God Acting! And God's actions are His words. "And His word cannot return unto Him void but it must accomplish that which He purposed, and prosper in the thing for which He sent it."

Well, what are you imagining? Whatever you are imagining, you are actually sending into being to be confronted with it. So if you really want a lovely life, be careful what you are imagining, because imagination is God. Imagining is God-in-action! So what are you imagining? That everything is going down? That the whole world is collapsing? Well then, if that is what you imagine, may I tell you? You will have the experience of a collapsed world, but others won't.

There are people today making fortunes out of the seeming collapsed market – fortunes, they are making! They held their cash. I read in the New York Times of last Sunday [June 14th] – I get the Sunday issue every week, and it came a little late this week. In the financial section this house – not one of the biggest houses, but a good house – and they are in the "black," they never once went into the "red." And the man's name is Gardener, and they are quoting him. He said, "In 1968, in the summer of '68, we knew this was coming, and we prepared for the recession. So we were not caught in it. We knew and prepared for it, for it had to come."

Well, that was an imaginal act. He was bringing it about within himself because he knew it had to come. It wasn't going to come in spite of some one imagining that it had to come. And so, he planned it within his own mind's eye. So then came 1970 and then came the radical, radical decline. They had cash; they could pick up all these things at the bottom. They've got to go back. This is a powerful land, for you and I are imaginative people.

Americans went to the moon. That's imagination. They will go to everything in this world that they want to go to, for this is a fabulous land. Well, you can't stop men imagining, and we do imagine in this country! We build the tallest – build all kinds of things because man here – you can't stop it. He is so constructed, he imagines all the time.

57

Well, you can't stop it going back; so he started the decline in his own mind's eye in the summer of '68, and waited patiently – waited and waited, and then came the inevitable crash. It will go back. But he had cash; waiting for what he knew was inevitable. So instead of buying it at 900, he now buys it in the 600's. It served him to wait a year and a half or two years, for what would he make now coming in at this bottom, when it starts moving again?

It's all within the imagination of man. But I am not an economist; I know nothing about economy. I am not interested in it. I get calls all the time saying, "Will you go into a business with me?" I am not interested. I got one yesterday. He cried on the phone when I would not come forward to buy a huge, large area of land for him because he wants to be a grower of trees. I said, "I'm not interested. I am not in business. I am telling you a principle and you don't have to turn to any one in this world to ask their assistance."

The whole vast world will rush to serve you if you assume a certain state and remain faithful to that assumption. If I dare to assume that I am the man that I want to be, the world has to come to my assistance and express it, for the world is David, and David is "a man after my heart who will do all my will."

And in the end, you will see him standing before you, not as humanity, but a single being – a glorified, glorious boy – a boy of about 12 or 13 at the most. And, oh! What a beauty he is. The sum total of all of humanity who did your will. So when you played all the parts, then you will know: "I came down from Heaven."

And they will say, "But I know your parents. I know your father and your mother."

Yes, they know my parents of the "garment" that I "wear," and they know my brothers and my sister, who are brothers and sisters of the "garment" that I "wear." But the wearer of the garment, they do not know. They do not know the Occupant of that garment. For that garment only serves the occupant for a purpose. And in this very moment he has completed the task.

I can say tonight, "I have accomplished the work which Thou sent me to do. Now return the glory that was mine, the glory that I had with Thee before that the world was." And may I tell you? He has, He has! I am not waiting for the return. But the mask hides it from those who have not in-current eyes to see it. But every one will see it. Every one will experience it. But while we are here, you play your part perfectly, not only for yourself; play it for every one in the world, for they are all "yourself pushed out" anyway.

So some one wants this, that or the other? As I said to my friend – he cried on the phone. I said, "I am speaking of a principle. I will 'hear' you tell me that you have your whatever acreage you want to plant your avocado pears, if you want to do that for a living, for they grow without effort on your part."

What he really wants – he doesn't want to do anything. He wants to have something planted that simply produces, like people buying stock. He is not interested in the Company, only in the little piece of paper, not the Company, what it is doing or the management of the Company. So he wants an area of avocado pears. Even though he doesn't want to work, I will still "hear" that he has it. I am not here to judge any one in the world. So he wants that? I will "hear" that he has it, and assume that he has it;' and may I tell you? He will have it. For the world will wait on him and the world will see that he has it; and he will never know, as told us in the very first chapter and the second chapter of Isaiah, that it was I who pray for him, because he cried and hung-up, he could not wait. But I did not. When he hung up crying, I did not until I had "heard" that he has what he wants.

But I need not be the medium through which he has whatever it takes to buy his "X" number of acres for his plants, because I am not in business. I am simply telling a story – an eternal story that is true. And the story is all for us in Scripture.

Jesus Christ is the true identity of every child born of woman. And Jesus Christ is the human imagination. "Through Him, all things were made, and without Him was not anything made that was made."

"He is in the world, and the world knows Him not"

[John 1:10]

So no one knows Him. He sits, and no one knows He is the Cause of the phenomena of life. And they turn to this place, that place, the other place; and here is one "treading out the wine press," knowing exactly what he is doing, allowing his will to express through humanity – humanity being David, the son of Jesse. And Jesse is I AM. It is any form of the verb "to be." "I AM" – that's the name of Jesse.

So, "Whose son are you?"

"I am the son of your servant."

"Jesse."

And "Now I have found in David, the son of Jesse, a man after my own heart, who will do all my will."

So humanity will do it. Every one will do it. And in the end, you will awaken, and you will discover that the whole drama started in your immortal head, and in that immortal head you dreamed the Dream of Life. And one day you heard a Voice, it was a wind – a strange wind, and you awoke form the Dream of Life to discover that you had dreamed it all. You were a dreamer and then you came out, and all the imagery of Scripture surrounds you. Everything about it surrounds you, and you are the One of whom it spoke in Scripture "born not of blood, nor of the will of man, nor of the will of the flesh, but of God." It was God re-born. You are the one destined to be re-born.

Don't let any one tell you that you began in your mother's womb or that you even began. There never was a time that you and I were not – never. Nor will there come a time when you and I shall cease to be. Before this whole vast world appeared to be, you and I were the creators of it. I know our scientists will question that and think me mad. It's perfectly all right. I will go along with Blake, based upon my visions.

"Eternity exists, and all things in Eternity,

Independent of Creation, which was an act of mercy."

[From "A Vision of the Last Judgment"]

And then what is that creation? All things exist. Humanity, the animal world, the plant world – everything exists in Eternity, and Eternity is in your own wonderful human imagination. That's Eternity!

All things exist now in the human imagination. Well now, what is the act of creation that I would bury myself in that which exists and return? That I could "die" – actually die – and return? For a seed must fall into the ground and die before it is made alive. If it does not fall into the ground and "die," it remains alone; but if it falls and dies, it brings forth much. So I "died," I fell into my own wonderful world that is -- it exists, and the world is "dead" – completely dead. And I could not pretend. I had to actually become this world of the "dead." So I became it, and then I passed through all the horrors of the world. For what purpose? To remember the glory that I saw before, that I gave up to come into this world.

"How long, how vast, how severe the anguish 'ere I find that glory were long to tell."

[Daniel 12:6]

But having gone through it all, then I remembered. And the only one that could actually bring me back to my memory of the glory that was mine was my "son," for "No one knows who the Father is except the Son, and non one knows who the Son is except the Father."

And so here the son stands before me and the memory – ancient, ancient memory returned. And I was the one who decided without any persuasion to lay myself down.

He said, "No one takes away my life. I lay it down myself. I have the power to lay it down, and the power to lift it up again." But while I lay it down:

"Then those in Great Eternity who contemplate on death

Said thus: What seems to be, is to those to whom

It seems to Be."

[From "Jerusalem"]

Here I am in a world. It seems that he is going to attack me. I am assuming that? Well then, he will attack me.

I assume that things are going to be bad, they will be bad.

I assume that things are going to break, and I am going to wait for it. So –

"What seems to Be, is, To those to whom It seems to Be, and is productive of the most dreadful Consequences to those to whom it seems to Be, even of Torments, Despair and Eternal Death; but the Divine Mercy Steps beyond and Redeems Man in the Body of Jesus."

So that act of mercy is the act of Creation, when I – the Eternal Being – gave up my Eternal Self and came down into a finite world and "died." And the act of creation is the redemptive act when I am brought back, because I am lost in a world where "what seems to be is, to those to whom it seems to be."

And when I have gone through the entire gamut of all the experiences of man, then I hear the Voice. The Voice is the wind – an unearthly wind; and you hear it within the immortal head where the drama started. And then you find yourself waking, and you awake within yourself, and then you come out of the tomb in which you were entombed. As you come out, the imagery of the birth of God surrounds you, and you are the star in the drama.

And from then on, three great events take place, and it's all over. The Descent of the Dove upon – the symbol of the Holy Spirit is completely satisfied with the journey, for the journey is now over; and "this is my beloved Son, in whom I am well pleased." [Matthew 3:17]

One of my sons has returned. When all the sons return, all the sons together from God the Father. We are the Elohim, and together we form Jehovah. But we are the gods – all of us are!

By the way, we got our contract today from the club. They finally came through with a contract. So will be returning the last week of September – same place, same time.

Now are there any questions, please?

QUESTIONS BY A LADY: Do you have any more understanding as to why we have to leave before some people experience the Power from on high?

NEVILLE: Well, we are told in Scripture: "Remain just where you are until you are clothed with Power from on high." All will be clothed in Power. But not very many – strangely enough, only the women saw him. All saw him after that, but the women saw him. Why, I do not know. They saw him in his transfigured state. He did take three into the state, but that is "before that the world was." He is not talking of anything in this world.

Everything that is said from the lips of the one called Jesus Christ is of another world – a world which is his true home, from which he came and to which he will return. But men misunderstood him. For they knew the early man, and they would say, "We know his father. His name is Joseph. We know his father and his mother and his brother and his sisters. How can he tell us, I have come down from heaven?" That's an insane statement for any man to make, but he was never speaking of anything of this world.

After you have the experiences, you will have the same social gathering that you've always had; but in the midst of the most intimate relationships, you know they are only brothers of your body that you "wear." Behind the garments that they wear, they are your eternal brothers; but they do not know that as yet. They know only the physical descent, but they do not know the spiritual beings that they are. So if you told them that you re the father of David of Biblical fame, they would be concerned and think, "We had better take good care of him, because he's not all here." So you don't tell them.

But in the midst of the gathering, you know Who-You-Are, and they don't know Who-You-Are; and so as you walk the street, you walk in the consciousness of being the Father of the Son of God.

Humanity seems so vast. Three and a half billion, and they are growing; and yet all this did you will through the centuries, that you dreamed the Dream of Life. And in the end, it formed itself into a single youth who called you "Father." So you walk in that consciousness.

If you could only get the accustomed aspect of things out of your eyes and drop in on yourselves as stranges, just like some visitor from Heaven! Here I drop in on myself, but Neville belongs to a certain family physically in this world; and then after the experience you get the accustomed aspect of things out of your eyes; and you walk not as the brother of this large, wonderful family of physical descent but you walk in the consciousness of being the Father of the Son of God!

Neville (no date)

YOU MUST EXPERIENCE GOD

God is known by experience or not at all. I have experienced God. I can no more deny it than I can the humblest evidence of my senses, so I feel qualified to tell you how you are going to experience God. There is only God in the world. When you say, "I am," *that's* God forever and forever.

Tonight you will know why the term "Judao-Christian" came to be hyphenated. The story as told in the Old Testament is a prophetic blueprint; that which is told in the New is its fulfillment. They are really two parts of one book – the prophecy and its fulfillment.

"God became as we are, that we may be as He is." [Blake, from "There Is No Natural Religion"] Every little child born of woman is aware that it *is*. Before it is aware of *what* it is, *who* it is, *where* it is, it is *aware that it is*. That's fundamental. That is God-*in*-that-child. It's the same God in the adult. It is the Dreamer in man. It has to be awakened, and when it awakes, it is the being in whom it awakes, and then he knows Who-He-Is.

We are told in Scripture that, "The hour is coming when all of those who are in the tomb will hear His voice and come forth." They hear the voice of the Son; it's called the voice of the child. And the voice of the child, like a tuning fork, sets the tone, and then the Dreamer awakes and knows that he is God. It's entirely up to the voice of the Son.

"When the time had fully come, God sent forth the Spirit of His Son into our hearts crying, Father."

He is crying, "Father," but we do not hear it – not until "the fullness of time has come."

We are told in the 44th Psalm, "Rouse Thyself. Why sleepest Thou, 0 Lord? Awake!" It is God who sleeps in man. It is God-*in*-man who does everything that man does – good, bad or indifferent. He actually became as I am – that's His name – that I may be as He is. And He is Father.

The day is coming, everyone will know the experience that I have had, for there is no other experience in Eternity that can convince you that you *are* God the Father, other than *this* experience. His Son must call you, and you must respond, and when you actually hear it and then look and see what is calling, and it is your *son* David, then everything returns. Memory returns, and you know exactly Who-You-Are – that you are God the Father, and your *son* is David.

This secret is told us in Scripture in the words "Jesus Christ" and you take it as one being – one being only, if you know that "I and my Father are one," but if you do not know that, here you find two beings.

Jesus is I AM. That's the Lord. "No one can say that Jesus is Lord, except by the Holy Spirit." The Holy Spirit is called the "Remembrancer."

"I will go, and I will send the Holy Spirit who will bring to your understanding all that you have heard from me." So, he brings back the memory that you lost. But "No one can say that Jesus is Lord, except by the Holy Spirit." So, when the Spirit comes and memory returns – but you will never know that you really are until you hear the voice of your own *son*, for you are suffering from complete and total amnesia. You do not know that you are God the Father! And you will never know it until you hear the Son's voice; he is calling and calling, but only when the moment is ripe do you hear it. Just as we have told you, like the tuning fork it sets the tone, and it wakes you, and you hear it. When you awake, standing before you is your *son*, and memory returns – the Remembrancer, the Holy Spirit. And then you know exactly Who-You-Are, and you are God the Father!

It is going to happen to every child born of woman. And therefore, every child born of woman is one with the speaker who has had that experience, because it is the identical *son* who is calling him "Father." And there is only one God, one Father of all, and only one Son. So, when he calls *you* "Father," and you know it because memory returns, and he has called *me* "Father," and I know it – then you and I are one.

So, "There is only one body, one spirit, one hope, one lord, one faith, one baptism, one God and Father of all, who is above all, through all, and in all." That's the mystery of Scripture. It hasn't a thing to do with secular history. It is all salvation history. It has not a thing to do with history as the world teaches it.

You and I are experiencing history – secular history, and my history is known to anyone who wants to investigate it. I wouldn't say that it is anything to write about. I was born in a simple little environment without any educational, social, financial background whatsoever. I am making a struggle, as all people make a struggle in the world – I have to pay rent and to buy food, and then to put the garments on the body. That's a struggle for everyone. They seem to have no time for the Spirit. But the day is coming, *all* will have this experience, regardless of the struggle, and no one will be greater than the other, because everyone is the *same* God the Father – the Father of the one and only Son, who is David.

So, you know why we hyphenate the name "Judao-Christian." Judaism is the foundation, and Christianity is its fulfillment. That is the fruit on the tree; that is the flower. Without that tree, it couldn't bear the fruit, so the whole thing is contained in that Old Testament, but it is adumbrated; it's a foreshadowing in a not altogether conclusive or immediately evident way. When it happens, it's not what the world thought should happen. They are expecting some being to come from without and save them, but He doesn't come that way. He comes to us as "one unknown," yet one who in the most ineffable mystery lets the individual to whom He comes *experience* who He is, and you will never experience who He is until He awakes by the voice of His Son who is calling Him, "Rouse Thyself. Why sleepest Thou, O Lord? Awake! Do not cast us off forever" – as you read it in the 44th Psalm, the 23rd verse.

So, as we are told in the 5th chapter of John, "And the hour is coming when all those who are in the tomb will hear His voice" – the Son's voice – "and come forth."

The *tomb* is your own wonderful skull. You are not buried in any cemetery in this world. Let them build all the great mausoleums they want. That's man. It is big business. Let them do it; let them build it. But you are "buried" in your skull! That's where *God* is buried! And out of that Golgotha He will rise, and He will rise while you walk the earth. You will sleep this night without knowing you will be awakened by the call of the voice.

The *voice* is a vibration. It is a sound. And so, David will *sound* the call. It will be in tune with you *if* the hour is right, and then you will awake to find yourself completely entombed within your own skull. And without any assistance from without, you will push the base of your skull and come out, just like a child being born from the womb of woman, only this is now being "born from above" – not from below. When you come out, all the symbolism of Scripture will surround you. The witnesses will be there. There are three – and the infant wrapped in swaddling clothes, which is only the *sign* of your exit from that heavenly *womb*. *You* are "born from above!"

And from then, you go to another scene, another scene, over a period of three and a half years, and your journey is then completed. You'll remain in this world long enough to tell of your experience – to tell of your own experience of God. And until God is experienced, you do not know Him. Let all the preachers do what they want; it's perfectly all right. They are sound asleep because God-in-them is sound asleep, and they are speculating. They are theorizing, based upon what they believe God *ought* to do. He should punish this one and punish that one, and they do not know everyone punished *is God being punished* for His dream. He is dreaming the Dream of Life. And many dreams are like nightmares, whether they be waking dreams or the dreams of sleep, they are nightmares. But nevertheless, it's still God dreaming.

Who is dreaming when he wakes in the morning? We will say, "Well, I had a dream," and you had a dream. "A horrible dream! I was" – and then he begins to describe it, but what is he saying? He is calling Him by the name of God. It was God who had the dream. When he wakes, "I am going to do so-and-so." Who is that saying, "I am going to do so-and-so"? That is God. There is nothing but God in the world. There is no room for anyone in the world but God and His only begotten Son. And His Son is David. That's His Son.

Jesus is the Lord God Jehovah, and "David in the spirit called him 'my lord.'" That's the son calling him "my lord." Here is Jesus of Scripture – the awakened God. He's not asleep. Here is the one who first awoke in the world. But then he calls us "Brothers." He said, "Go unto my brothers and tell them I am ascending unto my Father," but he said, "I and my Father are one" – "unto my God," and he also said, "My Father is *your* Father. My God is your God," and "I and my Father are one," and my Father is He Whom you call "God."

Here the mystery begins to unfold. Until you actually experience it, you do not know how wonderful Scripture is. Man must

71

experience Scripture before he can *begin* to understand how altogether wonderful it is. It's eternally true. From beginning to end, the whole thing is true, and it is not secular history. It's *divine* history.

So, I share with you what I know from experience. I am not theorizing. I am not speculating. It happened to me – a simple man, as you are simple, and I did not for one moment suspect this was the mystery until it actually unfolded within me and I experienced it.

When someone who supposedly lived three thousand years ago calls me "Father," I know exactly that I *am* his father; there was no uncertainty as to this relationship. I am looking into the face of the most heavenly youth, and he was the one who called me from my profound sleep, and when I awoke, it was God who awoke, for he is calling upon the Lord to awake, "Rouse Thyself. Why sleepest Thou, 0 Lord? Awake!" And then you awake as though you had never before been awake. It's a peculiar, strange awaking that takes place is you. And now you see this heavenly, eternal being who is the Son of God, and because he is going to wake you, you will know that he is your son, and he will know that you are God.

So, in the end, everyone will awake, and everyone will be God! So, it takes all of us to make the Lord. It's a compound unity – the word "Elohim." It is a plural word.

"In the beginning God" – that word is "Elohim." And "God said, Let *us* make man in our image." That word is "Elohim" – a compound unity – one made up of others. It takes *all* of us to make the *one* God. "Hear, O Israel, the Lord our God, the Lord is one" – not two.

So here, the only one who could ever rouse you and actually bring you from your profound sleep is your *son*, whose name is David.

"I will tell of the decree of the Lord," said David. "He said unto me, Thou art my son. Today I have begotten thee."

And so we have confused it with Jesus, and Jesus is the Lord. He is the Lord speaking. He is the Lord who inspired the prophets to write what they did. And finding no one to fulfill it, He Himself came into the world and became man. He became you! His name is I AM. That's the Lord God Jehovah that we call "Jesus" in Scripture. That's I AM.

"Do you not realize," said Paul, "that Jesus Christ is in you?" Don't you know that He is *in* you? Are you looking for Him to come from without, when He is within you? Well, he *is* within. You cannot say, "I am," and point elsewhere. Whether you are in a frightful dream, you are aware. To be aware is saying, "I am." And you can't point on the outside of self when you say, "I am," and "that is my name forever and forever." And that is the Lord Jesus in every being in the world.

But his Son plays such an important part – that Son called "David." You say he is the son of Jesse, and "Jesse" means "I AM." The word "Jesse" means, "Jehovah exists." It is any form of the verb "to be." In other words, I am. *That* is the Father of David.

And what I tell you I am telling you from experience. I am not the scholar who simply went through Scripture and combed it to bring forward this theory. It's not theory with me. I am not qualified to go through the Scriptures, knowing Greek, and knowing Latin, and knowing Aramaic, to do that. It has *happened* to me. It was all by revelation. So, let the scholars go on and try to find it. Let them go on. Until it's *revealed* to them, they do not know it.

Revealed truth cannot be actually, legally or – I would say – logically proven. It's all revealed. If it isn't revealed, well then speculate. And I am *not* speculating. I am telling you exactly Who-

God-Is. And until you *experience* God, you do not know Him. And I am telling you from my own experience, you *will* experience God, and then you will *know* Him. And you'll know why we hyphenate the words "Judao- Christian." It's one tree. The tree is Judaism; the fruit is Christianity. Christianity is simply the fulfillment of Judaism.

So here, he tells you, "I will not leave you desolate. I will come again." And then He becomes invisible. The story is told us in the pre-existence "before that the world was." And here, He becomes invisible, because He takes up His residence *in* us, and the darkest hour in the world, symbolized in Scripture as the three hours of darkness that descended – no. The darkest hour is when God became invisible. As He became invisible, he took up His residence in us, and man is looking for Him to come from without, and He cannot come from without. He will rise from within, but only at the call of His Son's voice.

So, in the fullness of time, He sent forth the Spirit of His Son into our hearts, crying what? "Father." And if you hear it, then you respond. Responding is waking. And you begin to awake within yourself, to find yourself entombed within your own skull – completely sealed, but you have an innate wisdom. You know exactly what to do, for He prepared the way before He set forth. You know exactly what to do – you push the base of your skull, and it gives, and then you come out. And the symbolism surrounds you. You know exactly Who-You-Are – but not quite until the Son appears. At first, only the infant wrapped in swaddling clothes, and you are told in Scripture that's only a *sign*, like the sign on the top of the White House.

I ask the guard, "Is the President in residence?"

And he looks. If his insignia is flying, he will say, "Yes, he is in residence." If it's not flying, the President is not in residence.

If the little child is found wrapped in swaddling clothes, then I ask, "Is God born?"

"Yes, here is His sign."

"This shall be a *sign* unto you. You shall find a child wrapped in swaddling clothes and lying on the floor." When that sign is found, the question is asked, "Is God born?" Yes, here is the *sign* of His "birth." But when the *child* comes – not the little infant – when the Son comes, then you hear his voice. And the voice is the voice of God's Son, who is Christ.

Christ is the Son of God, and the "Anointed" means Christ, and "Christ" means the "Anointed." And did he not say in the 89th Psalm, "I have anointed you with my holy oil"? Well, who is He speaking to? He is speaking to David. Did He not say in the 89th Psalm, "I have found David, and David has cried unto me, Thou art my Father, my God, and the Rock of my Salvation"? Did he not say in the 2nd Psalm, "Thou art my son? Today I have begotten thee"?

All these words were inspired by the One Being whom we call "Jesus, the Lord." He inspired it through his prophets, and then Himself came down and took upon himself humanity. I am speaking of the Cosmic God – of the Cosmic Son. So, He is buried in *every* child born of woman, but this is so unique He comes to us individually. He calls us, one by one, in season.

So, tonight could be *your* call. It may be tomorrow night. I hope it is not in the distant future. But He will call all, and when you take off this garment, having been called and having seen the Son, you have taken it off for the last time. Until it actually happens to you, *death* is not death. *Death* is nothing more than simply leaving a room and entering another room, simply like the room you left – the same terrestrial world. With all the struggles you left behind you? You'll find them there. You are restored to life, not as a baby, no

75

reincarnation. You are *restored* – a young man, a young woman, with not a thing missing. No need of anything to be added because nothing is missing, only you are young – about 20 years of age – to continue your journey in this world, to be confronted with all the problems that are here. Yes, and you marry there, too. You marry, and you grow old, and you "die" there, too. And if it hasn't yet happened, you are restored again to continue the journey until it happens. But it's going to happen to every being in the world. Not one can fail, because then *God* would fail, and that's impossible. So everyone will awaken from the Dream of Life, and it doesn't end at that moment in time that your senses cease to register that being and we speak of him as *dead*.

He is not *dead*. He's in a world just like this – restored to life in a world that is terrestrial, in a young, wholesome, healthy body, with all the problems that faced him; because in the Resurrection of which I speak, there is no marriage, no male, no female – a completely transformed being, who is God. But until then, there is still sex – very much so in that world. But I am telling you what I know. I see them – my father, my mother, my brother – so many friends who are gone. I see them. They are not *gone* at all. They are in a world just like this, with all their struggles.

Therefore, I ask you to live so that your mind can store a past worthy of recall, for you are taking that with you. Spend all of your time entertaining noble thoughts, for you are taking that with you into the world where you are headed, unless this thing happens before you make your departure from this world. If it does not happen before that, you are taking with you what you have actually entertained in this world. So, live so that your mind can store a past worthy of recall, because you are going to actually take it right into your world to resolve it. And that is a part of your struggle.

But the day is coming – everyone is going to have the experience that I have just told you. No one can avoid it. If others have other ideas, let them have it. I wouldn't raise a finger to change it. They have all these -isms in the world; let them have it – all kinds of concepts of what God *ought* to have done. What God ought to have done, He has already done! The drama is over. The Resurrection is taking place. It didn't take place once and forever two thousand years ago. It is taking place at every moment of time, but not everyone is articulate. Not everyone is sent to tell it after it takes place. So, they will go through their little exit from this world, not having told it to anyone.

On the other hand, I was not restrained. I had to tell it, like Jeremiah, "If I say I will not mention it, or speak any more in His name, then there is in me, as it were, a burning fire, all shut up in my bones, and I am tired of holding it in, and I cannot." So, I cannot restrain the impulse to talk about it. Others can. They are embarrassed even to bring it up, but I am not. It is part of my way of being, of thinking.

So, I tell you, the voice spoken of is a real voice, but like all voices, you are now interpreting the vibration that is coming from my mouth. It is all vibration, and then you actually translate it within yourself, because it is simply impinging upon you. Well, this is the same voice. It's just like the tuning fork. And then it sets a tone, and the tone rouses you if you are in tune with that tone, and then you are actually hearing Him call you. He is calling you "Father." And you awake to find standing before you this heavenly youth. And then, at that very moment, you know exactly who he is, and he is David, the sweet Psalmist David, and he is your *son*, and you know he is your son. Memory has returned.

So, "God became as we are, that we may be as He is." [Blake, from "There Is No Natural Religion"] Don't for one moment forget that. That is the great sacrifice. It was *God* Who "died."

"Unless I die, thou canst not live; but if I die, I shall arise again, and thou with me."

[Blake, from "Jerusalem"]

So, it is *God* who is crucified on these garments. And the God-in-you – His name is "I AM." And when you hear the voice and you awake, *who* awakes? *I* awake.

Who is waking? *I* am waking.

What is His name? "I AM," forever and forever.

And who is His Son's name? I am telling you, His Son's name is David, but because he has been anointed with the holy oil, he is the Christ. "Thou art the Christ, the Son of the Living God."

In the Old Testament the word "Christ" is not used, but the word "Messiah" is. He is the Messiah, for the Messiah simply means the "anointed one." And the word "Messiah" is used only in the book of John in the New Testament. He does speak of the Christ as the Messiah, and it is *not* Jesus. Jesus is the Lord. Yet the Son could say, "I and my Father are one." So, "When you see me, you see the Father." He is the image of the Father.

You are told, "It does not yet appear what we shall be, but we know that when he appears, we shall be like Him."

I am telling you that is exactly what is going to happen. Forget the mask that you are now wearing. Behind that mask is the Ancient of Days, the Eternal One who is the Lord God Jehovah. And David is the image of the Lord God Jehovah. He is the Eternal Youth, and the Lord is the Ancient of Days, without beginning, without end.

So, when you dwell tonight on it, treat it seriously. What I have told you this night is true. I haven't speculated. I haven't turned to anyone for support. I was never taught it. It's in the Bible, but I never saw it in the Bible until I experienced it. That is why I can tell you, until God is experienced, you do not know God. One must *experience* God to know Him. He is not deaf; you don't have to scream to have Him hear you. You need not utter anything. Your simple thought is heard because who is hearing it? "I AM." That's God.

The way they have all these prayers – Let us pray. They put on all these microphones and just blast the whole thing out calling upon God to hear them. That's not God. God is within you. And the God – the only Living God – is your own wonderful *human* imagination. When you say, "I am," that is God!

"By Him all things were made, and without Him was not anything made that was made." In His dream, naturally He makes mistakes. God makes mistakes? There is only one that can make a mistake, and that is God. There is only one that can make anything, and that's God. For, in a nightmare, well can you blame the man if he has the most horrible nightmare? You would console him in the morning if he told you of some horrible dream. You wouldn't condemn him. Well now, this is a waking dream, but it is still a dream.

So, in the end, everything is forgiven. Every being in the world is forgiven, for there is only God who did it all! So, the story is the Father and His Son, and there is no other being in the world. And *you* are the Father, and His Son is *your* son. And if he can say, "I and my Father are one," then he can say of you, "I and my Father are one."

When you look into the face and you see that beauty – you cannot describe the beauty of David. No artist could paint it. He is the image of you. But no one knows it, only the mask that you wear, for He is the image of the Invisible You, and He bears the express image of your Person. But your Person is not the thing that you *wear* as a mask. You are the Immortal Being. You are the Eternal Being.

When you hear it, and you really believe it, you will see why this Book of 66 books is really a library. When you have a Bible of both the Old and the New under one cover, you have a library. Very few homes have 66 books in them. If they have a Bible, they have 66 books, and they have the greatest library in the world in having the Bible. And one is the Old; the other is the New. One foreshadows, and the other tells you how it is fulfilled. But even though it is fulfilled, it still remains a mystery to those who have not experienced it. So, I tell you, He comes to us as One Unknown, yet one who in the most wonderful manner lets you experience Who-He-Is. And when you experience Who-*He*-Is, it's your Self. *That* is God!

What a sacrifice! He *literally* became, as I am, that I may be as He is. And that is true of every child born of woman.

Now, if you enjoy other things, enjoy them, but you will not in Eternity undo what I have told you. Not in Eternity will you disprove it; may I tell you? All the wisdom of the world cannot disprove what I have told you tonight. You may rise in opposition, and I wouldn't bat an eye to argue with you, for I know what I have experienced. So, let them argue. *I* will not argue.

They said he was silent. "You will not speak to me." Why argue the point? "So you were a king. The world says so."

"It's the Father's good pleasure to give me the Kingdom." Well, if He is going to give me the Kingdom, He is going to give me Himself, for He *is* the Kingdom. Read it in the 12th chapter of Luke, the 32nd verse, "It is your Father's good pleasure to give you" – you don't earn it; it's unmerited. It's grace – "to give you the Kingdom." And when He succeeds in giving me the Kingdom, He succeeds in giving me Himself, for He *is* the Kingdom.

The Kingdom is not a realm, as the world teaches. It is *God* – the character that is God – that is perfect, so wherever you are, clothed in that Perfect Character, everything is perfect. Everything is alive. Nothing is dead, and nothing is imperfect. Wherever you are *after* you have received the gift, you could walk through the Petrified Forest, and it would all suddenly burst into blossom. Walk through the desert, and the desert will bloom. Come into any place where they are imperfectly formed – eyes that are missing out of their sockets will come out of the Nowhere and fill the empty sockets, and they will be perfect. Arms missing? No, not in your presence when you receive the Kingdom; in the presence of You, the Perfect Man, *nothing* can remain imperfect, but you don't do it out of compassion. You don't even *do* anything. Your very presence does it! So, no matter where you are – go down into hell, "hell" is transformed into heaven. Wherever you are is perfect, because you are now the King. You have received the Kingdom. I am telling you from my own experience. You walk into a world, and the world is instantly transformed to be in harmony with the Perfection that is springing within you.

So, I tell you, "It is your Father's *good* pleasure to give you the Kingdom." That is a wonderful way of telling you it is your Father's good pleasure to give *you* Himself! That's how the Evangelist told it in the book of Luke, "It is your Father's good pleasure to give you Himself." And your Father is God. And God is Jesus. Jesus is the Lord. There is no other God! But He's a *father,* and because He's a father, He has a son. And I am telling you, in spite of the whole vast world, that Son is *David*, our sweet Psalmist of Biblical fame. And he will stand before you, and he too will call you "my Lord, my Father, the Rock of my Salvation."

Now let us go into the Silence.

Neville (03-10-1972)

YOU MUST EXPERIENCE GOD

God is known by experience or not at all. I have experienced God. I can no more deny it than I can the humblest evidence of my senses; so I feel qualified to tell you how you are going to experience God. There is only God in the world. When you say, "I am," that's God forever and forever.

Tonight you will know why the term "Judeo-Christian" came to be hyphenated. The story as told in the Old Testament is a prophetic blueprint; that which is told in the New is its fulfillment. They are really two parts of one book: the prophecy and its fulfillment.

"God became as we are, that we may be as He is." [Blake, from "There is No Natural Religion"] Every little child born of woman is aware that it is. Before it is aware of what it is, who it is, where it is, it is aware that it is. That's fundamental. That is God-in-that-child. It's the same God in the adult. It is the Dreamer in man. It has to be awakened; and when it awakes, it is the being in whom it awakes, and then he knows Who-He-Is.

We are told in Scripture that: "The hour is coming when all of those who are in the tomb will hear His voice and come forth." They hear the voice of the Son: it's called the voice of the child. And the voice of the child, like a tuning fork, sets the tone; and then the Dreamer awakes and knows that he is God. It's entirely up to the voice of the Son.

"When the time had fully come, God sent forth the Spirit of His Son into our hearts crying, Father." He is crying "Father," but we do not hear it – not until "the fullness of time has come."

We are told in the 44th Psalm: "Rouse Thyself. Why sleepest Thou, O Lord? It is God who sleeps in man. It is God-in-man who does everything that man does – good, bad or indifferent. He actually became as I am – that's His name – that I may be as He is. And He is Father.

The day is coming; every one will know the experience that I have had, for there is no other experience in Eternity that can convince you that you are God the Father, other than this experience. His Son must call you, and you must respond; and when you actually hear it and then look and see what is calling, and it is your "son" David, then everything returns. Memory returns, and you know exactly Who-You- Are: that you are God the Father, and you "son" is David.

This secret is told us in Scripture in the words "Jesus Christ," and you take it as one being – one being only, if you that "I and my Father are one;" but if you do not know that that, here you find two beings.

Jesus is I AM. That's the Lord. "No one can say that Jesus is Lord, except by the Holy Spirit." The Holy Spirit is called the "remembrancer."

"I will go, and I will send the Holy Spirit who will bring to your understanding all that you have heard from me." So he brings back the memory that you lost. But "No one can say that Jesus is Lord except by the Holy Spirit." So when the Spirit comes and memory returns – but you will never know that you really are until you hear the voice of your own "son," for you are suffering from complete and total amnesia. You do not know that you are God the Father! And you will never know it until you hear the Son's voice; he is calling and calling, but only when the moment is ripe do you hear it. Just as we have told you, like when the moment is ripe do you hear it. Just as we have told you, like the tuning fork it sets the tone, and it wakes you, and you hear it. When you awake, standing before you is your "son;" and memory returns – the Remembrancer, the Holy Spirit. And then you know exactly Who-You-Are, and you are God the Father!

It is going to happen to every child born of woman. And therefore, every child born of woman is one with the speaker who has had that experience, because it is the identical "son" who is calling him "Father." And there is only one God, one Father of all, and only Son. So when he calls you "Father," and you know it because memory returns, and he has called me "Father," and I know it – then you and I are one.

So "There is only one body, one spirit, one hope, one lord, one faith, one baptism, one God and Father of all, who is above all, through all, and in all." That's the mystery of Scripture. It hasn't a thing to do with secular history. It is all salvation history. It has not a thing to do with history as the world teaches it.

You and I are experiencing history – secular history; and my history is known to any one who wants to investigate it. I wouldn't say that it is anything to write about. I was born in a simple little environment without any educational, social, financial background whatsoever. I am making a struggle, as all people make a struggle in the world: I have to pay rent and to buy food, and then to put the garments on the body. That's a struggle for every one. They seem to have no time for the Spirit. But the day is coming, all will have this experience, regardless of the struggle; and no one will be greater than the other, because every one is the same God the Father – the Father of the one and only Son, who is David.

So you know why we hyphenate the name "Judeo-Christian." Judaism is the foundation, and Christianity is its fulfillment. That is the fruit on the tree; that is the flower. Without that tree, it couldn't bear the fruit; so the whole thing is contained in that Old Testament, but it is adumbrated; it's a foreshadowing in a not-altogether conclusive or immediately evident way. When it happens, it's not what the world thought should happen. They are expecting some being to come from without and save them, but He doesn't come that way. He comes to us as "one unknown," yet one who in the most ineffable mystery lets the individual to whom He comes experience who He is, and you will never experience who He is until He awakes by the voice of His Son who is calling Him: "Rouse Thyself. Why sleepest Thou, O Lord? Awake! Do not cast us off forever," – as you read it in the 44th Psalm, the 23rd verse.

So as we are told in the 5th Chapter of John: "And the hour is coming when all those who are in the tomb will hear His voice," – the Son's voice – "and come forth."

The "tomb" is your own wonderful skull. You are not buried in any cemetery in this world. Let them build all the great mausoleums they want. That's man. It is big business. Let them do it; let them build it. But you are "buried" in your skull! That's where God is buried! And out of the Golgotha He will rise, and He will rise while you walk the earth. You will sleep this night without knowing you will be awakened by the call of the voice.

The "voice" is a vibration. It is a sound. And so, David will sound the call. It will be in tune with you if the hour is right; and then you will awake to find yourself completely entombed within your own skull. And without any assistance from without, you will push the base of your skull and come out, just like a child being born from the womb of woman, only this is now being "born from above" – not from below. When you come out, all the symbolism of Scripture will surround you. The witnesses will be there. There are three – and the infant wrapped in swaddling clothes, which is only the sign of your exit from that heavenly "womb." You are "born from above!"

And from then, you go to another scene, another scene, over a period of three and a half years, and your journey is then completed. You'll remain in this world long enough to tell of your experience – to tell of your own experience of God. And until God is experienced, you do not know Him. Let all the preachers do what they want; it's perfectly all right. They are sound asleep because God-in-them is sound asleep, and they are speculating. They are theorizing, based upon what they believe God ought to do. He should punish this one and punish that one; and they do not know every one punished is God being punished for His dream. He is dreaming the Dream of Life. And many dreams are like nightmares; whether they be waking dreams or the dreams of sleep, they are nightmares. But nevertheless, it's still God dreaming.

Who is dreaming when he wakes in the morning? We will say, "Well, I had a dream:" and you had a dream. "A horrible dream! I was," – and then he begins to describe it: but what is he saying? He is calling Him by the name of God. It was God who had the dream. When he wakes, "I am going to do so-and-so." Who is that saying, "I am going to do so-and-so?" That is God. There is nothing but God in the world. There is no room for any one in the world but God and His only begotten Son. And His Son is David. That's His Son.

Jesus is the Lord God Jehovah, and "David in the spirit called him 'my lord.'" That's the son calling him "my lord." Here is Jesus of Scripture – the awakened God. He's not asleep. Here is the one who first awoke in the world. But then he calls us "Brothers." He said, "Go unto my brothers and tell them I am ascending unto my Father," but he said, "I and my Father are one,"—"unto my God," and he also said, "My Father is your Father. My God is your God;"

and "I and my Father are one;" and my Father is He Whom you call "God."

Here the mystery begins to unfold. Until you actually experience it, you do not know how wonderful Scripture is. Man must experience Scripture before he can begin to understand how altogether wonderful it is. It's eternally true. From beginning to end, the whole thing is true, and it is not secular history. It's divine history.

So I share with you what I know from experience. I am no theorizing. I am not speculating. It happened to me – a simple man, as you are simple; and I did not for one moment suspect this was the mystery until it actually unfolded within me and I experienced it.

When someone who supposedly lived three thousand years ago calls me "Father," I know exactly that I am his father; there was no uncertainty as to this relationship. I am looking into the face of the most heavenly youth, and he was the one who called me from my profound sleep; and when I awoke, it was God awoke, for he is calling upon the Lord to awake: "Rouse Thyself. Why sleepest Thou, O Lord? Awake!" And then you awake as though you had never been awake. It's a peculiar, strange awaking that takes place in you. And now you see this heavenly, eternal being who is the Son of God; and because he is going to wake you, you will know that he is your son, and he will know that you are God.

So in the end, every one will awake, and everyone will be God! So it takes all of us to make the Lord. It's a compound unity – the word "Elohim." It is a plural word.

"In the beginning God," – that word is "Elohim." And "God said, Let us make man in our image." That word is "Elohim" – a compound unity: one made up of others. It takes all of us to make the one God. "Hear, O Israel, the Lord our God, the Lord is one," – not two.

So here, the only one who could ever rouse you and actually bring you from your profound sleep is your "son," whose name is David.

"I will tell of the decree of the Lord," said David. "He said unto me, Thou art my son. Today I have begotten thee."

And so we have confused it with Jesus, and Jesus is the Lord. He is the Lord speaking. He is the Lord who inspired the prophets to write what they did. And finding no one to fulfill it, He Himself came into the world and became man. He became you! His name is I AM. That's the Lord God Jehovah that we call "Jesus" in Scripture. That's I AM.

"Do you not realize," said Paul, "that Jesus Christ is in you?" Don't you know that He is in you? Are you looking for Him to come from without, when He is within you? Well, He is within. You cannot say, "I am," and point elsewhere. Whether you are in a frightful dream, you are aware. To be aware is saying, "I am." And you can't point on the outside of self when you say, "I am;" and "that is my name forever and forever." And that is the Lord Jesus in every being in the world.

But his Son plays such an important part – that Son called "David." You say he is the son of Jesse and "Jesse" means "I AM." The word "Jesse" means "Jehovah exists." It is any form of the verb "to be." In other words, I am. That is the Father of David.

And what I tell you I am telling you from experience. I am not the scholar who simply went through Scripture and combed it to bring forward this theory. It's not theory with me. I am not qualified to go through the Scriptures, knowing Greek, and knowing Latin, and knowing Aramaic, to do that. It has happened to me. It was all revelation. So let the scholars go on and try to find it. Let them go on. Until it's revealed to them, they do not know it.

Revealed truth cannot be actually, legally or – I would say – logically proven. It's all revealed. If it isn't revealed, well then speculate. And I am not speculating. I am telling you exactly Who-God-Is. And until you experience God, you do not know Him. And I am telling you from my own experience, you will experience God; and then you will know Him. And you'll know why we hyphenate the words "Judeo-Christian." It's one tree. The tree is Judaism; the fruit is Christianity. Christianity is simply the fulfillment of Judaism.

So here, he tells you: "I will not leave you desolate. I will come again." And then He becomes invisible. The story is told us in the pre-existence "before that the world was." And here, He becomes invisible, because He takes up His residence in us; and the darkest hour in the world, symbolized in Scripture as the three hours of darkness that descended – no. The darkest hour is when God became invisible. As He became invisible, he took up His residence in us; and man is looking for Him to come from without, and He cannot come from without. He will rise from within, but only at the call of His Son's voice.

So in the fullness of time, He sent forth the Spirit of His Son into our hearts, crying what? "Father." And if you hear it, then you respond. Responding is waking. And you begin to awake within yourself, to find yourself entombed within your own skull – completely sealed; but you have an innate wisdom. You know exactly what to do, for He prepared the way before He set forth. You know exactly what to do: you push the base of your skull, and it gives; and then you come out. And the symbolism surrounds you. You know exactly Who-You-Are – but not quite until the Son appears. At first, only the infant wrapped in swaddling clothes; and you are told in Scripture that's only a sign, like the sign on the top of the White House.

I ask the guard, "Is the President in residence?"

And he looks. If his insignia is flying, he will say, "Yes, he is in residence." If it's not flying, the President is not in residence.

If the little child is found wrapped in swaddling clothes, then I ask, "Is God born?"

"Yes, here is His sign."

"This shall be a sign unto you. You shall find a child wrapped in swaddling clothes and lying on the floor." When that sign is found, the question is asked, "Is God born?" Yes, here is the sign of His "birth." But when the child comes – not the little infant – when the Son comes, then you hear his voice. And the voice is the voice of God's Son, who is Christ.

Christ is the Son of God; and the "Anointed" means Christ and "Christ" means the "Anointed." And did he not say in the 89th Psalm: "I have anointed you with my holy oil?" Well, who is He speaking to? He is speaking to David. Did He not say in the 89th Psalm: "I have found David, and David has cried unto me, Thou art my Father, my God, and the Rock of my Salvation?" Did he not say in the Second Psalm, "Thou art my son??" Today I have begotten thee?"

All these words were inspired by the One Being whom we call "Jesus, the Lord." He inspired it through his prophets, and then Himself came down and took upon himself humanity. I am speaking of the Cosmic God – of the Cosmic Son. So He is buried in every child born of woman, but this is so unique He comes to us individually. He calls us, one by one, in season.

So tonight could be your call. It may be tomorrow night. I hope it is not in the distant future. But He will call all; and when you take off this garment, having been called and having seen the Son, you have taken it off for the last time. Until it actually happens to you, "death" is not death. "Death" is nothing more than simply leaving a room and entering another room, simply like the room you left – the same terrestrial world. With all the struggles you left behind you? You'll find them there. You are restored to life, not as a baby; no reincarnation. You are restored – a young man, a young woman, with not a thing missing. No need of anything to be added because nothing is missing; only you are young – about 20 years of age – to continue your journey in this world, to be confronted with all the problems that are here. Yes, and you marry there, too. You marry, and you grow old, and you "die" there, too. And if it hasn't yet happened, you are restored again to continue the journey until it happens. But it's going to happen to every being in the world. Not one can fail, because then God would fail, and that's impossible. So every one will awaken from the Dream of Life, and it doesn't end at that moment in time that your senses cease to register that being and we speak of him as "dead."

He is not dead. He's in a world just like this – restored to life in a world that is terrestrial, in a young, wholesome, healthy body, with all the problems that faced Him; because in the Resurrection of which I speak, there is no marriage, no male, no female – a completely transformed being, who is God. But until then, there is still sex – very much so in that world. But I am telling you what I know. I see them – my father, my mother, my brother – so many friends who are gone. I see them. They are not "gone" at all. They are in a world just like this, with all their struggles.

Therefore, I ask you to live so that your mind can store a past worthy of recall, for you taking that with you. Spend all of your time entertaining noble thoughts, for you are taking that with you into the world where you are headed, unless this thing happens before you make your departure from this world. If it does not happen before that, you are taking with you what you have actually entertained in this world. So live so that your mind can store a past worthy of recall, because you are going to actually take it right into your world to resolve it. And that is a part of your struggle.

But the day is coming; everyone is going to have the experience that I have just told you. No one can avoid it. If others have other ideas, let them have it. I wouldn't raise a finger to change it. They have all these-isms in the world; let them have it – all kinds of concepts of what God ought to have done. What God ought to have done, He has already done! The drama is over. The Resurrection is taking place. It didn't take place once and forever two thousand years ago. It is taking place at every moment of time, but not every one is articulate. Not every one is sent to tell it after it takes place. So they will go through their little exit from this world, not having told it to any one.

On the other hand, I was not restrained. I had to tell it, like Jeremiah: "If I say I will not mention it, or speak any more in His name, then there is in me, as it were, a burning fire, all shut up in my bones, and I am tired of holding it in, and I cannot." So I cannot restrain the impulse to talk about it. Others can. They are embarrassed even to bring it up; but I am not. It is part of my way of being, of thinking.

So I tell you, the voice spoken of is a real voice, but like all voices, you are now interpreting the vibration that is coming from my mouth. It is all vibration; and then you actually translate it within yourself, because it is simply impinging upon you. Well, this is the same voice. It's just like the tuning fork. And then it sets a tone, and the tone rouses you if you are in tune with that tone; and then you are actually hearing Him call you. He is calling you "Father." And

93

you awake to find standing before you this heavenly youth. And then, at that very moment, you know exactly who he is, and he is David, the sweet Psalmist David; and he is your "son," and you know he is your son. Memory has returned.

So "God became as we are, that we may be as He is." [Blake, from "There Is No Natural Religion"] Don't for one moment forget that. That is the great sacrifice. It was God Who "died."

"Unless I die, thou canst not live; but if I die, I shall arise again, and thou with me."

[Blake, from "Jerusalem"]

So it is God who is crucified on these garments. And the God-in-you, -- His name is "I AM." And when you hear the voice and you awake, who awakes? I awake. Who is waking? I am waking.

And who is His Son's name? I am telling you, His Son's name is David; but because he has been anointed with the holy oil, he is the Christ. "Thou art the Christ, the Son of the Living God."

In the Old Testament, the word "Christ" is not used, but the word "Messiah" is. He is the Messiah, for the Messiah simply means the "anointed one." And the "Messiah" is used only in the Book of John in the New Testament. He does speak of the Christ as the Messiah, and it is not Jesus. Jesus is the Lord.

Yet the Son could say, "I and my Father are one." So "When you see me, you see the Father." He is the image of the Father.

You are told, "It does not yet appear what we shall be, but we know that when he appears, we shall be like Him."

I am telling you that is exactly what is going to happen. Forget the mask that you are now wearing. Behind that mask is the Ancient

94

of Days, the Eternal One who is the Lord God Jehovah. And David is the image of the Lord God Jehovah. He is the Eternal Youth, and the Lord is the Ancient of Days, without beginning, without end.

So when you dwell tonight on it, treat it seriously. What I have told you this night is true. I haven't speculated. I haven't turned to any one for support. I was never taught it. It's in the Bible, but I never saw it in the Bible until I experienced it. That is why I can tell you, until God is experienced, you do not know God. One must experience God to know Him. He is not deaf; you don't have to scream to have Him hear you. You need not utter anything. Your simple thought is heard because who is hearing it? "I AM." That's God.

The way they have all these prayers – Let us pray. They put on all these microphones and just blast the whole thing out calling upon God to hear them. That's not God. God is within you. And the God – the only Living God – is your own wonderful human imagination. When you say, "I am," that is God!

"By Him all things were made, and without Him was not anything made that was made." In His dream, naturally He makes mistakes. God makes mistakes? There is only one that can make a mistake, and that is God. There is only one that can make anything, and that's God. For in a nightmare, well can you blame the man if he has the most horrible nightmare? You would console him in the morning if he told you of some horrible dream. You wouldn't condemn him. Well now, this is a waking dream; but it is still a dream.

So in the end, everything is forgiven. Every being in the world is forgiven, for there is only God who did it all! So the story is the Father and His Son, and there is no other being in the world. And you are the Father, and His Son is your son. And if he can say, "I and my Father are one," then he can say of you, "I and my Father are one."

When you look into the face and you see that beauty – you cannot describe the beauty of David. No artist could paint it. He is the image of you. But no one knows it, only the mask that you wear, for He is the image of the Invisible You, and He bears the express image of your Person. But your Person is not the thing that you "wear" as a mask. You are the Immortal Being. You are the Eternal Being.

When you hear it and you really believe it, you will see why this Book of 66 books is really a library. When you have a Bible of both the Old and the New under one cover, you have a library. Very few homes have 66 books in them. If they have a Bible, they have 66 books, and they the greatest library in the world in having the Bible. And one is the Old; the other is the New. One foreshadows, and the other tells you how it is fulfilled. But even though it is fulfilled, it still remains a mystery to those who have not experienced it. So I tell you, He comes to us as One Unknown, yet one who in the most wonderful manner lets you experience Who-He-Is. And when you experience Who-He-Is, it's your Self. That is God!

What a sacrifice! He literally became as I am, that I may be as He is. And that is true of every child born of woman.

Now, if you enjoy other things, enjoy them; but you will not in Eternity undo what I have told you. Not in Eternity will you disprove it, may I tell you? All the wisdom of the world cannot disprove what I have told you tonight. You may rise in opposition, and I wouldn't bat an eye to argue with you, for I know what I have experienced. So let them argue. I will not argue.

They said he was silent. "You will not speak to me." Why argue the point? "So you were a king. The world says so."

"It's the Father's good pleasure to give me the Kingdom." Well, if He is going to give me the Kingdom, He is going to give me Himself, for He is the Kingdom. Read it in the 12th Chapter of Luke, the 32nd earn it; it's unmerited; it's grace – "to give you the kingdom." And when He succeeds in giving me the Kingdom, He succeeds in giving me Himself, for He is the Kingdom.

The Kingdom is not a realm, as the world teaches. It is God! – the character that is God, that is perfect; so wherever you are, clothed in that Perfect Character, everything is perfect. Everything is alive. Nothing is dead, and nothing is imperfect. Wherever you are after you have received the gift, you could walk through the Petrified Forest, and it would all suddenly burst into blossom. Walk through the desert, and the desert will bloom. Come into any place where they are imperfectly formed – eyes that are missing out of their sockets will come out of the Nowhere and fill the empty sockets, and they will be perfect. Arms missing? No, not in your presence when you receive the Kingdom. In the presence of You, the Perfect Man, nothing can remain imperfect; but you don't do it out of compassion. You don't even do anything. Your very presence does it! So no matter where you are – go down into hell, "hell" is transformed into heaven. Wherever you are is perfect, because are now the King. You have received the Kingdom. I am telling you from my own experience. You walk into a world, and the world is instantly transformed to be in harmony with the Perfection that is springing within you.

So I tell you, "It is your Father's good pleasure to give you the Kingdom." That is a wonderful way of telling you it is your Father's good pleasure to give you Himself! That's how the Evangelist told it in the Book of Luke: "It is your Father's good pleasure to give you Himself." And your Father is God. And God is Jesus. Jesus is the Lord. There is no other God! But He's a father, and because He's a father, He has a son. And I am telling you, in spite of the whole vast

97

world, that Son is David, our sweet Psalmist of Biblical fame. And he will stand before you, and he too will call you "my Lord, my Father, the Rock of my Salvation."

Now let us go into the silence.

Good, now are there any questions please? Any questions?

A gentleman asks, "Can I have two for the price of one?

Neville- "Yes".

Question- "In any of Blake's writings can you tell whether or not he had received the promise?

Neville- "As far as I am concerned meeting Blake, as I have met him in this wonderful risen world, Blake had everything described in scripture. When you meet him he is one of the most majestic creatures that you could meet.

Let me quote speaking of tonights lecture, it's taken from his book Urizen (The [First] Book of Urizen). I think it's the seventh chapter and, "The dead heard the voice of the child and began to awake from sleep. All things heard the voice of the child and began to awake to life."

So when God became Man he transformed death into sleep. God is Infinite Mercy and man is dead. God, in becoming Man, made Man a living soul. He transformed death into sleep and then in the dream he transformed the dream himself into Himself and raises him as Himself.

Oh know, Blake had it. But You've got to read like all things, when Blake, read between the lines because as he said to the Reverend (Trustler) that criticized him. The Reverend said to him, "You know You need someone to elucidate Your ideas."

Blake said is that so, "But you ought to know that What is Grand is necessarily obscure to Weak men. That which can be made Explicit to the Idiot is not worth my care. The wisest of the Ancients considered what is not too Explicit as the fittest for Instruction because it rouses the faculties to act."

Something that anyone can see, even the idiot, well then it isn't worth my care. So he told in the way he did, causing you to dig for it. You have to dig for it. But Blake to me is one of the giants, spiritual giants of the world.

I've had people say to me, "why didn't he have money?" Who wants money when you had what Blake had? All the money in the world today couldn't buy one single copy that is at Yale. He left behind him five copies of Jerusalem, only one he colored. It is now in Yale University under lock and key. When Blake sold it, I think he sold it for one hundred guineas. That would be equivalent to five hundred dollars when Blake sold it. You couldn't buy that copy today no matter what sort of money you brought for it. You couldn't buy it, it's the only copy in the world. He left five copies, four were not colored. This is the only colored copy that Blake left behind him. It's priceless.

(audio lecture title is "GOD IS KNOWN BY EXPERIENCE")

Neville (02-02-1968)

YOUR HUSBAND

Probably one of the most misunderstood verses in the Bible is recorded in the 3rd chapter of Genesis, the 16th verse: "The Lord said to the woman, 'I will greatly multiply your sorrow and in pain you shall bring forth children, yet your desire shall be for your husband and he shall rule over you."

In this fabulous world of ours, many accept this statement literally and believe that the children spoken of here come from the womb of woman and the male is the husband and ruler; however in the 54th chapter of Isaiah, you are told: "Your Maker is your husband, the Lord of hosts is his name."

Humanity (male and female) is God's emanation, yet his wife, 'til the sleep of death is past. Regardless of your sex you are the woman the Lord spoke to in this 3rd chapter of Genesis. Your children are not those brought forth from the womb of woman, but from your imagination! Your husband (the Lord of hosts) will sire every idea you fall in love with, no matter how horrible it may be. And being protean, God has the power to play every part and assume every shape in the world.

Let us take a vivid example. When Hitler and his Third Reich came into power, unnumbered happily married women who loved their husbands and children fell in love with the concept of a superior race - a Germanic race who would enslave humanity. And as the idea caught fire in their minds, these women had an affair with Hitler in their dreams. It was not the person, Hitler, that they had union with, but the state he personified - just as you, if you are completely honest with yourself, have fallen in love with an idea (a state) and met its personification in soft Beulah's night and had an affair. Then in the morning you have looked at your husband and experienced pain, for not understanding the mystery of Christ, you thought you had an affair with a person. But the man involved could have been playing cards, getting drunk, or sound asleep in his own bed and be completely oblivious to you as a person. He was merely the personification of a state which you accepted and yielded to in soft Beulah's night, but by that act you multiplied and replenished the earth with the same idea, the same state!

It is impossible to kill an idea, for the moment an idea is accepted, it is conceived and the earth replenished. You cannot kill a state by cutting off the occupant's head, shooting [him], or putting the man in prison. The occupant may depart, but the state remains for anyone to fall in love with. These are false gods, which will multiply your pain and cause you to go through literal hell as you bring forth these ideas as your children.

Look into your own mind, and if you are perfectly honest with yourself you will remember having had union with someone other than your mate in this world, not knowing he (or she) was only a state of consciousness personified. You do not have union with the person, but the state the person represents, for your Maker is your husband who is playing the part of the person.

If this night you really believe what I teach and fall in love with it, you may find yourself in soft Beulah's night having union with the being who personifies it. You may think it is with the personification called Neville, but it is union with the state. As Neville I may be entertaining someone at my home, enjoying a lovely drink, or reading the Bible as I do all through the day, and be totally oblivious of you and what you are doing. If you really believe what I say, accept it, and live by it, it is quite possible and highly probable that you will have union with this idea. And although he may wear my face, you are having union with God your Father, who is your own wonderful I Amness.

The Bible recognizes only one source, only one cause of all things. That one source is God, who - as a protean being - plays all the parts in history. He animates you, as you are his wife. And when you fall in love with something other than the true God and seek false gods, your sorrow is multiplied, and in pain you bring forth your children.

I recall a friend of mine who has now departed this world. Born in Boston to a very poor family, she hungered for the glamour of the theatrical life. Although she danced as one with two left feet, her mother brought her to New York City, where George M. Cohan was casting a show. Hiring a young dancer from Denmark, he was given the right to pick the girls for his chorus. Although this girl could not dance he chose her, and within a year they were married. This marriage produced three beautiful children.

The lovely girl had a desire for glamour, for pomp and circumstance, so during soft Beulah's night she had affair after affair after affair with everyone from the Pope to the Prince of Wales, thereby perpetuating the belief in pomp and circumstance. Now, don't blame the Pope, for he didn't know her - or the Prince of Wales, as they only personified the state she desired to express. She loved seeing the Pope being carried on the back of strong, strapping men, extending his hand to be kissed. Wanting to be part of that world, she was always having union with those who personified it.

Now, if you are Catholic you may be shocked, but don't think the Pope or the Prince of Wales is exempt from this action, as it is part of the great drama in which we all are cast. She has played her part and spent the last fifteen years of her life as a wino, giving her body to anyone for a bottle of wine. She wedded herself to a false god and greatly multiplied her sorrows. In pain she brought forth the children of her strange gods, yet her desire remained for her husband. God is your husband - your center and the very core of your being. No matter what you do, you are still seeking God. So while she was seeking wine for the last fifteen years of her life here, she was still seeking - not her husband, who came from Denmark, but her true husband, her Maker, who is the Lord of Hosts, the Father of the child!

In the 2nd chapter of Paul's 1st Letter to Timothy, the statement is made: "Woman is saved by the birth of children." This is false. The footnote in the Revised Standard Version gives you the Greek, and the true translation as: "by the birth of the child." It's not by bearing children (all these ideas) that one is saved, but by bearing the child! When you give yourself completely over to the gospel story you are ready, and God will assume the mask of the one who is expressing it at the moment. Then you will have union with that being and bear the child!

So when you have these dreams, don't feel strange and condemn yourself. Everyone has had similar experiences. If you resist the union in dream it is because the idea represented there is foreign to you; but when your desire is something you really want to make alive and it is expressed - be it good, bad, or indifferent - you will have union with it and feel no shame, in spite of the whole vast world looking on, for this is the world in which we live.

In the 9th chapter of Luke, Jesus asked his disciples: "Who do people say that I am?" And they answered: "John the Baptist, or Elijah, or one of the risen prophets." Then he turned to them and asked: "But who do you say that I am?" Peter then became the spokesman for the group and said: "You are the Christ of God." Commanding them to tell no one, he said: "The Son of man must suffer and be rejected by the elders, the chief priests, and the scribes. He must be killed, but on the third day he will rise again."

Jesus did not deny Peter's confession, but declined to make it public until he had reinterpreted the popular messianic concept in terms of his own experience. From time to time, one who has experienced the true story of salvation comes into the world and tells it. Then all the elders, scribes, and priests, who carry on the traditions of men, will deny it. This is eternally so; that is why he declined to make it public. The scribes, teaching the traditions of men, claim Christ is coming from without - but I tell you he comes from within! I tell you that God became your very "self" that you may become God.

Playing all the parts, God lets you go anywhere and meet anyone. And when you fall in love with a state, he will play the part of the state expressed, and in soft Beulah's night you will have an affair. He will play the part of a Stalin or a Hitler, a Pope or a prince, if you are in love with the state of consciousness. And you will give yourself willingly to him, thereby multiplying and perpetuating that state in the world. In the morning you may be ashamed of your act when you face the one who bears your name (or whose name you now bear), but at the time you had no choice in the matter, for God in you - who is your husband and Maker - played the part. Being protean, if you meet a dog or cat, see a bird or fish in your dreams, it is because God is playing their parts. No matter what the animal, remember: God is playing its part in order for you to become one, for in the end he will leave all others and cleave to you, his wife, until you become one being, one body, one Spirit, one hope, one God and Father of all.

Now let me share a letter I have been waiting to receive since the 15th of December. This lady's home is in a small, rustic canyon. One day she spent the afternoon in Los Angeles with a casual acquaintance, and had just returned home, when she heard the phone ringing. She was being called by the casual friend, who appeared to be quite distressed. Inviting the lady to join her for dinner, she returned to Los Angeles, where the lady asked her to spend the night. It seemed strange to her to agree, but after spending several hours reading aloud to the lady, they retired and she fell asleep. Then she said: "At 3:30 in the morning a peculiar, cold wind caused me to awake. The room contained an eerie light, when out of nowhere my two brothers - whom I haven't seen in over forty years - appeared, along with my landlord, who is like a brother to me. The three take their positions, two at my feet and one at my head. Picking up an infant wrapped in swaddling clothes, my older brother said: "She is too old to have a baby." Then he placed it in my arms, and as I looked at the child I began to smile. The child then responded and extended its arms toward me, when I awoke on the bed."

Then she continues: "About five months later, I saw a young boy in his teens coming toward me out of the canyons. He had blond hair and blue eyes, and as I looked at him I knew he was David. Passing me, he headed for the sea, and I watched until he was out of sight. I didn't have to ask him: 'Whose son are you?' because I knew he was mine.

"Four months later, again at 3:30 in the morning, I was awakened by the sound of an earthquake, followed by a loud bomb. Suddenly my entire being was broken from top to bottom. I felt myself outside of my body, looking at it as though I were another. The left shoulder had fallen a bit and when I returned to the body moments later, I felt pain on the left side. Now I await the fourth vision, which is the descent of the dove."

I can't tell you my thrill when I look over this audience and see how many are awakening. In the 9th chapter of Luke, it is said:

"Truly, truly I say unto you, there are some here who will not taste of death until they have seen the kingdom of God." The babe is the key to that kingdom! When Simeon held the child in his arms, he said: "Now Lord let thy servant depart in peace, for my eyes have seen the salvation of Israel." So to have held the child is to have witnessed the kingdom of God. This kingdom is a character, an entirely different concept of creative power- not a place in time or space! And you are that character when you are one with your creative power, there to create what you want!

The child is a symbol of your entrance, and there are some standing here who will not experience the phenomenon that men call death before experiencing the kingdom of God! Although this audience can be counted on your fingers, there are so many here who have experienced the truth and so many on the verge of it, that my joy is boundless; for if you owned the entire world and were not awake, what would it matter! No matter how wealthy you are here, the day will come when you will depart to discover that you have left your billions behind. You will be in a body like this one, only incredibly young, in a terrestrial world just like this to continue to have blind unions with strange gods, not knowing that your Maker is your husband - the Lord of hosts is his name.

The search for your real husband is on! You have gone into strange lands and had union with strange states personified by man. Falling in love with a state, its personification always confronts you in a dream, the mask being worn by your husband, who did it without the person's consent or knowledge. As an innocent bystander, the person will never know he was used. He was simply the personification of certain beliefs which inflamed your mind, and confronted by your real husband - who is the Lord of hosts - you submitted to them.

All of the characters in scripture are played by God. It is He who plays the part of the angel in the story of Abraham and Sarah. Read it carefully and you will notice that the voice changes from that of an angel to the voice of God. When Abraham is told: "Your wife will have a son," Sarah laughed because they were both so old and it had long ceased to be with her after the manner of women. Now, the child promised to the Sarah in everyone is the child of which I speak. You are God's emanation and he has promised that, in spite of your age, you will have a son. Blake put is so beautifully when he said:

"Whom God has afflicted for secret ends,

he comforts and heals and calls them friend."

Although you go astray, following false gods, false beliefs, God will always bring you back; but you will suffer, for you must experience the messianic pains of childbearing. Then one day you will find the one husband and fall in love with his promise. And you will meet someone who personifies salvation's story and have union with him. But he will be totally unaware of the fact that you so fell in love with the idea that he sponsors, and will never know of your experience unless you tell him.

Having been sent from on high to tell you who "I AM," you may believe me or resent my message; but I, a person called Neville, am totally unaware, totally innocent of anything that happens to you in your dreams. Leading you now toward what you believe in, your husband will assume my mask and play the role I personify in your dream. Change your beliefs and he will assume another mask and play that part, as you multiply and replenish the earth with ideas of which you are in love!

Don't think that communism or democracy can be destroyed. If I believe in democracy as a form of government, it is an idea. You can kill me, but you can never kill the ideas I entertain. This morning's paper tells of those who have been stealing from the government. Why should we be taken aback when we see dishonesty among officials? From the very beginning they are encouraged by example to make what gain they can from their positions. Seeing what their superiors did and got away with, they have union with the idea and awaken to that state of consciousness. Then they suffer, for this is bearing the children of a false god.

Examine your thoughts. Are they ones you want to bear in this world? Are they calling forth false gods? False ideas? If so, "I will multiply your pain in childbearing, yet your desire shall be for your husband." The Lord is always ruling, always willing to assume any role and play it for you as he leads you towards himself. And when you meet the true God you will discover that you were the actor all along, for you and He will be One. Blake said it so beautifully:

"Joy and woe have woven fine

a garment for my Soul divine."

In Blake's "Marriage of Heaven and Hell," he gave us this true revelation: "God only acts and Is in existing Beings or men." Let this thought burn itself into your mind. God is a thought in action! Imagine something and God is acting! God only acts and is. Every moment in time, whether in this the waking world or the world of sleep, God is and only God acts! At night in dream, God plays the part of the state you are attached to at the moment or falling in love with. If you like the state, God will assume its personification and you will yield to become one with him. Then in the morning you will awaken with the memory of what happened and multiply your world with the idea. You will give your life, if necessary, to get your idea over to the world, even though it is the most nonsensical thing possible. This you will continue to do until the child is born and your journey is over.

In the 16th chapter of John, we are told: "When a woman is in labor with all the pain that possesses her it is only because the hour has come. But after the child is delivered she no longer remembers the anguish, for joy that a child has been born into the world." Life consists of the children you have borne and are bearing, and life is very painful. You must pay rent or bear the consequences. You must buy food or go hungry. You must buy clothes or be embarrassed. You must pay taxes, drink water, and breathe air. Man has discovered how to tax the water you drink, but as yet has not found a way to tax the air you breathe. Give him time and I'm sure he will! We are already taxed to the bursting point. You go to work, and at the end of the year you pay taxes to someone who doesn't exist! We call him "Uncle Sam," but he is invisible! There is no Uncle Sam, yet he puts his hands in our pockets and takes from us what we could spend in a far better way than he does. So you see: that 3rd chapter, the 16th verse of Genesis is true: "I will greatly multiply your pain in child bearing." If you entertain the idea of war or famine, fame or fortune, you shall bring forth their children and your pain will be multiplied in child bearing, yet your desire will be for your husband who is the Lord, your Maker.

Even though you are not aware of it now, your husband is suffering with you and will continue to, until you hear the gospel with understanding and believe the incredible story that God actually became you that you could become God the Father. Then to prove that God actually gave himself to you, you will see his only son, David, and - like the lady - you will not have to ask: "Whose son are you?" You will know he is your son, and he will know that regardless of your sex here, you are his Father. When that experience is yours, you will stop giving yourself to false gods and obey your husband by fulfilling the divine formula of salvation.

Now let us go into the silence.

Neville (01-07-1969)

YOUR MAKER

Your maker is your husband, the Lord of Hosts is his name. By him all things are made, and although he is an unseen activity within you, without him is not anything made that is made. I ask you, as Paul asked the Corinthians, to examine yourselves to see if you are holding to your faith. To test yourselves. Do you not realize that Jesus Chris is in you? - unless, of course, you fail to meet the test. I tell you: Jesus Christ is a power within you, which you must find and test. Paul didn't say that Jesus Christ made only the good, but everything - be it good, bad, or indifferent. And Blake said: "I know of no other Christianity and of no other gospel than the liberty both of body and mind to exercise the divine arts of Imagination. Imagination, the real and external world into which we will live [sic] when these vegetable, mortal bodies are no more. The apostles knew of no other gospel."

Now, John Mills defines causation as the assemblage of phenomena, which occurring, some other phenomena commence to appear in the world. In other words, causation is the assemblage of an imaginal state implying the fulfillment of desire, which feeling will activate and produce in the world. And H. G. Wells put it this way: "Throughout the ages, life is nothing more than a continuing solution to a continuous synthetic problem," How many times have you said to yourself: if I only had x-number of dollars I could live comfortably, then inflation appears and you are forced to use your creative power to construct an imaginal solution to your new problem.

Webster defines a synthetic body as the compiling of separate elements which produce a new form. In this world you will never find permanency, for something will penetrate the state you are now occupying and force you to conceive a new solution. This is how it is done. Do not judge the problem - rather ask yourself what its solution would be. Suppose you were in jail. The solution would be to be out of jail, pardoned, and sleeping in your own home. So, while still confronted with the problem, and lying on your cot in jail, you would close your eyes to the cell and feel you are now home, as a free man. Then fall asleep allowing the maker of all things to create that which will be seen out of that which does not appear.

A few years ago, a lady in my San Francisco audience rose and said: "My brother is in the army. I do not know what he did to cause his punishment, but he has been sentenced to six months of hard labor, and I want him set free." After establishing the fact that he would go to her apartment if he were free, I urged her to imagine he was there now. That night, this lady imagined hearing the doorbell ring. Rushing down the stairs, she opened the door to find her brother standing there, a free man. She rehearsed that scene over and over again until it seemed natural to her. One week later, while sitting in her apartment, the doorbell rang. She ran downstairs, opened the door, and embraced her brother - who told her he was honorably discharged. Who brought the action against him, or who discharged him I do not know. I only know the brother did not run away from the punishment, for the lady came to my meeting the next Sunday and shared her story with all who were there. Now, if she hadn't known this principle and put it into practice, she would have remained at home, angry and frustrated for six months until her brother was released.

All things are made by your imagination, for without imagining, nothing is made. Imagination is not limited to this level of consciousness. There are levels and levels of imagination, as your dreams and visions prove. This world is sustained by Divine Imagining, which is human imagining on a higher level. Our imagination is keyed low, but we are called upon to exercise this power, to examine ourselves to see if we are keeping our faith. On this level, faith is not complete until, through experiment, it becomes experience. Experiment with this statement: "Whatever you desire, believe you have received it and you will." (Mark 11) If faith is not complete until, through experiment it becomes experience, you must take an unseen objective and place it in an assemblage of mental states which would imply its fulfillment. Then this desire must be activated by entering into its center, feeling its reality, and walking in the faith that it will happen. I tell you: in a way you could not devise, what you have assumed will come into your world.

You do not have to construct a bridge of incident to walk across; you simply move toward the fulfillment of what you have already prepared for yourself. Then fulfill another desire the same way, and when it appears you will know exactly what to do when confronted with any problem. You will simply turn your back upon it by constructing an imaginal scene which would imply the fulfillment of its solution. Activate it and let it come into being.

Unfortunately it is so easy to make the acceptance of Christianity a substitute for living by it. In New York City alone there are more than one million people on relief, and I dare say 90 per cent of them claim to be Christians, yet do not know the meaning of Christianity. Christ is not on the outside, but within you. And when He appears you will be like him. That is what we are promised in the Book of John. Will you see someone on the outside who looks like you? No! Christ is in you, and he makes all things. Test him and you will discover he is your imagination!

When I was a boy I lived in Barbados. Unschooled, with no background whatsoever, I dreamed of coming to America. I became so enamored with the idea, that at the age of 17 my parents put me on a boat to America with $600 in my pocket. They thought I would come back once the money was gone, but I wanted to live in America so badly I had to come and make it my home.

Are you willing to become enamored over a desire that much? Are you willing to fall in love with its fulfillment that you imagine it is yours now? If so, I promise you it will outpicture itself in your world. And when it does, you will have found Christ, for the words of scripture: "By him all things are made and without him is not anything made that is made," are false.

When you test your imagination you will find He who produced your desire and the Maker of all things! I have tested him numberless times. I have taught this principle to others who have tested him and shared their experiences with me. Now I know who Jesus Christ really is. The words, "Unless you believe that I am he, you will die in your sins," are not spoken on the outside, but on the inside. Now wearing a garment of flesh, my words appear to be coming from without, and one day I will seem to die and become a historical fact. But I am not speaking as an outer man. I am speaking as the true Jesus Christ, who comes in every individual by unfolding his story as recorded in scripture. There is only one story, and only one being to play the part. That being is God. It is he alone who acts and is in all things.

When the Old Testament fulfills itself in you - an individual - you will not be a spectator observing the drama, but the central actor. And, knowing it is God alone who acts, you know you are He. And when you tell your story, those who hear you will see the garment of flesh you wear, and think you have a devil and are blaspheming the name of God. But, knowing your father is he who men call God - you know your father, while men know not their God.

While wearing a garment of flesh, I know my origin and destiny, for scripture has unfolded itself in me. Many who hear my confession are not expecting this kind of revelation, so they shut me out as one who blasphemes God's name. But the words of scripture are spoken from within. This statement is one you are saying to yourself: "Unless I believe that I am he, I will die in my sins." To sin is to miss your desire. If you do not believe you are its creator, you are missing your mark. You must believe, to achieve! You must assume you already are the person you want to be, in order to become it. Although your assumption is denied by reason and your senses, if you will persist in your assumption, it will harden into fact. This is how something is made out of that which does not appear.

Knowing what you want, assume your desire is already fulfilled by imagining a circle of friends are congratulating you. Fall asleep knowing that those who would empathize with you have already witnessed your good fortune. Knowing you have put the fulfillment of your desire in motion, walk confident that what you are assuming is true. And when it happens, share your experience with others, in the hope that they will try it and it will work for them. It does not matter to me what others think, for I have found my Father - the one the world worships and calls God - to be my own wonderful human imagination!

People buy pictures of Jesus and hang them on the wall to bow before, yet the pictures are so unlike the artist who painted them. When Christ appears, you will be like him. This I know from experience. When Christ appeared in me, I was the one playing his part. Since only God acts and is in all men, God puts himself into the central role and unfolds the eternal drama in each individual, who then knows that he is God.

Last year I gave ten lectures in San Francisco. Just before the first meeting a lady told me she thought I was the greatest teacher of truth in the world. I thanked her and began my lecture by stating that man is all imagination and God is man. That the eternal body of man is the imagination, and that is God Himself. Then I told the story of a lady who found herself sitting in a chair in a very large room, when a self-propelled carriage appeared. The door opened and I stepped out, wearing a cape and carrying a briefcase. Personifying sheer power, I entered the room and began to proclaim the power of God. As she looked at me, she said to herself: "That is Neville, and yet it is God." Without giving her any sign of recognition, I finished my proclamation, turned, and - as though by appointment - the carriage appeared, I entered it, and vanished.

I continued by telling everyone that life itself is a glorious play, which was conceived by God, directed by God, and every part is being played by God. That this world is like a glorious poem, which exists not for itself, but for the one who conceived it. Falling in love with the world God had conceived, He wanted all of the characters to exist for themselves. But, finding no one to play the parts, God died to his true identity in order to take upon himself the limitation of the characters in his play. Now playing the part of every individual, God experiences all of the tribulations of being man, until He awakens in the character He is playing. I know I am Neville, a character in the play, but I also know I am God. This lady, who only a few minutes before had told me I was the greatest truth teacher in the world, was so shocked she never came back to the other lectures. She had expected me to conform to her little concept of God and I did not. Instead, I boldly proclaimed that we were all God, even though we are not all aware of it. Unless the story told in the gospels concerning Jesus Christ awakens and unfolds in the individual, that individual does not know that he is the Christ.

Paul found Christ to be his human imagination and urged everyone to test himself. Like Paul, I urge you to test your human imagination. You do not need the money or the time to go anywhere in your imagination, yet you can put yourself there, just as though you had made the trip. If you do, and your circumstances change so that the money and the time appears, allowing you to go, have you not found Jesus Christ to be your imagination? This is what scripture teaches, but man has personified the story and made Jesus Christ into a little idol to bow before, when the true God is the human imagination. All things are made by the human imagination. Imagine something that is not now a fact. Persist in your imaginal act, and when it becomes a fact, you have found God. And once you have found him, never let him go!

At the end of the drama it is said that one who knew Jesus betrayed him. Now, in order to betray someone, you must know his secret! So the one who knows the secret betrays him. That one is self! God is self-revealed. Unless God reveals himself to you, how will you ever know him? Turning to those who did not know him, Jesus said: "Now that you have found me, do not let me go, but let all these go." Let every belief of a power on the outside go, but do not let the belief in your powerful imagination go - for truth is within you. When you find the Maker in yourself, then no matter what arguments the priesthoods may give, do not believe them, for the Christ you seek is the human imagination.

Tomorrow you may forget and be penetrated by rumors which disturb your body and cause you to suffer. When this happens you must reestablish your harmony by imagining things are as you desire them to be. Living in this wonderful world, we cannot stop the penetration. To perceive another, that other must first penetrate your brain; therefore, he is within you as well as on the outside and independent of your perception. Cities, mountains, rivers and streams, must first penetrate your brain for you to be aware of them.

At that moment of awareness they are within you, even though they still maintain a certain independence of your perception and are without. Treat this inner penetration seriously and you will discover all you need to do is adjust your thinking. That you are all imagination and must be wherever you think you are. If you want to contact a friend, simply adjust yourself to his community by making there - here, and then - now. Visit him in his home by penetrating it within yourself. Give him your message and see his eyes light up with the pleasure of your words.

If God is in you, is there any place where God is not? And if there is no place where imagination is not, where would you go to be where you want to be? If everything penetrates you, then you must choose what you want and adjust yourself into the feeling that you are already there. You will know you have arrived when you view the world from there.

Motion can be detected only by a change of position relative to another object. While physically sitting in a chair you appear not to move, but because everything penetrates you, by a mental adjustment you can think from the awareness of being the person you want to be. How will you know you have changed? By the expression on the faces of your friends. If they now see the new you, then you have moved. So let them look at you until their faces tell you they are seeing that which you are assuming is true.

There must always be a frame of reference from which you move. Your frame is your friends, who would know of any change in your life. If I died, motion would be detected, as one friend would call another, who would call another, and finally dozens of people would know that Neville had died. If, on the other hand, I became a millionaire, that same chain reaction would occur.

After assuming you are now what you want to be, make your friends your frame of reference by hearing them congratulate you. Feel the reality of their actions. Relax in the peace of knowing it is done. And when it comes to pass, you have found Christ, for it is He who makes all things and without him is not a thing made that is made. You made your life change by finding Christ to be your imagination!

I tell you: God became you, with all of your weakness and limitations, that you may become Imagination. Becoming our imagination, God exists in us and we in him. Our eternal body is the imagination, and that is God Himself. And God alone acts! He can act the part of the fool, or the king, the poor, or the rich man. Every desire is a state. Move into your desire, and God will play that part - as you! If you desire riches, yet do not know this power, you will remain poor because you are looking for a God on the outside, trying to coerce him into giving you wealth for acquiring merit. You can spend your life acquiring merit and be so good the world will think you are wonderful, yet remain poor. Man must seek and find his true identity within himself, for he and he alone is the revealer and maker of everything in this world.

I have never seen Neville do anything. I was never a spectator, but the actor playing the part. Now wearing this garment of decay, called Neville, when I tell my story people are shocked. They think I am blasphemous by making these bold claims, yet I can no more deny my mystical experiences than I can deny the simplest evidence of my senses. I know what I ate tonight, yet its memory is not as vivid to me as my experiences of scripture. So I say to all: the one who makes everything is the human imagination. This may seem cruel to one who is now experiencing pain, but it is true. I have suffered. I have known physical pain. Even though I may say I caught the flu, I know I caught it within me. I read the paper where I learned that 50 per cent of the people had the flu, and - becoming a statistic - I made it fifty-one. I have experienced its aches and pains, and learned a lesson. Now I know that even though I have experienced the drama of Jesus Christ, I am still subject to everything man is subject to. I know that I cannot point to any other cause other than my own imagination, as cause cannot come from the outside. If I am in pain, the cause is mine. We are told in Galatians that God - your imagination - is not mocked. That as you sow, so shall you reap. "See yonder fields? The sesame was sesame, the corn was corn, the silence and the darkness knew, and so is a man's fate born."

So I repeat: Causation is the assemblage of mental states, which occurring produces that which the assemblage implies. Assemble a mental state which implies you are now what you want to be. Enter into that state. Remain there until you become one with it by performing inner acts as though they were outer ones. Continue to do so and watch, for your outer world will change as these inner acts become facts in your world. And don't think you will ever find a stopping place. No state you have ever created will endure unmoved, undisturbed, forever - because every moment of time you are being penetrated. Your idea of perfection and harmony today will be disturbed tomorrow, forcing you to use your talent to construct an imaginal change.

Your departure from this world will be so only to those who cannot follow you into another section of the same world. There you will continue to imagine, until the gospel story repeats itself in you. It will, for it is the story of God awakening and being born in man. Where God is not in man as his human imagination, the story could not be repeated. But when it erupts and Christ unfolds within the individual, he leaves a section of time to enter an entirely new age called the kingdom of God.

You can prove you are all imagination if you believe it, for you live by your beliefs. Lip service is not enough. Belief must become alive. Do you really believe your imagination makes all things? Then test yourself and see. When confronted with any problem, immediately construct an imaginal solution. Enter into that image and abide in its truth. Always remember who the maker is, for he makes things out of that which does not appear. He is like quicksilver, but you can test him best in a daydream.

Fawcett said: "Divine imagining is like pure imagining in ourselves. It lives in the very depth of our soul underlining all of our faculties, including perception, but streams into our surface mind least disguised in the form of creative fantasy." All dreams proceed from God whether they be in the day, or night. Everything is preceded by a dream, called an imaginal act!

Take me seriously and test the maker in you. "Examine yourselves to see if you are holding to your faith. Test yourselves. Do you not realize that Jesus Christ is in you? Unless, indeed, you fail to meet the test." (II Corinthians 13) I hope you will find out that you have not failed!

Now let us go into the silence.

Neville (1953)

YOUR SUPREME DOMINION

As you have been told, this morning's subject is "Your Supreme Dominion". As a man does not possess it or he does not know that he possesses it for he certainly is not exercising it. As we read in the very first chapter of the Book of Genesis, "And God made man in His own image, in the image of God made He him. He made them male and female, and God blessed them." And God said unto them, "Be fruitful and multiply and replenish the earth, and subdue it and have dominion over all the fish of the sea and all the fowls of the air, and every moving thing that moves upon the earth. And God saw all that He had done, all that He had done, all that He had made, and they were very good."

Now, you and I reading the Bible, not knowing it to be a psychological truth and seeing it as historical fact, we cannot understand the word. But when man knows the Bible is the greatest collection of psychological truths and was never intended to be seen as history or cosmology, then he gets a glimpse into this great wonderful book. For man himself is the great psychological earth that must be subdued. In man move all the passions, all the great emotions symbolized as creeping things and animals. In the deep of man actually live the invisible states symbolized as fish. In the deep of man actually live all the unnumbered infinite ideas symbolized as the fowls of the air. It is this man that must be self subdued, for subdue it, then comes the promise and have dominion over this vast wonderful country that is man. If man does not know that he himself is the earth spoken of, he thinks he must go out into the world and conquer it. The world reflects the work done on man. And so when he looks upon this wonderful world round about him, he thinks himself so little.

125

The Bible also tells us he calls himself a grasshopper, and referring to himself as a grasshopper, he sees giants in the land, the giants of industry, the giants of economics, the giants all round about him, and he feels smaller and smaller because he does not know how to go about actually subduing the earth, which is himself. When man knows it, he will realize that man as an individual is supreme within the circle of his own consciousness, for within the circle of his consciousness the entire drama of life is re-enacted over and over again. He has to start with self and then he will see this outer wonderful world, this visible world, is not what he thinks it to be, a place of exile from God; it is the living garment of the Father, and although to many of us its discordant harmony needs some interpretation, to the wise it has a voice and the voice speaks of hidden things behind the veil hidden things behind the veil of man's mind, for this whole vast wonderful world is a response to the arrangement of man's mind. For when he knows it he will look within for the hidden causes, look into the deep to see the fish and how they swim and how they are related, for this arrangement of the deep is going to project itself as circumstances and conditions of life.

And so today, if you haven't started, today is the time to start to really put into practice this teaching, and make of this violence a garden of God. It is called Eden and man was placed within it to keep it and to care it, for the garden of God is man. It is the mind of man. You never find a garden unless a man is present, for without a man there would be a forest of wilderness. But when a man is placed in it he begins to cut the trees or the seeds of wrong thinking; he clears the ground and he cultivates the ground, and then plants wisely. Then you will have dominion, for you will select the seed you will plant, the ideas you will entertain, and you will cultivate them. Knowing the outer world constantly bears witness of the inner arrangement of mind, you will only select the things you want to project into the living garment of your Father. For the whole vast world round about you is a living garment worn by your Father.

So how did he reap? He said He made man in His own image; well, the methods of mental and spiritual knowledge are entirely different. You and I can know a thing mentally by looking at it from the outside, by comparing it with other things, by analyzing it, by defining it, by even giving a description of it, but we can know a thing spiritually only by becoming it. We must be the thing itself if we would know that thing spiritually. We must be in love if we would know love. We must be God like if we would know what God is. For God made me, not out of something other than Himself; He made me perfect, so He made me by becoming me. There was no other way in the world that God could have made me unless He became me. So God became man that He may know man in the only way that He could know anything, for He knows all things spiritually and He calls them very good.

So He made me by becoming me, and now I am called upon to go and take care of the earth, and to subdue it, and take dominion. And I am the earth - I must learn to plant as He planted, and He planted the world by becoming the world. I must now plant as man, by becoming the man I want to be. So I will itemize all the things, name them, give a name to everything I want to express as a man, and then know it spiritually by becoming and I become it as He became me. I identify myself with it and live in that identity and I clothe it in flesh, I clothe it in fact. Not one thing in the world that is mine can be taken from me save by detachment from the state where that thing I love has its natural life. If I live in a world of beauty, if I live in a world of friendship, of comfort and all the lovely things that men enjoy, no power in the world can take one of them from me save I, who live among them, detach myself from the state where these lovely things have their natural life. When you and I know it, we begin to cultivate the earth, we actually weed the mind of all

127

negative states, all unlovely emotions, and we bring into subjection not the outer but the inner, and then the outer reflects that cultivation on self.

Now, how is it done? You are told in the first book of the Bible how it's done. For the promise is to the man who does it and the promise is a complete expansion beyond his wildest dreams of the state he plants. The one who first did it was called Jacob; well, I am Jacob. You are Jacob if you start to plant; every man is the potential Jacob, and Jacob did it by righteousness. As you are told, he did it through righteousness and he multiplied exceedingly, so that he increased a thousand fold his flocks, his cattle; he increased and grew beyond the measure of man in having all the maid servants and men servants and the camels. And this is what he said, "My righteousness shall speak for me in time to come."

Righteousness is right consciousness. The only right consciousness is the consciousness of already being the man you want to be, for that attaches you with an invisible state. You can't see it yet but you become attached to the state that you dare to assume you are, and you go fishing in the deep, you are beginning now to subdue the deep. You enter a state through the medium of feeling, through feeling that you are already what you want to be. And that is how you grow exceedingly great in your world, for you will be the Jacob expanding in your world.

The next one we come upon is Job. Here in the midst of all the trials and tribulations of a man, Job says, "I will hold fast to my righteousness and then my heart shall never judge me harshly as long as I live." He will hold fast to righteousness in the midst of storm, in the midst of all the problems of the world he will assume that he is free and hold fast to that right consciousness knowing that not in eternity could his heart ever judge him harshly.

Then we are told, "The meek of the earth seek righteousness and it is to the meek of the earth that the earth is given. As you are told the meek shall inherit the earth. You might have been taught to believe it meant the beaten man, the man who falls and grovels like the grasshopper; it doesn't. The word "meek" if translated actually means to be tamed as a wild animal is tamed. To the man who tames the mind, the man who tames his being that he can set it any task and have it execute that task, that man is meek and the meek inherit the earth. And the meek always seek righteousness, so if I today began to subdue this earth, I must make righteousness my watchword, and so if I were righteous I would now single out the nature of the trees I would plant, the nature of the flowers I would plant, the nature of the animals I would cultivate, the nature of the fish that I would catch, and I would name them as desirable states, called in the Bible beauty instead of ashes, called in the Bible the spirit of joy instead of mourning, called by all these lovely things. As you are told, all the things that are good, dwell on these things. To every good thing, for He called it very good. Every thing that I would call the good, which is a righteous judgment, will be the right judgment. I, in spite of the evidence of my senses that would deny it, in spite of reason that would tell me that it was impossible of realization, having discovered that I am the one planting my garden, that this is the only garden to cultivate, that this is the only earth to subdue, I would start now and boldly assume the good, first for myself - always start with Jerusalem - then go into the world and preach the goodness by knowing the goodness.

When you meet someone, regardless of what the appearance would reveal, know the truth for that one and set him free. Know that knowing as he ought to be known first by himself, but if he hasn't known it as true of himself, you at least know it for him. And though you never meet him in the flesh again keep on knowing the truth that sets man free by knowing he is already free, and you are cultivating your garden. You are bringing it into subjection, you are subduing it and then you shall have dominion. So you are supreme in your world if you only know the world that you really are; so man is the psychological earth on which this wonderful whirl of events takes place. Man is the psychological earth on which all the animals move; every emotion is symbolized as the animal. Every fowl of the air is truly the idea you entertain. Every fish of the deep is the invisible state that you could catch if you only knew how to cast your net on the right side. For you fish all night and catch nothing, but then comes one who knows, who is righteous, and he casts it on the right side, always that right side, and the right side is righteousness or right consciousness. And I will catch it; I may not see them, I don't have to see them. I don't have to wait for the evidence of my senses to confirm, for I am told, "And faith was accounted unto him for righteousness." So I will have faith in the reality of the deep; I will have faith in the reality of invisible states. So it's now invisible, I know it, it's a fish, but I have faith in the existence and the reality of the invisible state I want to externalize, knowing I can externalize it, for every time I externalize it I add to this wonderful garment of my Father, and that is my job, my duty.

So here, everyone of us, begin to believe that you are the only earth spoken of in the Bible. You are the one chosen to live in the center of the garden, but make it a garden, for the words are, "Keep it, keep it and plant it well". You have dominion over every idea in your mind. You say you haven't. Well, some may be to you disturbing, but you do have the choice of rejecting it or accepting it.

If you accept it, you identify with it and the state with which you are identified must, by the very law of your being, objectify itself within your world, that you may see by it how you plant that garden. Now, don't wait one second beyond the time that you observe weeds instead of flowers. Start right at the moment of observation, and start to replant the garden. Start really to subdue it. Become the meek and the meek is the bold. The meek is the bold of heart who does not ask assistance. He walks knowing he can do it. He can fish. He can actually bring into subjection every bird of the air, every idea of the mind. He will begin to know these things spiritually. He will know them in the only way that you and I should know anything, by becoming it, not to have a world of information concerning objective things, and knowing these things only mentally. I must learn to know things spiritually; I must learn to know what love is spiritually by being in love. I must learn to know what security is spiritually be becoming conscious of already being secure. I must learn to know what health is by becoming conscious of already being healthy, and sustain these states in the name of righteousness, knowing that my righteousness shall answer for me in time to come.

Make me no promise for when the father-in-law said to Jacob, "What promise should I make you?" "Just tell me that the offspring born in a certain manner shall be mine and no other promise, and no wages and no salary, all the spotted ones are mine. There isn't a spotted one among the parents but every offspring that is spotted though the parents are not, that is mine. That's my wage and my righteousness shall know it for me in time to come." And he begins to assume that his world is peopled with the spotted calves, and everyone born that was healthy was born spotted. And he increased beyond the wildest dream of a man.

Well, become that man, and start from the simple beginning as he started. There wasn't one thing in the world to encourage him that one calf could ever be born from parents that were not spotted and be a spotted calf. Yet he knew and he assumed that they had given birth to such things in numbers, they would come and they came a thousand fold. So in your case, maybe it's business, maybe the doctors have given you a final, final verdict and it's fatal. Well, I say in spite of this, and the doctor in his own way is doing his best, he would not have said it to hurt you or to frighten you. He firmly believed it, but you have another law and your law is that you can assume, in spite of that verdict, that you are well. And then, though tomorrow and the next day the tree doesn't appear, know that in time your righteousness shall speak for you, and like Job in the midst of all the storms, when he should have gone to the grave, he held fast to the consciousness of already being what he wanted to be, that his heart may not in time speak harshly against him. Well, it didn't - you know the story.

And so, all through we are told, "Break off the sins, break off missing marks by righteousness. Blessed are they that hunger and thirst after righteousness, for they shall be filled."

Now you are told, "Seek first the kingdom of God and His righteousness and all things shall be added unto you." Well, the kingdom of God is within you. You have been told that a number of times. The Bible affirms it over and over - "The Kingdom of God and the kingdom of heaven are within you." They aren't without. You see them seemingly without; that is the response to the within-ness where they are. Now, seek it and His righteousness. So assume within the mood that would be yours were you already the man that you want to be. Sustain that mood, occupy it as often as you can, and see how that righteousness shall draw things unto itself, and the things it draws are always in harmony with its nature. It never draws anything foreign to itself. If I assume that I am the man I want to be, I cannot then encounter events that are in conflict with my assumption. For my world mirrors the being I am.

So, here, today when you return read the whole chapter. It's beautiful. But I started with the 27th verse, "And God made man in his own image, in the image of God made He him. Male and female made He them." Then comes what is to be done. Then comes the promise if you do it. Then comes the judgment, "It is good and very good." So you start knowing that you are the earth on which you

132

now start to labor. If you do it, you shall be fruitful, and you will multiply, and you actually replenish this world, though it seemingly is barren you replenish it, if you subdue it. And the earth is self to be subdued, not by beating self as some people have misunderstood, not by isolating the self in some little secluded spot, not by running away from life, but in the midst of life is the opportunity to become meek: to take the violence that is man, it is individual man, and then bring it into the state of the meek, to transcend the violence by not fighting against conditions; know that conditions can only reflect what is within the one who observes that condition. So don't rage against it; leave it just as it is. If conditions remain the same, that is a sure, sure sign that you have not been faithful to righteousness.

Had you been faithful to the consciousness of already being the man you want to be, conditions would have to change in harmony with that righteousness. So don't rage against it; leave it as it is, and start today to take this wonderful earth, which is the foot stool of the Lord, which really is the mind of man, and start really to work upon it. Then you will not turn from left to right; you will keep the narrow path. You will go out knowing you can do it.

I know from experience it will not take long to see shoots appear; it will not take long to see the flowers appear. They will all appear, if you will take yourself in hand and by an uncritical observation of self watch the being you are; see the condition of the earth as it is now by the uncritical observation of your reactions to life. When you see who you are that is showing you the state of the earth as it is now. Don't condemn it, just start to subdue it, and know that you do have dominion over all the fish of the sea, the fowls of the air, and all the animals that move upon the earth. Knowing them to be the moods of thought, the desires, the passions that move in you, start to entertain only the good and the very good.

Dwell upon them and you will re-people your earth for you are supreme within the circle of your own consciousness. Now you may say it's a very little one; may I tell you that though you have a body and a life of your own, you are rooted in me, and you end in me, as I am rooted in God and end in God.

So every man can say the same thing no matter if you look into a world of 2,500,000,000 of them and every year they slip through the gates into the invisible state relative to this world, but as they come and go every man in the world is actually rooted in you and ends in you, and you are rooted in the ultimate that we call God, the Father. So the whole vast (world) is simply centered in you; start now to rearrange it that it may reflect the beauty that you want to live about and live in in this world. You do it by assuming the best. Always imagine the best of self; always imagine first with Jerusalem and then go out and radiate what you have given to self. If you live in that wonderful state yourself, you will only have the good to shower upon others, for you have one gift that is truly yours to give and that is yourself. You have no other gift. If you are good, you can give only the good. If you are not - well, whatever you are - that you give.

So the story is you may find today when you observe yourself, by observing your reactions, that it's not a very pleasant land but it is still a fertile land; it can be cleared of all these trees of traditional wrong thinking and can be replanted in harmony with the beauty that you desire. And in the immediate present it will bear fruit in harmony with the seeds you plant.

So let us go out determined to bring about a better arrangement of our mind that we may produce more noble garments for our Father to wear. For this wonderful, visible, objective universe is only the living garment of my Father, it's not a place of exile, as so many believe, talking about home and their going home, as though they are not now in the very midst of their Father. When you see me, you see my Father. Whenever you see me, you see the state of my mind, for you will see the world in which I live and the state of my mind, that inner arrangement, that's my Father. When you see me projected, you then call it the Son, and my world round about me tells me where I am. All these inner states are places in this fabulous psychological consciousness. Inner state is equal to place and where I stand within myself determines what I see when I look outside the self. So, when I look out upon the world, that area of my Father's garment, whether it be torn by reason of the inner place where I stand or whether it be lovely, I see only the inner arrangement of myself. I am forever surrounding myself with the true image of myself, and what I am in consciousness that only can I see. Knowing that, let me be determined today to seek righteousness, or right consciousness, that I may reap in the immediate present all the lovely things that I desire.

Now in summary, single out some noble aim in life. Having defined it clearly to yourself as a desirable state, the state you would like to externalize, ask yourself this very simple question, "What would the feeling be like were it true if I already embodied that noble state?" In response to your question will come a feeling; assume that feeling; it has reality outside of the present moment. Its being is in complete independence of present objective fact. It has real structure; it has reality in the deep of it. It came in response to your call when you said, "What would the feeling be like were it true?" And you named what you were thinking of - if it was security, if it was health, if it was any state, that fish came from the deep; it's located and you took the "I" and placed it in that feeling. You were actually standing upon it though it is invisible. Now remain on it.

If you remain in that state, you are told in the Bible three days, you will be "spewed out on dry land." "Three" doesn't mean three days; "three" means fullness, "three" means complete. So if I will live within that fish for three days until the whole thing seems natural and seems real, and it has the sensory vividness of reality. I will then be spewed out as something objective, and something that is commonly called in the Bible "land" or "dry land." But it does have reality, as you feel it, only people get away from it because it doesn't have immediate objective fact to confirm it. But you ride it for your three days and you will know what it was to enter that fish and remain in it until fullness was attained, until reality was attained within. In that state you were righteous and your righteousness will speak for you in time to come. It will not fail you; it cannot fail you.

Neville (09-18-1967)

YOURS FOR THE TAKING

There is only one cause for the phenomena of life. That cause is God. Housed in you, God is a person in the most literal sense of the word. Believe me, for I know this from experience. God, the only creator, is pure imagination working in the depth of your soul. God began a good work in you and He will bring it to completion on the day God's creative power is unveiled in you! God's creative power and wisdom is defined in scripture as Christ. When Christ unveils himself in you, you will know you are God's power and God's wisdom.

God, your own wonderful human imagination, underlies all of your faculties, including perception, and streams into your surface mind least disguised in the form of creative, productive fantasy. When you ask yourself what you can do to transcend your present limitation of life, you are dwelling upon the means. God does not ask you to consider the means, but to define the end. Speaking to you through the medium of desire, God asks the question: "What wantest thou of me?" Then he tells you not to be concerned with the ways and means, for his ways are unsearchable. They are inscrutable and past finding out. This statement you will find in the 11th chapter of the Book of Romans. So don't be concerned as to how God will fulfill the end, only know that He will. Can you believe your desire is fulfilled? Can you believe it is true? If you can, it is yours for the taking, for nothing is impossible to one who believes.

Now, let me share with you three stories which came to me during the summer. The first letter was from my friend Bennie. In it he told of lying prone on his bed, face down, when he felt as though someone grabbed his shoulders; and as he was lifted up he heard the words: "Take a stand!" Intuitively he knew he had to make the decision now as to whether he was going to believe that imagining creates reality or disbelieve it.

Scripture tells us, "He who is not with me is against me." There is no neutral ground, for "I have not come to bring peace, but a sword. To set a man against his father and a daughter against her mother." Why? Because a man's enemies are within him. Everyone must eventually take the stand that imagining creates reality and swim or sink with this concept.

Now, a few days later while in meditation, Bennie felt himself being held from behind by three men. As they raised him, he watched the sun rise and heard the words: "Look! Behold!" and "Recognition!" And he remembered a passage from my book, Your Faith Is Your Fortune: "Recognition of this truth will transform you from one who tries to make it so, into one who recognizes it to be so."

Soon after this, a friend asked Ben to pray for him. He wanted to be the property manager of the company he worked for. Although he had been passed by year after year, Bennie told him what to do, and imagined hearing the friend tell him the job was now his. A few months later the job was vacated and his friend was given the position with an increase in salary and greater responsibility, just as he had imagined. What did Bennie do? He imagined! To whom did he pray? To his own wonderful human imagination! God, the creator of all life, is like pure imagining in you, underlying all of your faculties - including perception. He streams into your surface mind least disguised in the form of productive fantasy. Bennie took a stand. He prayed for his friend and believed his prayer was answered. He tested himself, and the windows of heaven opened and poured forth blessings for all to see. Now Bennie knows that with God all things are possible.

God is your mightier self. Emptying himself, God took on the form of a slave and is now found in the likeness of man. Abdicating his power, Pure Imagination took upon himself the limitations of flesh, thereby becoming human. It is God who weaves your every desire into cubic reality, waiting upon you effectively and swiftly, regardless of whether your desire is for evil or for good. The one who conjures thoughts in the mind of a Hitler or Stalin is the same power as the one conjuring thoughts in the mind of a pope or the Arch Bishop of Canterbury. There aren't two Gods. There is only one!

The 14th and 53rd chapters of the Book of Psalms are identical, each telling us: "The fool says in his heart there is no God, but the Lord looks down from heaven upon the children of the many to see if there are any that act wise and seek the Lord." Here we find that in the eyes of God, wisdom is equated with seeking the Lord. And if God is all-wise and all powerful, then any search other than for the Lord is stupid. You may be the greatest mathematician or scientist, the most intelligent and honored man among men, but if your search is not for God, you are stupid in His eyes.

Called upon to look for the cause of creation, what are you doing losing yourself in the phenomena of life? When something happens, search your thoughts and you will discover your own wonderful human imagination to be the cause of your experience, because God is a person. At the present time He is wearing a mask called Neville, but the one speaking to you now knows himself to be the Ancient of Days. Every being in the world is a mask worn by God; for housed in man, is man's imagination.

A thought acted upon is an imaginal act. Think (imagine) a horrible earthquake and God will give it to you. Imagine (think of) a war and God will provide that, too. Imagine peace and you will have it. God will give you health if you will but imagine being healthy.

Imagine success and you will have it. The moment you think, you are feeding your imagination, which is a person. I use the word person deliberately, for you are a person. You are the mask God is now wearing, for God became you that you may become God.

Now let me share another letter with you. Last year this lady, living about sixty miles north of San Francisco, was possessed with the desire to come to Los Angeles and attend my lecture. Leaving word at her office, she drove her car to the San Francisco airport, where she took a plane to Los Angeles. There she was met by a friend and immediately came to the lecture. After the lecture she joined a group of four women and one man for coffee, where she expressed her hunger, having missed lunch and dinner that day. The gentleman sitting beside her then said, "I'd like to buy you a steak." And as she looked into his face she heard a voice within her say, "This is your husband."

Now, this lady has been married and divorced four times, so she had specific desires for a husband which she felt must be fulfilled. She wanted to be happily married to a man who lived by this truth. She wanted him to love and respect her as well as her seventeen-year-old son. Having imagined such a man in September, she attended my meeting in October, and married the gentleman she met here the following January.

The gentleman added his story to her letter, saying: "Having played with the idea of being married, I went to a pawn shop last September and purchased a plain gold band which I placed on the third finger of my left hand. Every day I wore the ring and every night I slept in the feeling of being happily married. (My friend thought he could not get the feeling of being married without a physical aid, but you don't need anything outside of your imagination to catch the mood.)

Having been an alcoholic, this gentleman imagined his wife never mentioned his past; for although he had not tasted alcohol for nine years, he had paid the price in his search for God. You see, the alcoholic is searching for truth. Thirsty, he finds a false spirit in the form of alcohol, while those who will not touch it - and criticize those who do - haven't even started their search. But I have news for them. One day they, too, will know a hunger which will not be satisfied by bread. They will know a thirst so great they will make the mistake of clothing it in the form of a bottle. But because it will be a false thirst, the thirst will remain. Then they will discover the true hunger and the true thirst, which is for the hearing of the word of God.

Now, in the third letter a gentleman writes: "Having borrowed from the bank, every month when I sent in my payment I reduced the total amount in my record book. One day, as I was writing my check and recording its payment, I closed my eyes and saw two zeros under the balance due column. Then I gave a sigh of relief because the note was paid. For the next thee months I persisted in seeing those double zeros and rejoicing in being debt-free. Then came an unexpected surprise! Our company paid us all a mid-year bonus which was so large I was able to pay all of my bills, including the bank loan, and deposit the rest in the bank."

Now I think this gentleman and I must be two peas in the same pod, because money seems to burn in his pocket, too. Instead of keeping the money in the bank as the rational mind would do, my friend began to think about how to spend it, so of course he found a way. He bought a tape recorder to bring and record my message!

To whom did my friend turn when he wanted the bank loan paid? He turned to God! He did not get down on his knees and ask some outside God to do it for him. He didn't go to church and consult a priest, rabbi or minister. He didn't contact a so-called truth teacher, but simply closed his eyes to the obvious and saw two zeros in the balance due column. Then for the first time in the history of his company a mid-year bonus was paid. This happened to him because of his use of the law, and his knowledge of who God is.

Not everyone who seeks God finds him, but there are those - like Philip -that when they find him, they bring their brother Nathanael. Andrew found Jesus and brought Peter. You, too, will find Jesus when you exercise your imagination, and bring those you love to his awareness. If great wealth befell you, would not your wife (or husband), your children, as well as those in your immediate circle benefit from your good fortune? And if it befell them, would it not befall you? So we benefit each other as we search out God and test him.

Revelation tells us to be either hot or cold, but never to be lukewarm. If you do not believe me to the point of testing the law, you are lukewarm. But one day, like Ben, you will take a stand. You will either be for me or against me. You will try to believe that imagining creates reality, or reject it. You will be hot or cold about it, and that is better than being lukewarm. I have discovered that those who hated me at first when I took from them their idols, the icon in their mind called Jesus, have become my finest students. So many people claim they believe in Jesus, but cannot define him. Unable to place him in time and space, they are defiant when I say: Christ in you is your hope of glory. Full of insults, they are cold. Some have even been violent. But one day they will find him of whom Moses and the prophets wrote, turn around, and be embraced by the Lord.

I started telling this story in the 1930's and here we are in the 1960's. During these thirty-odd years I have found those who really opposed me - those who were so moved and disturbed they were determined to disprove my words. But since they couldn't do it, they too have found God to be their own wonderful human imagination. The Bible is addressed only to the human imagination. In Blake's famous letter to the Rev. Dr. Trusler he makes this comment: "Why is the Bible more entertaining and instructive than any other book? Is it not because it is addressed to the imagination, which is spiritual sensation, and only immediately to the understanding, or reason?"

The Bible is imaginative instruction. When it unfolds in you it is more real than anything here, yet it is all imagined, for God is all imagination and so is man. The eternal body of man is the imagination, and that is God Himself. There is nothing but this one body called Jesus, who is the Lord God Jehovah.

I tell you, God became as we are that we may become as He is. No one took God's life. He laid it down himself saying: "I have the power to lay it down and the power to lift it up again. The fall into fragmented space was deliberate. And He who fell has the power to gather us all together, one by one, into that single body who is all love. His body is above the organization of sex. In it there is no Greek, no Jew, no bond, no free, no male, no female. When you wear it you understand Paul's statement: "I consider the sufferings of this present time not worth comparing to the glory that has been revealed in me." In that body you know yourself to be the real Man, and this fleshly body as nothing. You will realize that you were never male or female, but have always been God.

Remember, everything is yours for the taking. If you want it, take it. If you cannot claim it for yourself, ask a friend for help. If you want to be happily married, do what my friends did. You want to pay off all of your debts? Whatever you desire is yours. All you have to do is imagine you have it, for everything in life is yours for the taking!

Now let us go into the silence.

CONSCIOUSNESS IS THE ONLY REALITY

(Lesson 1)

This is going to be a very practical Course. Therefore, I hope that everyone in this class has a very clear picture of what he desires, for I am convinced that you can realize your desires by the technique you will receive here this week in these five lessons.

That you may receive the full benefit of these instructions, let me state now that the Bible has no reference at all to any persons who ever existed or to any event that ever occurred upon earth.

The ancient storytellers were not writing history but an allegorical picture lesson of certain basic principles which they clothed in the garb of history, and they adapted these stories to the limited capacity of a most uncritical and credulous people.

Throughout the centuries we have mistakenly taken personifications for persons, allegory for history, the vehicle that conveyed the instruction for the instruction, and the gross first sense for the ultimate sense intended.

The difference between the form of the Bible and its substance is as great as the difference between a grain of corn and the life germ within that grain. As our as similative organs discriminate between food that can be built into our system and food that must be discarded, so do our awakened intuitive faculties discover beneath allegory and parable, the psychological life-germ of the Bible; and, feeding on this, we, too, cast off the form which conveyed the message.

The argument against the historicity of the Bible is too lengthy; consequently, it is not suitable for inclusion in this practical psychological interpretation of its stories. Therefore, I will waste no time in trying to convince you that the Bible is not an historical fact.

Tonight I will take four stories and show you what the ancient story-tellers intended that you and I should see in these stories. The ancient teachers attached psychological truths to phallic and solar allegories. They did not know as much of the physical structure of man as do modern scientists, neither did they know as much about the heavens as do our modern astronomers. But the little they did know they used wisely and they built phallic and solar frames to which they tied the great psychological truths that they had discovered.

In the Old Testament you will find much of the Phallic worship. Because it is not helpful, I am not going to emphas ize it. I shall only show you how to interpret it.

Before we come to the first of the psychological dramas that you and I may use in a practical sense, let me state the two outstanding names of the Bible: the one you and I translate as GOD or JEHOVAH, and the one we call his son, which we have as JESUS.

The ancients spelled these names by using little symbols. The ancient tongue, called the Hebraic language, was not a tongue that you exploded with the breath. It was a mystical language never uttered by man. Those who understood it, understood it as rnathematicians understand symbols of higher mathematics. It is not something people used to convey thought as I now use the English language.

They said that God's name was spelled, JOD HE VAU HE. I shall take these symbols and in our normal, down to earth language, explain them in this manner.

The first letter, JOD in the name GOD is a hand or a seed, not just a hand, but the hand of the director. If there is one organ of man that discriminates and sets him apart from the entire world of creation it is his hand. What we call a hand in the anthropoid ape is not a hand. It is used only for the purpose of conveying food to the mouth, or to swing from branch to branch. Man's hand fashions, it molds. You cannot really express yourself without the hand. This is the builder's hand, the hand of the director; it directs, and molds, and builds within your world.

The ancient story-tellers called the first letter JOD, the hand, or the absolute seed out of which the whole of creation will come.

To the second letter, HE, they gave the symbol of a window. A window is an eye -- the window is to the house what the eye is to the body.

The third letter, VAU, they called a nail. A nail is used for the purpose of binding things together. The conjunction "and" in the Hebraic tongue is simply the third letter, or VAU. If I want to say 'man and woman', I put the VAU in the middle, it binds them together.

The fourth and last letter, HE, is another window or eye.

In this modern, down to earth language of ours, you can forget eyes and windows and hands and look at it in this manner. You are seated here now. This first letter, JOD, is your I AMness, your awareness. You are aware of being aware -- that is the first letter. Out of this awareness all states of awareness come.

The second letter, HE, called an eye, is your imagination, your ability to perceive. You imagine or perceive something which seems to be other than Self. As though you were lost in reverie and contemplated mental states in a detached manner, making the thinker and his thoughts separate entities.

The third letter, VAU, is your ability to feel you are that which you desire to be. As you feel you are it, you become aware of being it. To walk as though you were what you want to be is to take your desire out of the imaginary world and put the VAU upon it. You have completed the drama of creation. I am aware of something. Then I become aware of actually being that of which I was aware.

The fourth and last letter in the name of God is another HE, another eye, meaning the visible objective world which constantly bears witness of that which I am conscious of being. You do nothing about the objective world; it always molds itself in harmony with that which you are conscious of being

You are told this is the name by which all things are made, and without it there is nothing made that is made. The name is simply what you have now as you are seated here. You are conscious of being, aren't you? Certainly you are. You are also conscious of something that is other than yourself: the room, the furniture, the people.

You may become selective now. Maybe you do not want to be other than what you are, or to own what you see. But you have the capacity to feel what it would be like were you now other than what you are. As you assume that you are that which you want to be, you have completed the name of God or the JOD HE VAU HE. The final result, the objectification of your assumption, is not your concern. It will come into View automatically as you assume the consciousness of being it.

Now let us turn to the Son's name, for he gives the Son dominion over the world. You are that Son, you are the great Joshua, or Jesus, of the Bible. You know the name Joshua or Jehoshua we have Anglicized as Jesus.

The Son's name is almost like the Father's name. The first three letters of the Father's name are the first three letters of the Son's name, JOD HE VAU, then you add a SHIN and an AYIN, making the Son's name read, JOD HE VAU SHIN AYIN'.

You have heard what the first three are: JOD HE VAU. JOD means that you are aware; HE means that you are aware of something; and VAU means that you became aware of being that of which you were aware. You have dominion because you have the ability to conceive and to become that which you conceive. That is the power of creation.

But why is a SHIN put in the name of the Son? Because of the infinite mercy of our Father. Mind you, the Father and the Son are one. But when the Father becomes cons cious of being man he puts within the condition called man that which he did not give unto hims elf. He puts a SHIN for this purpose; a SHIN is symbolized as a tooth.

A tooth is that which consumes, that which devours. I must have within me the power to consume that which I now dislike.

I, in my ignorance, brought to birth certain things I now dislike and would like to leave behind me. Were there not within me the flames that would consume it, I would be condemned forever to live in a world of all my mistakes. But there is a SHIN, or flame, within the name of the Son, which allows that Son to become detached from states He formerly expressed within the world. Man is incapable of seeing other than the contents of his own consciousness.

If I now become detached in consciousness from this room by turning my attention away from it, then, I am no longer conscious of it. There is something in me that devours it within me. It can only live within my objective world if I keep it alive within my consciousness.

It is the SHIN, or a tooth, in the Son's name that gives him absolute dominion. Why could it not have been in the Father's name? For this simple reason: Nothing can cease to be in the Father. Even the unlovely things cannot cease to be. If I once give it expression, forever and ever it remains locked within the dimensionally greater Self which is the Father. But I would not like to keep alive within my world all of my mistakes. So I, in my infinite mercy gave to myself, when I became man, the power to become detached from these things that I, in my ignorance, brought to birth in my world.

These are the two names which give you dominion. You have dominion if, as you walk the earth, you know that your consciousness is God, the one and only reality. You become aware of something you would like to express or possess. You have the ability to feel that you are and possess that which but a moment before was imaginary. The final result, the embodying of your assumption, is completely outside of the offices of a three-dimensional mind. It comes to birth in a way that no man knows.

If these two names are clear in your mind's eye, you will see that they are your eternal names. As you sit here, you are this JOD HE VAU HE; you are the JOD HE VAU SHIN AYIN.

The stories of the Bible concern themselves exclusively with the power of imagination. They are really dramatizations of the technique of prayer, for prayer is the secret of changing the future. The Bible reveals the key by which man enters a dimensionally larger world for the purpose of changing the conditions of the lesser world in which he lives.

A prayer granted implies that something is done in consequence of the prayer, which otherwise would not have been done. Therefore, man is the spring of action, the directing mind, and the one who grants the prayer.

The stories of the Bible contain a powerful challenge to the thinking capacity of man. The underlying truth -- that they are psychological dramas and not historical facts -- demands reiteration, inasmuch as it is the only justification for the stories. With a little imagination we may easily trace the psychological sense in all the stories of the Bible.

"And God said, Let us make man in our image, and after our likeness: and let them have dominion over the fish of the sea, and over the fowl of the air, and over the cattle, and over all the earth, and over every creeping thing that creepeth upon the earth. So God created man in his own image, in the image of God created he him" Gen. 1:26, 27.

Here in the first chapter of the Bible the ancient teachers laid the foundation that God and man are one, and that man has dominion over all the earth. If God and man are one, then God can never be so far off as even to be near, for nearness implies separation.

The question arises: What is God? God is man's consciousness, his awareness, his I AMness. The drama of life is a psychological one in which we bring circumstances to pass by our attitudes rather than by our acts. The corner-stone on which all things are based is man's concept of himself. He acts as he does, and has the experiences that he does, because his concept of himself is what it is, and for no other reason. Had he a different concept of himself, he would act differently and have different experiences.

151

Man, by assuming the feeling of his wish fulfilled, alters his future in harmony with his assumption, for, assumptions though false, if sustained, will harden into fact.

The undisciplined mind finds it difficult to assume a state which is denied by the senses. But the ancient teachers discovered that sleep, or a state akin to sleep, aided man in making his assumption. Therefore, they dramatized the first creative act of man as one in which man was in a profound sleep. This not only sets the pattern for all future creative acts, but s hows us that man has but one substance that is truly his to use in creating his world and that is himself.

"And the Lord God (man) caused a deep sleep to fall upon Adam and he slept: and he took one of his ribs, and closed up the flesh instead thereof; and the rib, which the Lord God had taken from man, made he a woman." Gen. 2: 21, 22.

Before God fashions this woman for man he brings unto Adam the beasts of the field, and the fowls of the air and has Adam name them. "Whatsoever Adam called every living creature, that was the name thereof."

If you will take a concordance or a Bible dictionary and look up the word thigh as used in this story you will see that it has nothing to do with the thigh. It is defined as the soft parts that are creative in a man, that hang upon the thigh of a man.

The ancient story-tellers used this phallic frame to reveal a great ps ychological truth. An angel is a mes s enger of God. You are God, as you have jus t dis covered for your cons cious nes s is God, and you have an idea, a mes s age. You are wres tling with an idea, for you do not know that you are already that which you contemplate, neither do you believe you could become it. You would like to, but you do not believe you could.

Who wrestles with the angel? Jacob. And the word Jacob, by definition, means the supplanter.

You would like to transform yourself and become that which reas on and your senses deny. As you wrestle with your ideal, trying to feel that you are it, this is what happens. When you actually feel that you are it, something goes out of you. You may use the words, "Who has touched me, for I perceive virtue has gone out of me?"

You become for a moment, after a successful meditation, incapable of continuing in the act, as though it were a physical creative act. You are just as impotent after you have prayed successfully as you are after the physical creative act. When satisfaction is yours, you no longer hunger for it. If the hunger persists you did not explode the idea within you, you did not actually succeed in becoming conscious of being that which you wanted to be. There was still that thirst when you came out of the deep.

If I can feel that I am that which but a few seconds ago I knew I was not, but desired to be, then I am no longer hungry to be it. I am no longer thirsty because I feel satisfied in that state. Then something shrinks within me, not physically but in my feeling, in my conscious ness, for that is the creativeness of man. He so shrinks in desire, he loses the desire to continue in this meditation. He does not halt physically, he simply has no desire to continue the meditative act.

"When you pray believe that you have received, and you shall receive." When the physical creative act is completed, the sinew which is upon the hollow of man's thigh shrinks, and man finds himself impotent or is halted. In like manner when a man prays successfully he believes that he is already that which he desired to be, therefore he cannot continue desiring to be that which he is already conscious of being. At the moment of satisfaction, physical and psychological, something goes out which in time bears witness to man's creative power.

****

Our next story is in the 38th chapter of the book of Genesis. Here is a King whose name is Judah, the first three letters of whose name also begins JOD HE VAU. Tamar is his daughter-in-law.

The word Tarmar means a palm tree or the most beautiful, the most comely. She is gracious and beautiful to look on and is called a palm tree. A tall, stately palm tree blossoms even in the desert --- wherever it is there is an oasis. When you see the palm tree in the desert, there will be found what you seek most in that parched land. There is nothing more desirable to a man moving across a desert than the sight of a palm tree.

In our case, to be practical, our objective is the palm tree. That is the stately, beautiful one that we seek. Whatever it is that you and I want, what we truly desire, is personified in the story as Tamar the beautiful.

We are told she dresses herself in the veils of a harlot and sits in the public place. Her father-in-law, King Judah, comes by; and he is so in love with this one who is veiled that he offers her a kid to be intimate with her. She said, "What will you give me as a pledge that you will give me a kid?"

Looking around he said, "What do you want me to give as a pledge?"

She answered, "Give me your ring, give me your bracelets, and give me your staff."

Whereupon, he took from his hand the ring, and the bracelet, and gave them to her along with his sceptre. And he went in unto her and knew her, and she bore him a son.

That is the story; now for the interpretation. Man has one gift that is truly his to give, and that is himself. He has no other gift, as told you in the very first creative act of Adam begetting the woman out of himself. There was no other substance in the world but himself with which he could fashion the object of his desire. In like manner Judah had but one gift that was truly his to give -- himself, as the ring, the bracelets and the staff symbolized, for these were the symbols of his kingship.

Man offers that which is not himself, but life demands that he give the one thing that symbolizes himself. "Give me your ring, give me your bracelet, give me your sceptre." These make the King. When he gives them he gives of himself.

You are the great King Judah. Before you can know your Tamar and make her bear your likeness in the world, you must go in unto her and give of self. Suppose I want security. I cannot get it by knowing people who have it. I cannot get it by pulling strings. I must become conscious of being secure.

Let us say I want to be healthy. Pills will not do it. Diet or climate will not do it. I must become conscious of being healthy by assuming the feeling of being healthy.

Perhaps I want to be lifted up in this world. Merely looking at kings and presidents and noble people and living in their reflection will not make me dignified. I must become conscious of being noble and dignified and walk as though I were that which I now want to be.

When I walk in that light I give of myself to the image that haunted my mind, and in time she bears me a child; which means I objectify a world in harmony with that which I am conscious of being.

You are King Judah and you are also Tamar. When you become conscious of being that which you want to be you are Tamar. Then you crystallize your desire within the world round about you.

No matter what stories you read in the Bible, no matter how many characters these ancient story-tellers introduced into the drama, there is one thing you and I must always bear in mind -- they all take place within the mind of the individual man. All the characters live in the mind of the individual man.

As you read the story, make it fit the pattern of self. Know that your consciousness is the only reality. Then know what you want to be. Then assume the feeling of being that which you want to be, and remain faithful to your assumption, living and acting on your conviction. Always make it fit that pattern.

****

Our third interpretation is the story of Isaac and his two sons: Esau and Jacob. The picture is drawn of a blind man being deceived by his second son into giving him the blessing which belonged to his first son. The story stresses the point that the deception was accomplished through the sense of touch.

"And Isaac said unto Jacob, Come near, I pray thee that I may feel thee, my son, whether thou be my very son Esau or not. And Jacob went near unto Isaac his father; and he felt him.... And it came to pass, as soon as Isaac had made an end of blessing Jacob, and Jacob was yet scarce gone out from the presence of Isaac his father, that Es au his brother came in from his hunting." Gen. 27:21, 30.

156

This story can be very helpful if you will re-enact it now. Again bear in mind that all the characters of the Bible are personifications of abstract ideas and must be fulfilled in the individual man. You are the blind father and both sons.

Isaac is old and blind, and sensing the approach of death, calls his first son Esau a rough hairy boy, and sends him into the woods that he may bring in some venison.

The second son, Jacob, a smooth skin boy, overheard the request of his father. Desiring the birthright of his brother, Jacob, the smooth skinned son, slaughtered one of his father's flock and skinned it. Then, dressed in the hairy skins of the kid he had slaughtered, he came through subtlety and betrayed his father into believing that he was Esau.

The father said, "Come close my son that I may feel you. I cannot see, but come that I may feel." Note the stress that is placed upon feeling in this story.

He came close and the father said to him, "The voice is Jacob's voice, but the hands are the hands of Esau." And feeling this roughness, the reality of the son Esau, he pronounced the blessing and gave it to Jacob.

You are told in the story that as Isaac pronounced the blessing and Jacob had scarcely gone out from his presence, that his brother Esau came in from his hunting.

This is an important verse. Do not become distressed in our practical approach to it, for as you sit here you, too, are Isaac. This room in which you are seated is your present Esau. This is the rough or sensibly known world, known by reason of your bodily organs. All of your senses bear witness to the fact that you are here in this room. Everything tells you that you are here, but perhaps you do not want to be here.

You can apply this toward any objective. The room in which you are seated at any time -- the environment in which you are placed, this is your rough or sensibly known world or son which is personified in the story as Esau. What you would like in place of what you have or are is your smooth skinned state or Jacob, the supplanter.

You do not send your visible world hunting, as so many people do, by denial. By saying it does not exist you make it all the more real. Instead, you simply remove your attention from the region of sensation which at this moment is the room round about you, and you concentrate your attention on that which you want to put in its place, that which you want to make real.

In concentrating on your objective, the secret is to bring it here. You must make elsewhere here and then now imagine that your objective is so close that you can feel it.

Suppose at this very moment I want a piano here in this room. To see a piano in my mind's eye existing elsewhere does not do it. But to visualize it in this room as though it were here and to put my mental hand upon the piano and to feel it solidly real, is to take that subjective state personified as my second son Jacob and bring it so close that I can feel it.

Isaac is called a blind man. You are blind because you do not see your objective with your bodily organs, you cannot see it with your objective senses. You only perceive it with your mind, but you bring it so close that you can feel it as though it were solidly real now. When this is done and you lose yourself in its reality and feel it to be real, open your eyes.

When you open your eyes what happens? The room that you had shut out but a moment ago returns from the hunt. You no sooner gave the blessing -- felt the imaginary state to be real -- than the objective world, which seemingly was unreal, returns. It does not speak to you with words as recorded of Esau, but the very room round about you tells you by its presence that you have been self-deceived.

It tells you that when you lost yourself in contemplation, feeling that you were now what you wanted to be, feeling that you now possess what you desire to possess, that you were simply deceiving self. Look at this room. It denies that you are elsewhere.

If you know the law, you now say: "Even though your brother came through subtlety and betrayed me and took your birthright, I gave him your blessing and I cannot retract."

In other words, you remain faithful to this subjective reality and you do not take back from it the power of birth. You gave it the right of birth and it is going to become objective within this world of yours. There is no room in this limited space of yours for two things to occupy the same space at the same time. By making the subjective real it resurrects itself within your world.

Take the idea that you want to embody, and assume that you are already it. Lose yourself in feeling this assumption is solidly real. As you give it this sense of reality, you have given it the blessing which belongs to the objective world, and you do not have to aid its birth any more than you have to aid the birth of a child or a seed you plant in the ground. The seed you plant grows unaided by a man, for it contains within itself all the power and all the plans necessary for self-expression.

You can this night re-enact the drama of Isaac blessing his second son and see what happens in the immediate future in your world. Your present environment vanishes, all the circumstances of life change and make way for the coming of that to which you have given your life. As you walk, knowing that you are what you wanted to be, you objectify it without the assis tance of another.

****

The fourth story for tonight is taken from the last of the books attributed to Moses. If you need proof that Moses did not write it, read the story carefully. It is found in the 34th chapter of the book of Deuteronomy. Ask any priest or rabbi, 'who is the author of this book?', and they will tell you that Moses wrote it.

In the 34th chapter of Deuteronomy you will read of a man writing his own obituary, that is, Moses wrote this chapter. A man may sit down and write what he would like to have placed upon his tombstone, but here is a man who writes his own obituary. And then he dies and so completely rubs himself out that he defies posterity to find where he has buried himself.

"So Moses the servant of the Lord died there in the land of Moab, according to the word of the Lord. And he buried him in a valley in the land of Moab, over against Beth-poer: but no man knoweth of his sepulchre unto this day. And Moses was an hundred and twenty years old when he died: his eye was not dim, nor his natural force abated." Deut. 34:5, 6, 7.

You must this night -- not tomorrow -- learn the technique of writing your own obituary and so completely die to what you are that no man in this world can tell you where you buried the old man. If you are now ill and you become well, and I know you by reason of the fact that you are ill, where can you point and tell me you buried the sick one?

If you are impoverished and borrow from every friend you have, and then suddenly you roll in wealth, where did you bury the poor man? You so completely rub out poverty in your mind's eye that there is nothing in this world you can point to and claim, that is where I left it. A complete transformation of consciousness rubs out all evidence that anything other than this ever existed in the world.

The most beautiful technique for the realizing of man's objective is given in the first verse of the 34th chapter of Deuteronomy:

"And Moses went up from the Plains of Moab unto the mountain of Nebo, to the top of Pisgah, that is over against Jericho. And the Lord shewed him all the land of Gilead, unto Dan."

You read that verse and say, "So what?" But take a concordance and look up the words. The first word, Moses, means to draw out, to rescue, to lift out, to fetch. In other words, Moses is the personification of the power in man that can draw out of man that which he seeks, for everything comes from within, not from without. You draw from within yourself that which you now want to express as something objective to yourself.

You are Moses coming out of the plains of Moab. The word Moab is a contraction of two Hebraic words, Mem and Ab, meaning mother-father. Your consciousness is the mother-father, there is no other cause in the world. Your I AMness, your awareness, is this Moab or mother-father. You are always drawing something out of it.

The next word is Nebo. In your concordance Nebo is defined as a prophecy. A prophecy is something subjective. If I say, "So-and-so will be," it is an image in the mind; it is not yet a fact. We must wait and either prove or disprove this prophecy.

In our language Nebo is your wish, your desire. It is called a mountain because it is something that appears difficult to ascend and is therefore seemingly impossible of realization. A mountain is something bigger than you are, it towers over you. Nebo personifies that which you want to be in contrast to that which you are.

The word Pisgah, by definition, is to contemplate. Jericho is a fragrant odor. And Gilead means the hills of witnesses. The last word is Dan the Prophet.

Now put them all together in a practical sense and see what the ancients tried to tell us. As I stand here, having discovered that my consciousness is God, and that I can by simply feeling that I am what I want to be transform myself into the likeness of that which I am assuming I am; I know now that I am all that it takes to scale this mountain.

I define my objective. I do not call it Nebo, I call it my desire. Whatever I want, that is my Nebo, that is my great mountain that I am going to scale. I now begin to contemplate it, for I shall climb to the peak of Pisgah.

I must contemplate my objective in such a manner that I get the reaction that satisfies. If I do not get the reaction that pleases then Jericho is not seen, for Jericho is a fragrant odor. When I feel that I am what I want to be I cannot suppress the joy that comes with that feeling.

I must always contemplate my objective until I get the feeling of satisfaction personified as Jericho. Then I do nothing to make it visible in my world; for the hills of Gilead, meaning men, women, children, the whole vast world round about me, come bearing witness. They come to testify that I am what I have assumed myself to be, and am sustaining within myself. When my world conforms to my assumption the prophecy is fulfilled.

If I now know what I want to be, and assume that I am it, and walk as though I were, I become it and becoming it I so completely die to my former concept of self that I cannot point to any place in this world and say: that is where my former self is buried. I so completely died that I defy posterity to ever find where I buried my old self.

There must be someone in this room who will so completely transform himself in this world that his close immediate circle of friends will not recognize him.

For ten years I was a dancer, dancing in Broadway shows, in vaudeville, night clubs, and in Europe. There was a time in my life when I thought I could not live without certain friends in my world. I would spread a table every night after the theatre and we would all dine well. I thought I could never live without them. Now I confess I could not live with them. We have nothing in common today. When we meet we do not purposely walk on the opposite side of the street, but it is almost a cold meeting because we have nothing to discuss. I so died to that life that as I meet these people they cannot even talk of the old times.

But there are people living today who are still living in that state, getting poorer and poorer. They always like to talk about the old times. They never buried that man at all, he is very much alive within their world.

Moses was 120 years, a full, wonderful age as 120 indicates. One plus two plus zero equals three, the numerical symbol of expression. I am fully conscious of my expression. My eyes are undimmed and the natural functions of my body are not abated. I am fully conscious of being what I do not want to be.

But knowing this law by which a man transforms himself, I assume that I am what I want to be and walk in the assumption that it is done. In becoming it, the old man dies and all that was related to that former concept of self dies with it. You cannot take any part of the old man into the new man. You cannot put new wine in old bottles or new patches on old garments. You must be a new being completely.

As you assume that you are what you want to be, you do not need the assistance of another to make it so. Neither do you need the assistance of anyone to bury the old man for you. Let the dead bury the dead. Do not even look back, for no man having put his hand to the plow and then looking back is fit for the kingdom of heaven.

Do not ask yourself how this thing is going to be. It does not matter if your reason denies it. It does not matter if all the world round about you denies it. You do not have to bury the old. "Let the dead bury the dead." You will so bury the past by remaining faithful to your new concept of Self that you will defy the whole vast future to find where you buried it. To this day no man in all of Israel has discovered the sepulchre of Moses.

****

These are the four stories I promised you tonight. You must apply them every day of your life. Even though the chair on which you are now seated seems hard and does not lend itself to meditation you can, by imagination, make it the most comfortable chair in the world.

Let me now define the technique as I want you to employ it. I trust each one of you came here tonight with a clear picture of your desire. Do not say it is impossible. Do you want it? You do not have to use your moral code to realize it. It is altogether outside the reach of your code.

Consciousness is the one and only reality. Therefore, we must form the object of our desire out of our own consciousness.

People have a habit of slighting the importance of simple things, and the suggestion to create a state akin to sleep in order to aid you in assuming that which reason and your senses deny, is one of the simple things you might slight.

However, this simple formula for changing the future, which was discovered by the ancient teachers and given to us in the Bible, can be proved by all.

The first step in changing the future is Desire, that is, define your objective -- know definitely what you want.

Second: construct an event which you believe you would encounter FOLLOWING the fulfillment of your desire - an event which implies fulfillment of your desire - something which will have the action of Self predominant.

The third step is to immobilize the physical body and induce a state akin to sleep. Then mentally feel yourself right into the proposed action, imagine all the while that you are actually performing the action HERE AND NOW. You must participate in the imaginary action, not merely stand back and look on, but FEEL that you are actually performing the action, so that the imaginary sensation is real to you.

It is important always to remember that the proposed action must be one which FOLLOWS the fulfillment of your desire, one which implies fulfillment. For example, suppose you desired promotion in office. Then being congratulated would be an event you would encounter following the fulfillment of your desire.

Having selected this action as the one you will experience in imagination to imply promotion in office, immobilize your physical body and induce a state bordering on sleep, a drowsy state, but one in which you are still able to control the direction of your thoughts, a state in which you are attentive without effort. Then visualize a friend standing before you. Put your imaginary hand into his. Feel it to be solid and real, and carry on an imaginary conversation with him in harmony with the FEELING OF HAVING BEEN PROMOTED.

You do not visualize yourself at a distance in point of space and at a distance in point of time being congratulated on your good fortune. Instead, you MAKE elsewhere HERE and the future NOW. The difference between FEELING yourself in action, here and now, and visualizing yourself in action, as though you were on a motion-picture screen, is the difference between success and failure.

The difference will be appreciated if you will now visualize yourself climbing a ladder. Then, with eyelids closed imagine that a ladder is right in front of you and FEEL YOURSELF ACTUALLY CLIMBING IT.

Experience has taught me to restrict the imaginary action which implies fulfillment of the des ire, to condense the idea into a single act, and to re-enact it over and over again until it has the feeling of reality. Otherwise, your attention will wander off along an associational track, and hosts of associated images will be presented to your attention, and in a few seconds they will lead you hundreds of miles away from your objective in point of space and years away in point of time.

If you decide to climb a particular flight of stairs, because that is the likely event to follow the fulfillment of your desire, then you must restrict the action to climbing that particular flight of stairs.

Should your attention wander off, bring it back to its task of climbing that flight of stairs, and keep on doing so until the imaginary action has all the solidity and distinctness of reality.

The idea must be maintained in the mind without any sensible effort on your part. You must, with the minimum of effort permeate the mind with the feeling of the wish fulfilled.

Drowsiness facilitates change because it favors attention without effort, but it must not be pushed to the state of sleep in which you no longer are able to control the movements of your attention. But a moderate degree of drowsiness in which you are still able to direct your thoughts.

A most effective way to embody a desire is to assume the feeling of the wish fulfilled and then, in a relaxed and drowsy state, repeat over and over again like a lullaby, any short phrase which implies fulfillment of your desire, s uch as, "Thank you, thank you, thank you" as though you addressed a higher power for having given you that which you desired.

I know that when this course comes to an end on Friday many of you here will be able to tell me you have realized your objectives. Two weeks ago I left the platform and went to the door to shake hands with the audience. I am safe in saying that at least 35 out of a class of 135 told me that which they desired when they joined this class they had already realized. This happened only two weeks ago. I did nothing to bring it to pass save to give them this technique of prayer. You need do nothing to bring it to pass - save apply this technique of prayer.

With your eyes closed and your physical body immobilized induce a state akin to sleep and enter into the action as though you were an actor playing the part. Experience in imagination what you would experience in the flesh were you now in possession of your objective. Make elsewhere HERE and then NOW. And the greater you, using a larger focus will use all means, and call them good, which tend toward the production of that which you have assumed.

You are relieved of all responsibility to make it so, because as you imagine and feel that it is so your dimensionally larger self determines the means. Do not think for one moment that some one is going to be injured in order to make it so, or that some one is going to be disappointed. It is still not your concern. I must drive this home. Too many of us, schooled in different walks of life, are so concerned about the other.

You ask, 'If I get what I want will it not imply injury to another?' There are ways you know not of, so do not be concerned.

Close your eyes now because we are going to be in a long silence. Soon you will become so lost in contemplation, feeling that you are what you want to be, that you will be totally unconscious of the fact that you are in this room with others.

You will receive a shock when you open your eyes and discover we are here. It should be a shock when you open your eyes and discover that you are not actually that which, a moment before, you felt you were, or felt you possessed. Now we will go into the deep.

SILENCE PERIOD.........

****

I need not remind you that you are now that which you have assumed that you are. Do not discuss it with anyone, not even self. You cannot take thought as to the HOW, when you know that you ARE already.

Your three-dimensional reasoning, which is a very limited reasoning indeed should not be brought into this drama. It does not know. What you have just felt to be true is true.

Let no man tell you that you should not have it. What you feel that you have, you will have. And I promise you this much, after you have realized your objective, on reflection you will have to admit that this conscious reasoning mind of yours could never have devised the way.

You are that and have that which this very moment you appropriated. Do not discuss it. Do not look to someone for encouragement because the thing might not come. It has come. Go about your Father's business doing everything normally and let these things happen in your world.

ASSUMPTIONS HARDEN INTO FACT

(Lesson 2)

This Bible of ours has nothing to do with history. Some of you may yet be inclined tonight to believe that, although we can give it a psychological interpretation, it still could be left in its present form and be interpreted literally. You cannot do it. The Bible has no reference at all to people or to events as you have been taught to believe. The sooner you begin to rub out that picture the better.

We are going to take a few stories tonight, and again I am going to remind you that you must re-enact all of these stories within your own mind.

Bear in mind that although they seem to be stories of people fully awake, the drama is really between you, the sleeping one, the deeper you, and the conscious waking you. They are personified as people, but when you come to the point of application you must remember the importance of the drowsy state.

All creation, as we told you last night, takes place in the state of sleep, or that state which is akin to sleep -- the, sleepy drowsy state.

We told you last night the first man is not yet awakened. You are Adam, the first man, still in the profound sleep. The creative you is the fourth-dimensional you whose home is simply the state you enter when men call you asleep.

****

Our first story for tonight is found in the Gospel of John. As you hear it unfold before you, I want you to compare it in your mind's eye to the story you heard last night from the book of Genesis. The first book of the Bible, the bock of Genesis, historians claim is the record of events which occurred on earth some 3,000 years before the events recorded in the book of John. I ask you to be rational about it and see if you do not think the same writer could have written both stories. You be the judge as to whether the same inspired man could not have told the same story and told it differently.

This is a very familiar story, the story of the trial of Jesus. In this Gospel of John it is recorded that Jesus was brought before Pontius Pilate, and the crowd clamored for his life, they wanted Jesus. Pilate turned to them and said:

"But ye have a custom, that I should release unto you one at the Passover; will ye therefore that I release unto you the King of the Jews? Then cried they all again, saying, Not this man, but Barabbas. Now Barabbas was a robber." John 18:39, 40

You are told that Pilate had no choice in the matter, he was only a judge interpreting law, and this was the law. The people had to be given that which they requested. Pilate could not release Jesus against the wishes of the crowd, and so he released Barabbas and gave unto them Jesus to be crucified.

Now bear in mind that your consciousness is God. There is no other God. And you are told that God has a son whose name is Jesus. If you will take the trouble to look up the word Barabbas in your concordance, you will see that it is a contraction of two Hebraic words: BAR, which means a daughter or son- or child, and ABBA, which means father. Barabbas is the son of the great father. And Jesus in the story is called the Saviour, the Son of the Father.

We have two sons in this story. And we have two sons in the story of Esau and Jacob. Bear in mind that Isaac was blind, and justice to be true must be blind folded. Although in this case Pilate is not physically blind, the part given to Pilate implies that he is blind

172

because he is a judge. On all the great law buildings of the world we see the lady or the man who represents justice as being blindfolded.

"Judge not according to the appearance, but judge righteous judgment."

John 7:24.

Here we find Pilate is playing the same part as Isaac. There are two sons. All the characters as they appear in this story can apply to your own life. You have a son that is robbing you this very moment of that which you could be.

If you came to this meeting tonight conscious of wanting something, desiring something, you walked in the company of Barabbas.

For to desire is to confess that you do not now possess what you desire, and because all things are yours, you rob yourself by living in the state of desire. My saviour is my desire. As I want something I am looking into the eyes of my saviour. But if I continue wanting it, I deny my Jesus, my saviour, for as I want I confess I am not and "except ye believe that I AM He ye die in your sins." I cannot have and still continue to desire what I have. I may enjoy it, but I cannot continue wanting it.

Here is the story. This is the feast of the Passover. Something is going to change right now, something is going to passover. Man is incapable of passing over from one state of consciousness into another unless he releases from consciousness that which he now entertains, for it anchors him where he is.

You and I may go to physical feasts year after year as the sun enters the great sign of Aries, but it means nothing to the true mystical Passover. To keep the feast of the Passover, the

173

psychological feast, I pass from one state of consciousness into another. I do it by releasing Barabbas, the thief and robber that robs me of that state which I could embody within my world.

The state I seek to embody is personified in the story as Jesus the Saviour. If I become what I want to be then I am saved from what I was. If I do not become it, I continue to keep locked within me a thief who robs me of being that which I could be.

These stories have no reference to any persons who lived nor to any event that ever occurred upon earth. These characters are everlasting characters in the mind of every man in the world. You and I perpetually keep alive either Barabbas or Jesus. You know at every moment of time who you are entertaining.

Do not condemn a crowd for clamoring that they should release Barabbas and crucify Jesus. It is not a crowd of people called Jews. They had nothing to do with it.

If we are wise, we too should clamor for the release of that state of mind that limits us from being what we want to be, that restricts us, that does not permit us to become the ideal that we seek and strive to attain in this world.

I am not saying that you are not tonight embodying Jesus. I only remind you, that if at this very moment you have an unfulfilled ambition, then you are entertaining that which denies the fulfillment of the ambition, and that which denies it is Barabbas.

To explain the mystical, psychological transformation known as the Passover, or the crossing over, you must now become identified with the ideal that you would serve, and you must remain faithful to the ideal. If you remain faithful to it, you not only crucify it by your faithfulness, but you resurrect it unaided by a man.

As the story goes, no man could rise early enough to roll away the stone. Unaided by a man the stone was removed, and what seemingly was dead and buried was resurrected unassisted by a man.

You walk in the consciousness of being that which you want to be, no one sees it as yet, but you do not need a man to roll away the problems and the obstacles of life in order to express that which you are conscious of being. That state has its own unique way of becoming embodied in this world, of becoming flesh that the whole world may touch it.

Now you can see the relationship between the story of Jesus and the story of Isaac and his two sons, where one transplanted the other, where one was called the Supplanter of the other. Why do you think those who compiled the sixty odd books of our Bible made Jacob the forefather of Jesus?

They took Jacob, who was called the Supplanter, and made him father of twelve, then they took Judah or praise, the fifth son and made him the forefather of Joseph, who is supposed to have fathered in some strange way this one called Jesus. Jesus must supplant Barabbas as Jacob must supplant and take the place of Esau.

Tonight you can sit right here and conduct the trial of your two sons, one of whom you want released. You can become the crowd who clamors for the release of the thief, and the judge who willingly releases Barabbas, and sentences Jesus to fill his place. He was crucified on Golgotha, the place of the skull, the seat of the imagination.

To experience the Passover or passage from the old to the new concept of self, you must release Barabbas, your present concept of self, which robs you of being that which you could be, and you must assume the new concept which you desire to express.

The best way to do this is to concentrate your attention upon the idea of identifying yourself with your ideal. Assume you are already that which you seek and your assumption, though false, if sustained, will harden into fact.

You will know when you have succeeded in releasing Barabbas, your old concept of self, and when you have successfully crucified Jesus, or fixed the new concept of self, by simply looking MENTALLY at the people you know. If you see them as you formerly saw them, you have not changed your concept of self, for all changes of concepts of self result in a changed relationship to your world.

We always seem to others an embodiment of the ideal we inspire. Therefore, in meditation, we must imagine that others see us as they would see us were we what we desire to be.

You can release Barabbas and crucify and resurrect Jesus if you will first define your ideal. Then relax in a comfortable arm chair, induce a state of consciousness akin to sleep and experience in imagination what you would experience in reality were you already that which you desire to be.

By this simple method of experiencing in imagination what you would experience in the flesh were you the embodiment of the ideal you serve, you release Barabbas who robbed you of your greatness, and you crucify and resurrect your saviour, or the ideal you desired to express.

Now let us turn to the story of Jesus in the garden of Gethsemane. Bear in mind that a garden is a properly prepared plot of ground, it is not a wasteland. You are preparing this ground called Gethsemane by coming here and studying and doing something about your mind. Spend some time daily in preparing your mind by reading good literature, listening to good music and entering into conversations that ennoble.

We are told in the Epistles, "Whatsoever things are true, whatsoever things are honest, whatsoever things are just, whatsoever things are pure, whatsoever things are lovely, whatsoever things are of good report; if there be any virtue, and if there be any praise, think on these things." Phil. 4:8

Continuing with our story, as told in the 18th chapter of John, Jesus is in the garden and suddenly a crowd begins to seek him. He is standing there in the dark and he says, "Whom seek ye?"

The spokesman called Judas answers and says, "We seek Jesus of Nazareth."

A voice answers, "I am He."

At this instant they all fall to the ground, thousands of them tumbled. That in itself should stop you right there and let you know it could not be a physical drama, because no one could be so bold in his claim that he is the one sought, that he could cause thousands who seek him to fall to the ground.

But the story tells us they all fell to the ground. Then when they regained their composure they asked the same question.

"Jesus answered, I have told you that I am He: if therefore ye seek me, let these go their way."

John 18:8.

"Then said Jesus unto him, That thou doest, do quickly."

John 13:27

Judas, who has to do it quickly, goes out and commits suicide.

177

Now to the drama. You are in your garden of Gethsemane or prepared mind if you can, while you are in a state akin to sleep, control your attention and not let it wander away from its purpose. If you can do that you are definitely in the garden.

Very few people can sit quietly and not enter a reverie or a state of uncontrolled thinking. When you can restrict the mental action and remain faithful to your watch, not permitting your attention to wander all over the place, but hold it without effort within a limited field of presentation to the state you are contemplating, then you are definitely this disciplined presence in the garden of Gethsemane.

The suicide of Judas is nothing more than changing your concept of yourself. When you know what you want to be you have found your Jesus or saviour. When you assume that you are what you want to be you have died to your former concept of self (Judas committed suicide) and are now living as Jesus. You can become at will detached from the world round about you, and attached to that which you want to embody within your world.

Now that you have found me, now that you have found that which would save you from what you are, let go of that which you are and all that it represents in the world. Become completely detached from it. In other words, go out and commit suicide.

You completely die to what you formerly expressed in this world, and you now completely live to that which no one saw as true of you before. You are as though you had died by your own hand, as though you had committed suicide. You took your own life by becoming detached in consciousness from what you formerly kept alive, and you begin to live to that which you have discovered in your garden. You have found your saviour.

It is not men falling, not a man betraying another, but you detaching your attention, and refocusing your attention in an entirely new direction. From this moment on you walk as though you were that which you formerly wanted to be. Remaining faithful to your new concept of yourself you die or commit suicide. No one took your life, you laid it down yourself.

You must be able to see the relation of this to the death of Moses, where he so completely died that no one could find where he was buried. You must see the relationship of the death of Judas. He is not a man who betrayed a man called Jesus.

The word Judas is praise; it is Judah, to praise, to give thanks, to explode with joy. You do not explode with joy unless you are identified with the ideal you seek and want to embody in this world. When you become identified with the state you contemplate you cannot suppress your joy. It rises like the fragrant odor described as Jericho in the Old Testament.

I am trying to show you that the ancients told the same story in all the stories of the Bible. All that they are trying to tell us is how to become that which we want to be. And they imply in every story that we do not need the assistance of another. You do not need another to become now what you really want to be.

****

Now we turn to a strange story in the Old Testament; one that very few priests and rabbis will be bold enough to mention from their pulpits. Here is one who is going to receive the promise as you now receive it. His name is Jesus, only the ancients called him Joshua, Jehoshua Ben Nun, or saviour, son of the fish, the Saviour of the great deep. Nun means fish, and fish is the element of the deep, the profound ocean. Jehoshua means Jehovah saves, and Ben means the offspring or son of. So he was called the one who brought the fish age.

179

This story is in the 6th book of the Bible, the book of Joshua. A promise is made to Joshua as it is made to Jesus in the Anglicized form in the gospels of Matthew, Mark, Luke and John.

In the gospel of John, Jesus says, "All things whatsoever thou hast given me are of thee." John 17:7. "And all mine are thine, and thine are mine." John 17:10.

In the Old Testament in the book of Joshua it is said in these words: "Every place that the sole of your foot shall tread upon, that have I given unto you." Joshua 1:3

It does not matter where it is; analyze the promise and see if you can accept it literally. It is not physically true but it is psychologically true. Wherever you can stand in this world mentally that you can realize.

Joshua is haunted by this promise that wherever he can place his foot (the foot is understanding), wherever the sole of his foot shall tread, that will be given unto him. He wants the most desirable state in the world, the fragrant city, the delightful state called Jericho.

He finds himself barred by the impassable walls of Jericho. He is on the outside, as you are now on the outside. You are functioning three-dimensionally and you cannot seem to reach the fourth-dimensional world where your present desire is already a concrete objective reality. You cannot seem to reach it because your senses bar you from it. Reason tells you it is impossible, all things round about you tell you it is not true.

Now you employ the services of a harlot and a spy, and her name is Rahab. The word Rahab simply means the spirit of the father. RACE means the breath or spirit, and AB the father. Hence we find that this harlot is the spirit of the father and the father is man's awareness of being aware, man's I AMness, man's consciousness.

Your capacity to feel is the great spirit of the father, and that capacity is Rahab in this story. She has two professions that of a spy and that of a harlot.

The profession of a spy is this: to travel secretly, to travel so quietly that you may not be detected. There is not a single physical spy in this world who can travel so quietly that he will be altogether unseen by others. He may be very wise in concealing his ways, and he may never be truly apprehended, but at every moment of time he runs the risk of being detected.

When you are sitting quietly with your thoughts, there is no man in the world so wise that he can look at you and tell you where you are mentally dwelling.

I can stand here and place myself in London. Knowing London quite well, I can close my eyes and assume that I am actually standing in London. If I remain within this state long enough, I will be able to surround myself with the environment of London as though it were a solid concrete objective fact.

Physically I am still here, but mentally I am thousands of miles away and I have made elsewhere here. I do not go there as a spy, I mentally make elsewhere here, and then now. You cannot see me dwelling there, so you think I have just gone to sleep and that I am still here in this world, this three-dimensional world that is now San Francisco. As far as I am physically concerned, I am here but no one can tell me where I am when I enter the moment of meditation.

Rahab's next profession was that of a harlot, which is to grant unto men what they ask of her without asking man's right to ask. If she be an absolute harlot, as her name implies, then she possesses all and can grant all that man asks of her. She is there to serve, and not to question man's right to seek what he seeks of her.

You have within you the capacity to appropriate a state without knowing the means that will be employed to realize that end and you assume the feeling of the wish fulfilled without having any of the talents that men claim you must possess in order to do so. When you appropriate it in consciousness you have employed the spy, and because you can embody that state within yourself by actually giving it to yourself, you are the harlot, for the harlot satisfies the man who seeks her.

You can satisfy self by appropriating the feeling that you are what you want to be. And this assumption though false, that is, although reason and the senses deny it, if persisted in will harden into fact. By actually embodying that which you have assumed you are, you have the capacity to become completely satisfied. Unless it becomes a tangible, concrete reality you will not be satisfied; you will be frustrated.

You are told in this story that when Rahab went into the city to conquer it, the command given to her was to enter the heart of the city, the heart of the matter, the very center of it, and there remain until I come. Do not go from house to house, do not leave the upper room of the house into which you enter. If you leave the house and there be blood upon your head, it is upon your head. But if you do not leave the house and there be blood, it shall be upon my head.

Rahab goes into the house, rises to the upper floor, and there she remains while the walls crumble. That is, we must keep a high mood if we would walk with the highest. In a very veiled manner, the story tells you that when the walls crumbled and Joshua entered, the only one who was saved in the city was the spy and the harlot whose name was Rahab.

This story tells what you can do in this world. You will never lose the capacity to place yourself elsewhere and make it here. You will never lose the ability to give unto yourself what you are bold enough to appropriate as true of self. It has nothing to do with the woman who played that part.

The explanation of the crumbling of the walls is simple. You are told that he blew upon the trumpet seven times and at the seventh blast the walls crumbled and he entered victoriously into the state that he sought.

Seven is a stillness, a rest, the Sabbath. It is the state when man is completely unmoved in his conviction that the thing is. When I can assume the feeling of my wish fulfilled and go to sleep, unconcerned, undisturbed, I am at rest mentally, and am keeping the Sabbath or am blowing the trumpet seven times. And when I reach that point the walls crumble. Circumstances alter then remold themselves in harmony with my assumption. As they crumble I resurrect that which I have appropriated within. The walls, the obstacles, the problems, crumble of their own weight if I can reach the point of stillness within me.

The man Who can fix within his own mind's eye an idea, even though the world would deny it, if he remains faithful to that idea he will see it manifested. There is all the difference in the world between holding the idea, and being held by the idea. Become so dominated by an idea that it haunts the mind as though you were it. Then, regardless of what others may say, you are walking in the direction of your fixed attitude of mind. You are walking in the direction of the idea that dominates the mind.

As we told you last night, you have but one gift that is truly yours to give, and that is yourself. There is no other gift; you must press it out of yourself by an appropriation. It is there within you now for creation is finished. There is nothing to be that is not now. There is nothing to be created for all things are already yours, they are all finished.

Although man may not be able to stand physically upon a state, he can always stand mentally upon any desired state. By standing mentally I mean that you can now, this very moment, close your eyes and visualize a place other than your present one, and assume that you are actually there. You can FEEL this to be so real that upon opening your eyes you are amazed to find that you are not physically there.

This mental journey into the desired state, with its subsequent feeling of reality, is all that is necessary to bring about its fulfillment. Your dimensionally greater Self has ways that the lesser, or three-dimensional you, know not of. Furthermore, to the greater you, all means are good which promote the fulfillment of your assumption.

Remain in the mental state defined as your objective until it has the feeling of reality, and all the forces of heaven and earth will rush to aid its embodiment. Your greater Self will influence the actions and words of all who can be used to aid the production of your fixed mental attitude.

****

Now we turn to the book of Numbers and here we find a strange story. I trust that some of you have had this experience as described in the bock of Numbers. They speak of the building of a tabernacle at the command of God; that God commanded Israel to build him a place of worship.

He gave them all the specifications of the tabernacle. It had to be an elongated, movable place of worship, and it had to be covered with skin. Need you be told anything more? Isn't that man?

"Know ye not that ye are the temple of God, and that the Spirit of God dwelleth in you?"

I Cor. 3:16

There is no other temple. Not a temple made with hands, but a temple eternal in the heavens. This temple is elongated, and it is covered with skin, and it moves across the desert.

"And on the day that the tabernacle was reared up the cloud covered the tabernacle, namely, the tent of the testimony: and at even there was upon the tabernacle as it were the appearance of fire, until the morning. So it was always: the cloud covered it by day, and the appearance of fire by night."

Num.9:15, 16

The command given to Israel was to tarry until the cloud ascended by day and the fire by night. "Whether it were two days, or a month, or a year, that the cloud tarried upon the tabernacle, remaining thereon, the children of Israel abode in their tents, and journeyed not: but when it was taken up, they journeyed." Num. 9:22

You know that you are the tabernacle, but you may wonder, what is the cloud. In meditation many of you must have seen it. In meditation, this cloud, like the sub-soil waters of an artesian well, springs spontaneously to your head and forms itself into pulsating, golden rings. Then, like a gentle river they flow from your head in a stream of living rings of gold.

In a meditative mood bordering on sleep the cloud ascends. It is in this drowsy state that you should assume that you are that which you desire to be, and that you have that which you seek, for the cloud will assume the form of your assumption and fashion a world in harmony with itself. The cloud is simply the garment of your consciousness, and where your consciousness is placed, there you will be in the flesh also.

This golden cloud comes in meditation. There is a certain point when you are approaching sleep that it is very, very thick, very liquid, and very much alive and pulsing. It begins to ascend as you reach the drowsy, meditative state, bordering on sleep. You do not strike the tabernacle; neither do you move it until the cloud begins to ascend.

The cloud always ascends when man approaches the drowsiness of sleep. For when a man goes to sleep, whether he knows it or not, he slips from a three-dimensional world into a fourth-dimensional world and that which is ascending is the consciousness of that man in a greater focus; it is a fourth-dimensional focus.

What you now see ascending is your greater self. When that begins to ascend you enter into the actual state of feeling you are what you want to be. That is the time you lull yourself into the mood of being what you want to be, by either experiencing in imagination what you would experience in reality were you already that which you want to be, or by repeating over and over again the phrase that implies you have already done what you want to do. A phrase such as, "Isn't it wonderful, isn't it wonderful," as though some wonderful thing had happened to you.

"In a dream, in a vision of the night, when deep sleep falleth upon men, in slumberings upon the bed. Then he openeth the ears of men, and sealeth their instruction. "

186

Job 33: 15, 16

Use wisely the interval preceding sleep. Assume the feeling of the wish fulfilled and go to sleep in this mood. At night, in a dimensionally larger world, when deep sleep falleth upon men, they see and play the parts that they will later on play on earth. And the drama is always in harmony with that which their dimensionally greater selves read and play through them. Our illusion of free will is but ignorance of the causes which make us act.

The sensation which dominates the mind of man as he falls asleep, though false, will harden into fact. Assuming the feeling of the wish fulfilled as we fall asleep, is the command to this embodying process saying to our mood, "Be thou actual." In this way we become through a natural process what we desire to be.

I can tell you dozens of personal experiences where it seemed impossible to go elsewhere, but by placing myself elsewhere mentally as I was about to go to sleep, circumstances changed quickly which compelled me to make the journey. I have done it across water by placing myself at night on my bed as though I slept where I wanted to be. As the days unfolded things began to mold themselves in harmony with that assumption and all things that must happen to compel my journey did happen. And I, in spite of myself, must make ready to go toward that place which I assumed I was in when I approached the deep of sleep.

As my cloud ascends I assume that I am now the man I want to be, or that I am already in the place where I want to visit. I sleep in that place now. Then life strikes the tabernacle, strikes my environment and reassembles my environment across seas or over land and reassembles it in the likeness of my assumption. It has nothing to do with men walking across a physical desert. The whole vast world round about you is a desert.

From the cradle to the grave you and I walk as though we walk the desert. But we have a living tabernacle wherein God dwells, and it is covered with a cloud which can and does ascend when we go to sleep or are in a state akin to sleep. Not necessarily in two days, it can ascend in two minutes. Why did they give you two days? If I now become the man I want to be, I may become dissatisfied tomorrow. I should at least give it a day before I decide to move on.

The Bible says in two days, a month, or a year: whenever you decide to move on with this tabernacle let the cloud ascend. As it ascends you start moving where the cloud is. The cloud is simply the garment of your consciousness, your assumption. Where the consciousness is placed you do not have to take the physical body; it gravitates there in spite of you. Things happen to compel you to move in the direction where you are consciously dwelling.

"In my Father's house are many mansions: if it were not so, I would have told you. I go to prepare a place for you. And if I go and prepare a place for you, I will come again, and receive you unto myself; that where I am, there ye may be also."

John 14:2, 3

The many mansions are the unnumbered states within your mind, for you are the house of God. In my Father's house are unnumbered concepts of self. You could not in eternity exhaust what you are capable of being.

If I sit quietly here and assume that I am elsewhere, I have gone and prepared a place. But if I open my eyes, the bilocation which I created vanishes and I am back here in the physical form that I left behind me as I went to prepare a place. But I prepared the place nevertheless and will in time dwell there physically.

You do not have to concern yourself with the ways and the means that will be employed to move you across space into that place where you have gone and mentally prepared it. Simply sit quietly, no matter where you are, and mentally actualize it.

But I give you warning, do not treat it lightly, for I am conscious of what it will do to people who treat it lightly. I treated it lightly once because I just wanted to get away, based only upon the temperature of the day. It was in the deep of winter in New York, and I so desired to be in the warm climate of the Indies, that I slept that night as though I slept under palm trees. Next morning when I awoke it was still very much winter.

I had no intentions of going to the Indies that year, but distressing news came which compelled me to make the journey. It was in the midst of war when ships were being sunk right and left, but I sailed out of New York on a ship 48 hours after I received this news. It was the only way I could get to Barbados, and I arrived just in time to see my mother and say a three-dimensional "Good-bye" to her.

In spite of the fact that I had no intentions of going, the deeper Self watched where the great cloud descended. I placed it in Barbados and this tabernacle (my body) had to go and make the journey to fulfill the command, "Wherever the sole of your foot shall tread that have I given unto you." Wherever the cloud descends in the desert, there you reassemble that tabernacle.

I sailed from New York at midnight on a ship without taking thought of submarines or anything else. I had to go. Things happened in a way that I could not have devised.

I warn you, do not treat it lightly. Do not say, "I will experiment and put myself in Labrador, just to see if it will work." You will go to your Labrador and then you will wonder why you ever came to this class. It will work if you dare assume the feeling of your wish fulfilled as you go to sleep.

Control your moods as you go to sleep. I cannot find any better way to describe this technique than to call it a "controlled waking dream." In a dream you lose control, but try preceding your sleep with a complete controlled waking dream, entering into it as you do in dream, for in a dream you are always very dominant, you always play the part. You are always an actor in a dream, and never the audience. When you have a controlled waking dream you are an actor and you enter into the act of the controlled dream. But do not do it lightly, for you must then reenact it physically in a three-dimensional world.

Now before we go into our moment of silence there is something I must make very clear, and that is this effort we discussed last night. If there is one reason in this whole vast world why people fail it is because they are unaware of a law known to psychologists today as the law of reverse effort.

When you assume the feeling of your wish fulfilled it is with a minimum of effort. You must control the direction of the movements of your attention. But you must do it with the least effort. If there is effort in the control, and you are compelling it in a certain way you are not going to get the results. You will get the opposite results, what ever they might be.

That is why we insist on establishing the basis of the Bible as Adam slept. That is the first creative act, and there is no record where he was ever awakened from this profound sleep. While he sleeps creation stops.

You change your future best when you are in control of your thoughts while in a state akin to sleep, for then effort is reduced to its minimum. Your attention seems to completely relax, and then you must practice holding your attention within that feeling, without using force, and without using effort.

Do not think for a moment that it is will power that does it. When you release Barabbas and become identified with Jesus, you do not will yourself to be it, you imagine that you are it. That is all you do.

Now as we come to the vital part of the evening, the interval devoted to prayer, let me again clarify the technique. Know what you want. Then construct a single event, an event which implies fulfillment of your wish. Restrict the event to a single act.

For instance, if I single out as an event, shaking a man's hand, then that is the only thing I do. I do not shake it, then light a cigarette and do a thousand other things. I simply imagine that I am actually shaking hands and keep the act going over and over and over again until the imaginary act has all the feeling of reality.

The event must always imply fulfillment of the wish. Always construct an event which you believe you would naturally encounter following the fulfillment of your desire. You are the judge of what event you really want to realize.

There is another technique I gave you last night. If you cannot concentrate on an act, if you cannot snuggle into your chair and believe the chair is elsewhere, just as though elsewhere were here, then do this: Reduce the idea, condense it to a single, simple phrase like, "Isn't it wonderful." or, "Thank you." or, "It's done." or, "It's finished."

There should not be more than three words. Something that implies the desire is already realized. "Isn't it wonderful", or "Thank you," certainly imply that. These are not all the phrases you could use. Make up out of your own vocabulary the phrase which best suits you. But make it very, very short and always use a phrase that implies fulfillment of the idea.

When you have your phrase in mind, lift the cloud. Let the cloud ascend by simply inducing the state that borders on sleep. Simply begin to imagine and feel you are sleepy, and in this state assume the feeling of the wish fulfilled. Then repeat the phrase over and over like a lullaby. Whatever the phrase is, let it imply that the assumption is true, that it is concrete, that it is already a fact and you know it.

Just relax and enter into the feeling of actually being what you want to be. As you do it you are entering Jericho with your spy who has the power to give it. You are releasing Barabbas and sentencing Jesus to be crucified and resurrected. All these stories you are re-enacting if now you begin to let go and enter into the feeling of actually being what you want to be. Now we can go.....

SILENCE PERIOD

****

If your hands are dry, and if your mouth is dry at the end of this meditation, that is positive proof that you did succeed in lifting the cloud. What you were doing when the cloud was lifted is entirely your business. But you did lift the cloud if your hands are dry.

I will give you another phenomena which is very strange and one I cannot analyze. It happens if you really go into the deep. You will find on waking that you have the most active pair of kidneys in the world. I have discussed it with doctors and they cannot explain it.

Another thing you may observe in meditation is a lovely liquid blue light. The nearest thing on earth to which I can compare it is burning alcohol. You know when you put alcohol on the plum pudding at Christmas time and set it a flame, the lovely liquid blue flame that envelopes the pudding until you blow it out. That flame is the nearest thing to the blue light which comes on the forehead of a man in meditation.

Do not be distressed. You will know it when you see it. It is like two shades of blue, a darker and a lighter blue in constant motion, just like burning alcohol, which is unlike the constant flame of a gas jet. This flame is alive, just as spirit would be alive.

Another thing that may come to you as it did to me. You will see spots before your eyes. They are not liver spots as some people will tell you who know nothing about it. These are little things that float in space like a mesh, little circles all tied together. They start with a single cell and come in groups in different geometrical patterns, like worms, like trailers, and they float all over your face. When you close your eyes you still see them, proving that they are not from without, they are from within.

When you begin to expand in consciousness all these things come. They may be your blood stream objectified by some strange trick of man that man does not quite understand. I am not denying that it is your blood stream made visible, but do not be distressed by thinking it is liver spots or some other silly thing that people will tell you.

If these various phenomena come to you, do not think you are doing something wrong. It is the normal, natural expansion that comes to all men who take themselves in tow and try to develop the garden of Gethsemane.

The minute you begin to discipline your mind by observing your thoughts and watching your thoughts throughout the day, you become the policeman of your thoughts. Refuse to enter into conversations that are unlovely, refuse to listen attentively to anything that tears down.

Begin to build within your own mind's eye the vision of the perfect virgin rather than the vision of the foolish virgin. Listen only to the things that bring joy when you hear them. Do not give a willing ear to that which is unlovely, which when you heard it you wish you had not. That is listening and seeing things Without oil in your lamp, or joy in your mind.

There are two kinds of virgins in the Bible: five foolish and five wise virgins. The minute you become the wise virgin, or try to make an attempt to do it, you will find all these things happen. You will see these things, and they interest you so that you have not time to develop the foolish sight, as many people do. I hope that no one here does. Because no one should be identified with this great work who can still find great joy in a discussion of another that is unlovely.

THINKING FOURTH-DIMENSIONALLY

(Lesson 3)

There are two actual outlooks on the world possessed by every man, and the ancient story tellers were fully conscious of these two outlooks. They called the one "the carnal mind," and the other "the mind of Christ."

We recognize these two centers of thought in the statement: "The natural man receiveth not the things of the Spirit of God: for they are foolishness unto him: neither can he know them, because they are spiritually discerned." I Cor. 2:14

To the natural mind, reality is confined to the instant called now; this very moment seems to contain the whole of reality, everything else is unreal. To the natural mind, the past and the future are purely imaginary. In other words my past, when I use the natural mind, is only a memory image of things that were. And to the limited focus of the carnal or natural mind the future does not exist. The natural-mind does not believe that it could revisit the past and see it as something that is present, something that is objective and concrete to itself, neither does it believe that the future exists.

To the Christ mind, the spiritual mind, which in our language we will call the fourth-dimensional focus, the past, the present, and the future of the natural mind are a present whole. It takes in the entire array of sensory impressions that man has encountered, is encountering, and will encounter.

The only reason you and I are functioning as we are today, and are not aware of the greater outlook, is simply because we are creatures of habit, and habit renders us totally blind to what

195

otherwise we should see; but habit is not law. It acts as though it were the most compelling force in the world, yet it is not law.

We can create a new approach to life. If you and I would spend a few minutes every day in withdrawing our attention from the region of sensation and concentrating it on an invisible state and remain faithful to this contemplation, feeling and sensing the reality of an invisible state, we would in time become aware of this greater world, this dimensionally larger world. The state contemplated is now a concrete reality, displaced in time.

Tonight as we turn to our Bible you be the judge as to where you stand in your present unfoldment.

****

Our first story for tonight is from the 5th chapter of the Gospel of Mark. In this chapter there are three stories told as though they were separate experiences of the dominant characters.

In the first story we are told that Jesus came upon an insane man, a naked man who lived in the cemetery and hid himself behind the tombs. This man appealed to Jesus not to cast out the devils that bedeviled him.

But Jesus said unto him, "Come out of the man, thou unclean spirit." Mark 5:8.

Thus Jesus cast out the devils that they may now destroy themselves, and we find this man, for the first time, clothed and in his right mind and seated at the feet of the Master. We will get the psychological sense of this chapter by changing the name Jesus to that of enlightened reason or fourth-dimensional thinking.

As we progress in this chapter we are told that Jesus now comes upon the High Priest whose name is Jairus, and Jairus the High

Priest of the Synagogue has a child who is dying. She is 12 years old, and he appeals to Jesus to come and heal the child.

Jesus consents, and as he starts toward the home of the High Priest a woman in the market place touched his garment.

"And Jesus, immediately knowing in himself that virtue had gone out of him, turned him about in the press, and said, Who touched my clothes?"

Mark 5:30.

The woman who was healed of an issue of blood that she had had for 12 years confessed that she had touched him. "And he said unto her, Daughter, Thy faith hath made thee whole; go in peace." Mark 5:34

As he continues toward the home the High Priest he is told that the child is dead and there is no need to go to resurrect her. She is no longer asleep, but is now dead.

"As soon as Jesus heard the word that was spoken, he saith unto the ruler of the synagogue, Be not afraid, only believe."

Mark 5:36

"And when he was come in, he saith unto them, Why make ye this ado, and weep? The damsel is not dead, but sleepeth."

Mark 5:39

With this the entire crowd mocked and laughed, but Jesus, closing the doors against the mocking crowd, took with him into the household of Jairus, his disciples and the father and mother of the dead child.

They entered into the room where the damsel was lying. "And he took the damsel by the hand, and said unto her, Damsel, I say unto thee, arise." Mark 5:41

"From this deep sleep she awoke and arose and walked, and the High Priest and all the others were astonished. And he changed them straightly that no man should know it; and he commanded that something should be given her to eat."

Mark 5:43

You are this very night, as you are seated here, pictured in this 5th chapter of Mark. A cemetery is for one purpose: it is simply a record of the dead. Are you living in the dead past?

If you are living among the dead, your prejudices, your superstitions, and your false beliefs that you keep alive are the tombstones behind which you hide. If you refuse to let them go you are just as mad as the mad man of the Bible who pleaded with enlightened reason not to cast them out. There is no difference. But enlightened reason is incapable of protecting prejudice and superstition against the inroads of reason.

There is not a man in this world who has a prejudice, regardless of the nature of the prejudice, who can hold it up to the light of reason. Tell me you are against a certain nation, a certain race, a certain "ism," a certain anything -- I do not care what it is -- you cannot expose that belief of yours to the light of reason and have it live. In order that it may be kept alive in your world you must hide it from reason. You cannot analyze it in the light of reason and have it live. When this fourth-dimensional focus comes and shows you a new approach to life and casts out of your own mind all these things that bedeviled you, you are then cleansed and clothed in your right mind. And you sit at the foot of understanding, called the feet of the Master.

Now clothed and in your right mind you can resurrect the dead. What dead? The child in the story is not a child. The child is your ambition, your desire, the unfulfilled dreams of your heart. This is the child housed within the mind of man. For as I have stated before, the entire drama of the Bible is a psychological one. The Bible has no reference at all to any person who ever existed, or any event that ever occurred upon earth. All the stories of the Bible unfold in the minds of the individual man.

In this story Jesus is the awakened intellect of man. When your mind functions outside of the range of your present senses, when your mind is healed of all the former limitations, then you are no longer the insane man; but you are this presence personified as Jesus, the power that can resurrect the longings of the heart of man.

You are now the woman with the issue of blood. What is this issue of blood? A running womb is not a productive womb. She held it for 12 years, she was incapable of conceiving. She could not give form to her longing because of the running of the issue of blood. You are told her faith closed it. As the womb closes it can give form to the seed or idea.

As your mind is cleansed of your former concept of Self, you assume you are what you want to be, and remaining faithful to this assumption, you give form to your assumption or resurrect your child. You are the woman cleansed of the issue of blood, and you move towards the house of the dead child.

The child or state you desired is now your fixed concept of yourself. But now having assumed that I am what formerly I desired to be, I cannot continue desiring what I am conscious of being. So I do not discuss it. I talk to no one concerning what I am. It is so obvious to me that I am what I wanted to be that I walk as though I were.

Walking as though I am what formerly I wanted to be, my world of limited focus does not see it and thinks I no longer desire it. The child is dead within their world; but I, who know the law, say, "The child is not dead." The damsel is not dead, she but sleepeth. I now awaken her. I, by my assumption, awaken and make visible in my world what I assume, for assumptions if sustained invariably awaken what they affirm.

I close the door. What door? The door of my senses. I simply shut out completely all that my senses reveal. I deny the evidence of my senses. I suspend the limited reason of the natural man and walk in this bold assertion that I am what my senses deny.

With the door of my senses closed, what do I take into that disciplined state? I take no one into that state but the parents of the child and my disciples. I close the door against the mocking, laughing crowd. I no longer look for confirmation. I completely deny the evidence of my senses, which mock my assumption and do not discuss with others whether my assumption is possible or not.

Who are the parents? We have discovered that the father-mother of all creation is man's I AMness. Man's consciousness is God. I am conscious of the state. I am the father-mother of all my ideas and my mind remains faithful to this new concept of self. My mind is disciplined. I take into that state the disciples, and I shut out of that state everything that would deny it.

Now the child, unaided by a man, is resurrected. The condition which I desired and assumed that I had, becomes objectified within my world and bears witness to the power of my assumption.

You be the judge, I cannot judge you. You are either living now in the dead past, or you are living as the woman whose issue of blood has been stanched. Could you actually answer me if I asked you the question:

"Do you believe now that you, without the assistance of another, need only assume that you are what you want to be, to make that assumption real within your world? Or do you believe that you must first fulfill a certain condition imposed upon you by the past, that you must be of a certain order, or a certain something?'

I am not being critical of certain churches or groups, but there are those who believe that anyone outside of their church or group is not yet saved. I was born a Protestant. You talk to a Protestant, there is only one Christian, a Protestant. You talk to a Catholic, why there is nothing in the world that is a Christian but a Catholic. You talk to a Jew, and the Christians are heathens, and the Jews are the chosen. You talk to a Mohammedan, Jews and Christians are the infidels. You talk to someone else and all these are the untouchables. It does not matter to whom you talk, they are always the chosen ones.

If you believe that you must be one of these in order to be saved, you are still an insane man hiding behind these superstitions and these prejudices of the past, and you are begging not to be cleansed.

Some of you say to me, "Do not ask me to give up my belief in Jesus the man, or in Moses the man, or in Peter the man. When you ask me to give up my belief in these characters you are asking too much. Leave me these beliefs because they comfort me. I can believe that they lived upon earth and still follow your psychological interpretation of their stories."

I say, Come out of the dead past. Come out of that cemetery and walk, knowing that you and your Father are one, and your Father, who men call GOD, is your own consciousness. That is the only creative law in the world.

Of what are you conscious of being? Although you cannot see your objective with the limited focus of your three-dimensional mind, you are now that which you have assumed you are. Walk in that assumption and remain faithful to it.

Time in this dimension of your being, beats slowly and you may not, even after you objectify your assumption, remember there was a time when this present reality was but an attitude of mind. Because of the slowness of the beat of time here you often fail to see the relationship between your inner nature and the outer world that bears witness to it.

You be the judge of the position you now occupy in this 5th chapter of Mark. Are you resurrecting the dead child? Are you still in need of having that womb of your mind closed? Is it still running and therefore cannot be fertile? Are you now the insane man living in the dead past? Only you can be the judge and answer these questions.

****

Now we turn to a story in the 5th chapter of the Gospel of John. This will show you how beautifully the ancient story tellers told of the two distinct outlooks on this world- one, the limited three-dimensional focus, and the other, the fourth-dimensional focus.

This story tells of an impotent man who is quickly healed. Jesus comes to a place called Bethesda, which by definition means the House of Five Porches. On these Five Porches are unnumbered impotent folk- lame, blind, halt, withered, and others. Tradition had it that at certain seasons of the year an angel would descend and disturb the pool which was near these Five Porches. As the Angel disturbed the pool, the first one in was always healed. But only the first one, not the second.

Jesus, seeing a man who was lame from his mother's womb, said to him, "Wilt thou be made whole?" John 5:6

"The impotent man answered him, Sir, I have no man, when the water is troubled, to put me into the pool - but while I am coming, another steppeth down before me."

John 5:7

"Jesus saith unto him, Rise, take up thy bed, and walk."

John 5:8

"And immediately the man was made whole, and took up his bed, and walked, and on the same day was the Sabbath."

John 5:9

You read this story and you think some strange man who possessed miraculous power suddenly said to the lame man, "Rise and walk." I cannot repeat too often that the story, even when it introduces numberless individualities, takes place within the mind of the individual man.

The pool is your consciousness. The angel is an idea, called the messenger of GOD. Consciousness being God, when you have an idea you are entertaining an angel. The minute you are conscious of a desire your pool has been disturbed. Desire disturbs the mind of man. To want something is to be disturbed.

The very moment you have an ambition, or a clearly defined objective, the pool has been disturbed by the angel, which was the desire. You are told that the first one into the disturbed pool is always healed.

My closest companions in this world, my wife and my little girl, are to me when I address them, second. I must speak to my wife as, "you are." I must speak to anyone, no matter how close they are, as "You are." And after that the third person, "He is." There is only one person in this world with whom I can use the first person present and that is self. "I am," can be said only of myself, it cannot be said of another.

Therefore, when I am conscious of some desire that I want to be, but seemingly am not, the pool being disturbed, who can get into that pool before me? I alone possess the power of the first person. I am that which I want to be. Except I believe I am what I want to be, I remain as I formerly was and die in that limitation.

In this story you need no man to put you into the pool as your consciousness is disturbed by desire. All you need do is to assume you are already that which formerly you wanted to be and you are in it, and no man can get in before you. What man can get in before you when you become conscious of being that which you want to be? No one can be before you when you alone possess the power to say I AM.

These are the two outlooks. You are now what your senses would deny. Are you bold enough to assume that you are already that which you want to be? If you dare assume you are already that which your reason and your senses now deny, then you are in the pool and, unaided by a man, you, too, will rise and take your couch and walk.

You are told it happened on the Sabbath. The Sabbath is only the mystical sense of stillness, when you are unconcerned, when you are not anxious, when you are not looking for results, knowing that signs follow and do not precede.

The Sabbath is the day of stillness wherein there is no working. When you are not working to make it so you are in the Sabbath. When you are not at all concerned about the opinion of others, when you walk as though you were, you cannot raise one finger to make it so, you are in the Sabbath. I cannot be concerned as to how it will

204

be, and still say I am conscious of being it. If I am conscious of being free, secure, healthy, and happy, I sustain these states of consciousness without effort or labor on my part. Therefore, I am in the Sabbath; and because it was the Sabbath he rose and walked.

'*****

Our next story is from the 4th chapter of the Gospel of John, and it is one you have heard time and time again. Jesus comes to the well and there is a woman called the woman of Samaria, and he said to her, "Give me to drink." John 4:7

"Then saith the woman of Samaria unto him, How is it that thou, being a Jew, asketh drink of me, which am a woman of Samaria? For the Jews have no dealings with the Samaritans."

John 4:9

"Jesus answered and said unto her, If thou knewest the gift of God, and who it is that saith to thee, Give me to drink; thou wouldest have asked of him, and he would have given thee living water."

John 4:10

"The woman seeing that he has nothing with which to draw the water, and knowing the well is deep, says: Art thou greater than our father Jacob, which gave us the well, and drank thereof himself, and his children, and his cattle?"

John 4:12

"Jesus answered and said unto her, Whosoever drinketh of this water shall thirst again- But whosoever drinketh of the water that I shall give him shall never thirst; but the water that I shall give him shall be in him a well of water springing up into everlasting life." John 4:13, 14

Then he tells her all concerning herself and asks her to go and call her husband. She answered and said, "I have no husband." John 4:17

"Jesus said unto her, Thou hast well said, I have no husband: For thou hast had five husbands; and he whom thou now hast is not thy husband."

John 4: 17, 18

The woman, knowing this to be true, goes into the market-place and tells the other, "I have met the Messiah."

They ask her, "How do you know you have met the Messiah?"

"Because he told me all things that I have ever done." she replies. Here is a focus that takes in the entire past at least, and tells her now concerning the future.

Continuing with the story, the disciples come to Jesus and say, "Master, eat." John 4:31

"But he said unto them, I have meat to eat that ye know not of."

John 4:32

When they speak of a harvest in four months, Jesus replies, "Say not ye, There are yet four months, and then cometh harvest? Behold, I say unto you, lift up your eyes, and look on the fields; for they are white already to harvest." John 4:35

He sees things that people wait four months for, or wait four years for; he sees them as now in a dimensionally larger world, existing now, taking place now.

Let us go back to the first part of the story. The woman of Samaria is the three-dimensional you, and Jesus at the well is the fourth-dimensional you. The argument starts between what you want to be, and what reason tells you that you are. The greater you tells you that if you would dare assume you are already what you want to be, you would become it.

The lesser you, with its limited focus, tells you, "Why you haven't a bucket, you haven't a rope and the well is deep. How could you ever reach the depth of this state without the means to that end?"

You answer and say, "If you only knew who asks of you to drink you would ask of him." If you only knew what in yourself is urging upon you the embodiment of the state you now seek, you would suspend your little sight and let him do it for you.

Then he tells you that you have five husbands, and you deny it. But he knows far better than you that your five senses impregnate you morning, noon, and night with their limitations. They tell you what children you will bear tonight, tomorrow, and the days to come. For your five senses act like five husbands who constantly impregnate your consciousness, which is the great womb of GOD; and morning, noon, and night they suggest to you, and dictate to you that which you must accept as true.

He tells you the one you would like to have for your husband is not your husband. In other words the sixth has not yet impregnated you. What you would like to be is denied by these five, and they hold the power, they dictate what you will accept as true. What you would like to accept has not yet penetrated your mind and impregnated your mind with its reality. He whom you call husband is really not your husband. You are not bearing his likeness. To bear his likeness is proof that you are his wife, at least you have known him intimately. You are not bearing the likeness of the sixth; you are only bearing the likeness of the five.

Then one turns to me and tells me all that I have ever known. I go back in my mind's eye and reason tells me that all through my life I have always accepted the limitations of my senses, I have always looked upon them as fact; and morning, noon, and night I have born witness to this acceptance.

Reason tells me I have only known these five from the time I was born. Now I would like to step outside the limitation of my senses but I have not yet found within myself the courage to assume I am what these five would deny that I am. So here I remain, conscious of my task, but without the courage to step beyond the limitations of my senses, and that which my reason denies.

He tells these, "I have meat ye know not of. I am the bread that droppeth down from heaven. I am the wine." I know what I want to be, and because I am that bread I feast upon it. I assume that I am, and instead of feasting upon the fact that I am in this room talking to you and you are listening to me, and that I am in Los Angeles, I feast upon the fact that I am elsewhere and I walk here as though I were elsewhere. And gradually I become what I feast upon.

****

Let me give you two personal stories. When I was a boy I lived in a very limited environment, in a little island called Barbados. Feed for animals was very, very scarce and very expensive because we had to import it. I am one of a family of 10 children and my grandmother lived with us making 13 at the table.

Time and again I can remember my mother saying to the cook in the early part of the week, "I want you to put away three ducks for Sunday's dinner." This meant that she would take from the flock in the yard three ducks and coop them up in a very small cage and feed them, stuff them morning, noon, and night with corn and all the things she wanted the ducks to feast upon.

This was an entirely different diet from what we regularly fed the ducks, because we kept those birds alive by feeding them fish. We kept them alive and fat on fish because fish were very cheap and plentiful; but you could not eat a bird that fed upon fish, not as you and I like a bird.

The cook would take three ducks, put them in a cage and for seven days stuff them with corn, sour milk and all the things we wanted to taste in the birds. Then when they were killed and served for dinner seven days later they were luscious, milk fed, corn fed birds.

But occasionally the cook forgot to put away the birds, and my father, knowing we were having ducks, and believing that she had carried out the command, did not send anything else for dinner, and three fish came to the table. You could not touch those birds for they were so much the embodiment of what they fed upon.

Man is a psychological being, a thinker. It is not what he feeds upon physically, but what he feeds upon mentally that he becomes. We become the embodiment of that which we mentally feed upon.

Now those ducks could not be fed corn in the morning and fish in the afternoon and something else at night. It had to be a complete change of diet. In our case we cannot have a little bit of meditation in the morning, curse at noon, and do something else in the evening. We have to go on a mental diet, for a week we must completely change our mental food.

"Whatsoever things are true, whatsoever things are honest, whatsoever things are just, whatsoever things are pure, whatsoever things are of good report; if there be any virtue, and if there be any praise, think on these things."

Phil. 4:8

209

As a man thinketh in his heart so is he. If I could now single out the kind of mental food I want to express within my world and feast upon it, I would become it.

Let me tell you why I am doing what I am doing today. It was back in 1933 in the city of New York, and my old friend Abdullah, with whom I studied Hebrew for five years, was really the beginning of the eating of all my superstitions. When I went to him I was filled with superstitions. I could not eat meat, I could not eat fish, I could not eat chicken, I could not eat any of these things that were living in the world. I did not drink, I did not smoke, and I was making a tremendous effort to live a celibate life.

Abdullah said to me, "I am not going to tell you 'you are crazy' Neville, but you are you know. All these things are stupid." But I could not believe they were stupid.

In November, 1933, I bade goodbye to my parents in the city of New York as they sailed for Barbados. I had been in this country 12 years with no desire to see Barbados. I was not successful and I was ashamed to go home to successful members of my family. After 12 years in America I was a failure in my own eyes. I was in the theatre and made money one year and spent it the next month.

I was not what I would call by their standards nor by mine a successful person.

Mind you when I said goodbye to my parents in November I had no desire to go to Barbados. The ship pulled out, and as I came up the street, something possessed me with a desire to go to Barbados.

It was the year 1933, I was unemployed and had no place to go except a little room on 75th Street. I went straight to my old friend Abdullah and said to him "Ab, the strangest feeling is possessing me.

For the first time in 12 years I want to go to Barbados."

If you want to go Neville, you have gone." he replied.

That was very strange language to me. I am in New York City on 72nd Street and he tells me I have gone to Barbados. I said to him, "What do you mean, I have gone, Abdullah?"

He said, "Do you really want to go?"

I answered "yes."

He then said to me, "As you walk through this door now you are not walking on 72nd Street, you are walking on palm lined streets, coconut lined streets; this is Barbados. Do not ask me how you are going to go. You are in Barbados. You do not say 'how' when you 'are there'. You are there. Now you walk as though you were there."

I went out of his place in a daze. I am in Barbados. I have no money, I have no job, I am not even well clothed, and yet I am in Barbados.

He was not the kind of a person with whom you would argue, not Abdullah. Two weeks later I was no nearer my goal than on the day I first told him I wanted to go to Barbados. I said to him, "Ab, I trust you implicitly but here is one time I cannot see how it is going to work. I have not one penny towards my journey, I began to explain."

You know what he did. He was as black as the ace of spades, my old friend Abdullah, with his turbaned head. As I sat in his living room he rose from his chair and went towards his study and slammed the door, which was not an invitation to follow him. As he went through the door he said to me, "I have said all that I have to say."

On the 3rd of December I stood before Abdullah and told him again I was no nearer my trip. He repeated his statement, "You are in Barbados."

The very last ship sailing for Barbados that would take me there for the reason I wanted to go, which was to be there for Christmas, sailed at noon on December 6th, the old Nerissa.

On the morning of December 4th, having no job, having no place to go, I slept late. When I got up there was an air mail letter from Barbados under my door. As I opened the letter a little piece of paper flickered to the floor. I picked it up and it was a draft for $50.00.

The letter was from my brother Victor and it read, "I am not asking you to come, Neville, this is a command. We have never had a Christmas when all the members of our family were present at the same time. This Christmas it could be done if you would come. "

My oldest brother Cecil left home before the youngest was born and then we started to move away from home at different times so never in the history of our family were we ever all together at the same time.

The letter continued, "You are not working, I know there is no reason why you cannot come, so you must be here before Christmas. The enclosed $50.00 is to buy a few shirts or a pair of shoes you may need for the trip. You will not need tips; use the bar if you are drinking. I will meet the ship and pay all your tips and your incurred expenses. I have cabled Furness, Withy & Co. in New York City and told them to issue you a ticket when you appear at their office. The $50.00 is simply to buy some little essentials. You may sign as you want aboard the ship. I will meet it and take care of all obligations."

I went down to Furness, Withy & Co. with my letter and let them read it. They said, "We received the cable Mr. Goddard, but unfortunately we have not any space left on the December 6th sailing. The only thing available is 3rd Class between New York and St. Thomas. When we get to St. Thomas we have a few passengers who are getting off. You may then ride 1st Class from St. Thomas to Barbados. But between New York and St. Thomas you must go 3rd Class, although you may have the privileges of the 1st Class dining room and walk the decks of the 1st Class."

I said, "I will take it."

I went back to my friend Abdullah on the afternoon of December 4th and said, "It worked like a dream." I told him what I had done, thinking he would be happy.

Do you know what he said to me? He said, "Who told you that you are going 3rd Class? Did I see you in Barbados, the man you are, going 3rd Class? You are in Barbados and you went there 1st Class."

I did not have one moment to see him again before I sailed on the noon of December 6th. When I reached the dock with my passport and my papers to get aboard that ship the agent said to me, "We have good news for you, Mr. Goddard. There has been a cancellation and you are going 1st Class."

Abdullah taught me the importance of remaining faithful to an idea and not compromising. I wavered, but he remained faithful to the assumption that I was in Barbados and had traveled 1st Class.

****

Now back to the significance of our two Bible stories. The well is deep and you have no bucket, you have no rope. It is four months to the harvest and Jesus says, "I have meat to eat ye know not of. I am the bread of heaven. "

Feast on the idea, become identified with the idea as though you were already that embodied state. Walk in the assumption that you are what you want to be. If you feast on that and remain faithful to that mental diet, you will crystallize it. You will become it in this world.

When I came back to New York in 1934, after three heavenly months in Barbados, I drank, I smoked, and did everything I had not done in years.

I remembered what Abdullah had said to me, "After you have proven this law you will become normal, Neville. You will come out of that graveyard, you will come out of that dead past where you think you are being holy. For all you are really doing you know, you are being so good, Neville, you are good for nothing"

I came back walking this earth a completely transformed person. From that day, which was in February 1934, I began to live more and more. I cannot honestly tell you I have always succeeded. My many mistakes in this world, my many failures would convict me if I told you that I have so completely mastered the movements of my attention that I can at all times remain faithful to the idea I want to embody.

But I can say with the ancient teacher, although I seem to have failed in the past, I move on and strive day after day to become that which I want to embody in this world. Suspend judgment, refuse to accept what reason and the senses now dictate, and if you remain faithful to the new diet, you will become the embodiment of the ideal to which you remain faithful.

If there is one place in the world that is unlike my little island of Barbados, it is New York City. In Barbados the tallest building is three stories, and the streets are lined with palm trees and cocoanut trees and all sorts of tropical things. In New York City you must go to a park to find a tree.

Yet I had to walk the streets of New York as though I walked the streets of Barbados. To one's imagination all things are possible. I walked, feeling that I was actually walking the streets of Barbados, and in that assumption I could almost smell the odor of the cocoanut lined lanes. I began to create within my mind's eye the atmosphere I would physically encounter were I in Barbados.

As I remained faithful to this assumption, somebody canceled passage and I received it. My brother in Barbados, who never thought of my coming home, has the commanding urge to write me a strange letter. He had never dictated to me, but this time he dictated, and thought that he originated the idea of my visit.

I went home and had three heavenly months, returned 1st Class, and brought back quite a sum of cash in my pocket, a gift. My trip, had I paid for it, would have been $3,000, yet I did it without a nickel in my pocket.

"I have ways ye know not of. My ways are past finding out." The dimensionally greater self took my assumption as the command and influenced the behaviour of my brother to write that letter, influenced the behaviour of someone to cancel that 1st Class passage, and did all the things necessary that would tend toward the production of the idea with which I was identified.

I was identified with the feeling of being there. I slept as though I were there, and the entire behaviour of man was molded in harmony with my assumption. I did not need to go down to Furness, Withy & Co. and beg them for a passage, asking them to cancel some one who was booked 1st Class. I did not need to write my brother and beg him to send me some money or buy me a passage. He thought he originated the act. Actually, to this day, he believes that be initiated the desire to bring me home.

My old friend Abdullah simply said to me, "You are in Barbados, Neville. You want to be there; wherever you want to be, there you are. Live as though you are and that you shall be."

These are the two outlooks on the world possessed by every man. I do not care who you are. Every child born of woman, regardless of race, nation, or creed, possesses two distinct outlooks on the world.

You are either the natural man who receiveth not the things of the Spirit of God, because to you in the natural focus they are foolishness unto you. Or you are the spiritual man who perceiveth things outside of the limitations of your senses because all things are now realities in a dimensionally larger world. There is no need to wait four months to harvest.

You are either the woman of Samaria or Jesus at the well. You are the man waiting on the Five Porches for the disturbance and someone to push him in; or you are the one who can command yourself to rise and walk in spite of others who wait.

Are you the man behind the tombstones in the cemetery waiting and begging not to be clean, because you do not want to be cleansed of your prejudices? One of the most difficult things for man to give up is his superstitions, his prejudice. He holds on to these as though they were the treasure of treasures.

When you do become cleansed and you are free, then the womb, your own mind is automatically healed. It becomes the prepared ground where seeds, your desires, can take root and grow into manifestation. The child you now bear in your heart is your present objective. Your present longing is a child that is as though it were sick. If you assume you are now what you would like to be, the child for a moment becomes dead because there is no disturbance any more.

You cannot be disturbed when you feel you are what you want to be because if you feel you are what you wanted to be, you are satisfied in that assumption. To others who judge superficially you seem no longer to desire, so to them the desire or damsel is dead. They think you have lost your ambition because you no longer discuss your secret ambition. You have completely adjusted yourself to the idea. You have assumed that you are what you want to be. You know, "She is not dead, she but sleepth." "I go to awaken her."

I walk in the assumption that I am, and as I walk, I quietly awaken her. Then when she awakens I will do the normal, natural thing, I will give her to eat. I will not brag about it and tell others I simply go and tell no man. I feed this state I now like with my attention. I keep it alive within my world by becoming attentive to it.

Things that I am not attentive to fade and wither within my world, regardless of what they are. They are not just born and then remain unfed. I gave them birth by reason of the fact that I became conscious of being them. When I embody them within my world that is not the end. That is the beginning. Now I am a mother who must keep alive this state by being attentive to it. The day that I am not attentive, I have withdrawn my milk from it, and it fades from my world, as I become attentive to something else in my world.

You can either be attentive to the limitations and feed these and make them mountains, or you can be attentive to your desires; but to become attentive you must assume you are already that which you wanted to be.

Although today we speak of a third-dimensional and a fourth-dimensional focus, do not think for one moment these ancient teachers were not fully conscious of these two distinct centers of thought within the minds of all men. They personified these two, and they tried to show man that the only thing which robs him of the man he could be, is habit. Although it is not law, every psychologist will tell you that habit is the most inhibiting force in the world. It completely restricts man and binds him and makes him totally blind to what otherwise he should be.

Begin now to mentally see and feel yourself as that which you want to be, and feast upon that sensation morning, noon, and night. I have scoured the Bible for a time interval that is longer than three days and I have not found it.

"Jesus answered and said unto them, Destroy this temple, and in three days I will raise it Up."

John 2:19

"Prepare you victuals; for within three days ye shall pass over this Jordan, to go in to possess the land, which the Lord your God giveth you to possess it."

Joshua 1:11

If I could completely saturate my mind with one sensation and walk as though it were already a fact, I am promised (and I cannot find any denial of it in this great book) that I do not need more than a three day diet if I remain faithful to it. But I must be honest about it. If I Change my diet in the course of the day, I extend the time interval.

You ask me, "But how do I know about the interval?" You, yourself determine the interval.

We have today in our modern world a little word which confuses most of us. I know it confused me until I dug deeper. The word is "action." Action is supposed to be the most fundamental thing in the world. It is not an atom, it is more fundamental. It is not a part of an atom like an electron, it is more fundamental than that. They call it the fourth-dimensional unit. The most fundamental thing in the world is action.

You ask, "What is action?" Our physicists tell us that it is energy multiplied by time. We become more confused and say, "Energy multiplied by time, what does that mean?', They answer, "There is no response to a stimulus, no matter how intense the stimulus, unless it endures for a certain length of time." There must be a minimum endurance to the stimulus or there is no response. On the other hand there is no response to time unless there is a minimum degree of intensity. Today the most fundamental thing in the world is called action, or simply energy multiplied by time.

The Bible gives it as three days; the duration is three days for response in this world. If I would now assume I am what I want to be, and if I am faithful to it and walk as though I were, the very longest stretch given for its realization is three days.

If there is something tonight that you really want in this world, then experience in imagination what you would experience in the flesh were you to realize your goal and deafen your ears, and blind your eyes to all that denies the reality of your assumption.

If you do this you would be able to tell me before I leave this city of Los Angeles that you have realized what was only a wish when you came here. It will be my joy to rejoice with you in the knowledge that the child which was seemingly dead is now alive.

This damsel really was not dead, she was only asleep. You fed her in this silence because you have meat no one else knows of. You gave her food and she became a resurrected living reality within your world. Then you can share your joy with me and I can rejoice in your joy.

The purpose of these lessons is to remind you of the law of your own being, the law of consciousness; you are that law. You were only unconscious of its operation. You fed and kept alive the things you did not wish to express within this world.

Take my challenge and put this philosophy to the test. If it does not work you should not use it as a comforter. If it is not true, you must completely discard it. I know it is true. You will not know it until you try either to prove or disprove it.

Too many of us have joined "isms" and we are afraid to put them to the test because we feel we might fail; and, then, where are we? Not really wanting to know the truth concerning it, we hesitate to be bold enough to put it to the test. You say, "I know it would work in some other way. I do not want to really test it. While I have not yet disproved it, I can still be comforted by it.

Now do not fool yourself, do not think for one second be that you are wise.

Prove or disprove this law. I know that if you attempt to disprove it, you will prove it, and I will be the richer for your proving it, not in dollars, not in things, but because you become the living fruit of what I believe I am teaching in this world. It is far better to have you a successful, satisfied person after five days of instruction than to have you go out dissatisfied. I hope you will be bold enough to challenge this instruction and either prove or disprove it.

Now before we go into the silence period I shall briefly explain the technique again. We have two techniques in applying this law. Everyone here must now know exactly what he wants. You must know that if you do not get it tonight you will still be as desirous tomorrow concerning this objective.

When you know exactly what you want, construct in your mind's eye a single, simple event which implies fulfillment of your desire, an event where in self predominates. Instead of sitting back and looking at yourself as though you were on the screen, you be the actor in the drama.

Restrict the event to one single action. If you are going to shake a hand because that implies fulfillment of your desire then do that and that only. Do not shake hands and then wander off in your imagination to a dinner party or to some other place. Restrict your action to simply shaking hands and do it over and over again, until that handshake takes on the solidity and the distinctness of reality.

If you feel you cannot remain faithful to an action, I want you now to define your objective, and then condense the idea, which is your desire, into a single phrase, a phrase which implies fulfillment of your desire, some phrase such as, "Isn't it wonderful?"

Or if I felt thankful because I thought someone was instrumental in bringing my desire to pass, I could say, "Thank you," and repeat it with feeling over and over again like a lullaby until my mind was dominated by the single sensation of thankfulness.

We will now sit quietly in these chairs with the idea which implies fulfillment of our desire condensed to a single phrase, or to a single act. We will relax and immobilize our physical bodies. Then let us experience in imagination the sensation which our condensed phrase or action affirms.

If you imagine yourself shaking another person's hand, do not use your physical hand, let it remain immobilized. But imagine that housed within your hand is a more subtle, more real hand, which can be extracted in your imagination. Put your imaginary hand into the imaginary hand of your friend who stands before you and feel the handshake. Keep your physical body immobilized even though you become mentally active in what you are now about to do.

Now we will go into the silence.

NO ONE TO CHANGE BUT SELF

(Lesson 4)

May I take just a minute to clarify what was said last night. A lady felt from what I said last night that I am anti one nation. I do hope that I am not anti any nation, race or belief. If perchance I used a nation, it was only to illustrate a point.

What I tried to tell you was this -- we become what we contemplate. For it is the nature of love, as it is the nature of hate, to change us into the likeness of that which we contemplate. Last night I simply read a news item to show you that when we think we can destroy our image by breaking the mirror, we are only fooling ourselves.

When, through war or revolution, we destroy titles which to us represent arrogance and greed, we become in time the embodiment of that which we thought we had destroyed. So today the people who thought they destroyed the tyrants are themselves that which they thought they had destroyed.

That I may not be misunderstood, let me again lay the foundation of this principle. Consciousness is the one and only reality. We are incapable of seeing other than the contents of our own consciousness

Therefore, hate betrays us in the hour of victory and condemns us to be that which we condemn. All conquest results in an exchange of characteristics, so that conquerors become like the conquered foe. We hate others for the evil which is in ourselves. Races, nations, and religious groups have lived for centuries in intimate hostility, and it is the nature of hatred, as it is the nature of love, to change us into the likeness of that which we contemplate.

223

Nations act toward other nations as their own citizens act toward each other. When slavery exists in a state and that nation attacks another it is with intent to enslave. When there is a fierce economic competition between citizen and citizen, then in war with another nation the object of the war is to destroy the trade of the enemy. Wars of domination are brought about by the will of those who within a state are dominant over the fortunes of the rest.

We radiate the world that surrounds us by the intensity of our imagination and feeling. But in this third-dimensional world of ours time beats slowly. And so we do not always observe the relationship of the visible world to our inner nature.

Now that is really what I meant. I thought I had said it. That I may not be misunderstood, that is my principle. You and I can contemplate an ideal, and become it by falling in love with it.

On the other hand we can contemplate something we heartily dislike and by condemning it we will become it. But because of the slowness of time in this three-dimensional world, when we do become what we contemplated we have forgotten that formerly we set out to worship or destroy it.

Tonight's lesson is the capstone of the Bible, so do give me your attention. The most important question asked in the Bible will be found in the 16th chapter of the Gospel of St. Matthew.

As you know, all of the Bible stories are your stories; its characters live only in the mind of man. They have no reference at all to any person, who lived in time and space, or to any event that ever occurred upon earth.

****

The drama related in Matthew takes place in this manner Jesus turns to his disciples and asks them, "Whom do men say that I the Son of man am?" Matt. 16:13

"And they said, Some say that thou art John the Baptist: some, Elias; and others, Jeremiah, or one of the prophets."

"He saith unto them, But whom say ye that I am?"

"And Simon Peter answered and said, Thou are the Christ, the Son of the living God."

"And Jesus answered and said unto him, Blessed art thou, Simon Bar-Jonah: for flesh and blood hath not revealed it unto thee, but my Father which is in heaven."

"And I say also unto thee that thou art Peter, and upon this rock I will build my church."

Matt. 16:14-18

Jesus turning to his disciples is man turning to his disciplined mind in self-contemplation. You ask yourself the question, "Whom do men say that I am?" In our language, "I wonder what men think of me?"

You answer, "Some say John come again, Some say Elias, others say Jeremiah, and still others a Prophet of old come again."

It is very flattering to be told that you are, or that you resemble, the great men of the past, but enlightened reason is not enslaved by public opinion. It is only concerned with the truth so it asks itself another question, "But whom say ye that I am?" In other words, "Who am I?"

If I am bold enough to assume that I am Christ Jesus, the answer will come back, "Thou are Christ Jesus."

225

When I can assume it and feel it and boldly live it, I will say to myself, "Flesh and blood could not have told me this. But my Father which is in Heaven revealed it unto me." Then I make this concept of Self the rock on which I establish my church, my world.

"If ye believe not that I am He, ye shall die in your sins."

John 8:24

Because consciousness is the only reality I must assume that I am already that which I desire to be. If I do not believe that I am already what I want to be, then I remain as I am and die in this limitation.

Man is always looking for some prop on which to lean. He is always looking for some excuse to justify failure. This revelation gives man no excuse for failure. His concept of himself is the cause of all the circumstances of his life. All changes must first come from within himself; and if he does not change on the outside it is because he has not changed within. But man does not like to feel that he is solely responsible for the conditions of his life.

"From that time many of his disciples went back, and walked no more with him."

"Then said Jesus unto the twelve, Will ye also go away?"

"Then Simon Peter answered him, Lord, to whom shall we go? Thou hast the words of eternal life."

John 6:66-68

I may not like what I have just heard, that I must turn to my own consciousness as to the only reality, the only foundation on which all phenomena can be explained. It was easier living when I could blame another. It was much easier living when I could blame society for my ills, or point a finger across the sea and blame another nation. It was easier living when I could blame the weather for the way I feel.

But to tell me that I am the cause of all that happens to me that I am forever molding my world in harmony with my inner nature, that is more than man is willing to accept. If this is true, to whom would I go? If these are the words of eternal life, I must return to them, even though they seem so difficult to digest.

When man fully understands this, he knows that public opinion does not matter, for men only tell him who he is. The behaviour of men constantly tell me who I have conceived myself to be.

If I accept this challenge and begin to live by it, I finally reach the point that is called the great prayer of the Bible. It is related in the 17th chapter of the Gospel of St. John, "I have finished the work which thou gavest me to do." John 17:4

"And now, O Father, glorify thou me with thine own self with the glory which I had with thee before the world was."

John 17:5

"While I was with them in the world, I kept them in thy name: those that thou gavest me I have kept, and none of them is lost, but the son of perdition."

John 17:12

It is impossible for anything to be lost. In this divine economy nothing can be lost, it cannot even pass away. The little flower which has bloomed once, blooms forever. It is invisible to you here with your limited focus, but it blooms forever in the larger dimension of your being, and tomorrow you will encounter it.

All that thou gavest me I have kept in thy name, and none have I lost save the son of perdition. The son of perdition means simply the belief in loss. Son is a concept, an idea. Perdido is loss. I have only truly lost the concept of loss, for nothing can be lost.

I can descend from the sphere where the thing itself now lives, and as I descend in consciousness to a lower level within myself it passes from my world. I say, "I have lost my health. I have lost my wealth. I have lost my standing in the community. I have lost faith. I have lost a thousand things." But the things in themselves, having once been real in my world, can never cease to be. They never become unreal with the passage of time.

I, by my descent in consciousness to a lower level, cause these things to disappear from my sight and I say, "They have gone; they are finished as far as my world goes." All I need do is to ascend to the level where they are eternal, and they once more objectify themselves and appear as realities within my world.

The crux of the whole 17th chapter of the Gospel of St. John is found in the 19th verse, "And for their sake I sanctify myself, that they also might be sanctified through the truth."

Heretofore I thought I could change others through effort. Now I know I cannot change another unless I first change myself. To change another within my world I must first change my concept of that other; and to do it best I change my concept of self. For it was the concept I held of self that made me see others as I did.

Had I a noble, dignified concept of myself, I never could have seen the unlovely in others.

Instead of trying to change others through argument and force, let me but ascend in consciousness to a higher level and I will automatically change others by changing self. "There is no one to change but self; that self is simply your awareness, your consciousness and the world in which it lives is determined by the concept you hold of self. It is to consciousness that we must turn as to the only reality. For there is no clear conception of the origin of phenomena except that consciousness is all and all is consciousness.

You need no helper to bring you what you seek. Do not for one second believe that I am advocating escape from reality when I ask you to simply assume you are now the man or the lady that you want to be.

If you and I could feel what it would be like were we now that which we want to be, and live in this mental atmosphere as though it were real, then, in a way we do not know, our assumption would harden into fact. This is all we need do in order to ascend to the level where our assumption is already an objective, concrete reality.

I need change no man, I sanctify myself and in so doing I sanctify others. To the pure all things are pure. "There is nothing unclean of itself: but to him that esteemeth anything to be unclean, to him it is unclean." Rom. 14:14. There is nothing in itself unclean, but you, by your concept of self, see things either clean or unclean.

"I and my Father are one."

John 10:30.

"If I do not the works of my Father, believe me not."

"But if I do, though ye believe not me, believe the works: that ye may know, and believe, that the Father is in me, and I in him."

John 10:37, 38

He made himself one with God and thought it not strange or robbery to do the works of God. You always bear fruit in harmony with what you are. It is the most natural thing in the world for a pear tree to bear pears, an apple tree to bear apples, and for man to mold the circumstances of his life in harmony with his inner nature.

"I am the vine, ye are the branches." John 15:5. A branch has no life save it be rooted in the vine. All I need do to change the fruit is to change the vine.

You have no life in my world save that I am conscious of you. You are rooted in me and, like fruit, you bear witness of the vine that I am. There is no reality in the world other than your consciousness. Although you may now seem to be what you do not want to be, all you need do to change it, and to prove the change by circumstances in your world, is to quietly assume that you are that which you now want to be, and in a way you do not know you will become it.

There is no other way to change this world. "I am the way." My I AMness, my consciousness is the way by which I change my world. As I change my concept of self, I change my world. When men and women help or hinder us, they only play the part that we, by our concept of self, wrote for them, and they play it automatically. They must play the parts they are playing because we are what we are.

You will change the world only when you become the embodiment of that which you want the world to be. You have but one gift in this world that is truly yours to give and that is yourself. Unless you yourself are that which you want the world to be, you will never see it in this world. "Except ye believe not that I am he, ye shall die in your sins." John 8:24

Do you know that no two in this room live in the same world. We are going home to different worlds tonight. We close our doors on entirely different worlds. We rise tomorrow and go to work, where we meet each other and meet others, but we live in different mental worlds, different physical worlds.

I can only give what I am, I have no other gift to give. If I want the world to be perfect, and who does not, I have failed only because I did not know that I could never see it perfect until I myself become perfect. If I am not perfect I cannot see perfection, but the day that I become it, I beautify my world because I see it through my own eyes. "Unto the pure all things are pure." Titus 1:15

No two here can tell me that you have heard the same message any one night. The one thing that you must do is hear what I say through that which you are. It must be filtered through your prejudices, your superstitions, and your concept of self. Whatever you are, it must come through that, and be colored by what you are.

If you are disturbed and you would like me to be something other than what I appear to be, then you must be that which you want me to be. We must become the thing that we want others to be or we will never see them be it.

Your consciousness, my consciousness, is the only true foundation in the world. This is that which is called Peter in the Bible, not a man, this faithfulness that cannot turn to anyone, that cannot be flattered when you are told by men you are John come again. That is very flattering to be told you are John the Baptist come again, or the great Prophet Elias, or Jeremiah.

Then I deafen my ears to this very flattering little bit of news men would give me and I ask myself, "But honestly who am I?"

If I can deny the limitations of my birth, my environment, and the belief that I am but an extension of my family tree, and feel within myself that I am Christ, and sustain this assumption until it takes a central place and forms the habitual center of my energy, I will do the works attributed to Jesus. Without thought or effort I will mold a world in harmony with that perfection which I have assumed and feel springing within me.

When I open the eyes of the blind, unstop the ears of the deaf, give joy for mourning and beauty for ashes, then and only then, have I truly established this vine deep within. That is what I would automatically do were I truly conscious of being Christ. It is said of this presence, He proved that He was Christ by His works.

Our ordinary alterations of consciousness, as we pass from one state to another, are not transformations, because each of them is so rapidly succeeded by another in the reverse direction; but whenever our assumption grows so stable as to definitely expel its rivals, then that central habitual concept defines our character and is a true transformation.

Jesus, or enlightened reason, saw nothing unclean in the woman taken in adultery. He said to her, "Hath no man condemned thee?" John 8:10

"She said, No man, Lord. And Jesus said unto her, neither do I condemn thee; go, and sin no more."

John 8:11

No matter what is brought before the presence of beauty, it sees only beauty. Jesus was so completely identified with the lovely that He was incapable of seeing the unlovely.

When you and I really become conscious of being Christ, we too will straighten the arms of the withered, and resurrect the dead hopes of men. We will do all the things that we could not do when we felt ourselves limited by our family tree. It is a bold step and should not be taken lightly, because to do it is to die. John, the man of three dimensions is beheaded, or loses his three-dimensional focus that Jesus, the fourth-dimensional Self may live.

Any enlargement of our concept of Self involves a somewhat painful parting with strongly rooted hereditary conceptions. The ligaments are strong that hold us in the womb of conventional limitations. All that you formerly believed, you no longer believe. You know now that there is no power outside of your own consciousness. Therefore you cannot turn to anyone outside of self.

You have no ears for the suggestion that something else has power in it. You know the only reality is God, and God is your own consciousness. There is no other God. Therefore on this rock you build the everlasting church and boldly assume you are this Divine Being, self-begotten because you dared to appropriate that which was not given to you in your cradle, a concept of Self not formed in your mother's womb, a concept of self conceived outside of the offices of man.

The story is beautifully told us in the Bible using the two sons of Abraham: one the blessed, Isaac, born outside of the offices of man and the other, Ishmael, born in bondage.

Sarah was much too old to beget a child, so her husband Abraham went in unto the bondservant Hagar, the pilgrim, and she conceived of the old man and bore him a son called Ishmael. Ishmael's hand was against every man and every man's hand against him.

Every child born of woman is born into bondage, born into all that his environment represents, regardless of whether it be the throne of England, the White House, or any great place in the world. Every child born of woman is personified as this Ishmael, the child of Hagar.

But asleep in every child is the blessed Isaac, who is born outside of the offices of man, and is born through faith alone. This second child has no earthly father. He is Self-begotten.

What is the second birth? I find myself man, I cannot go back into my mother's womb, and yet I must be born a second time. "Except a man be born again he cannot enter the kingdom of God." John 3:3

I quietly appropriate that which no man can give me, no woman can give me. I dare to assume that I am God. This must be of faith, this must be of promise. Then I become the blessed, I become Isaac.

As I begin to do the things that only this presence could do, I know that I am born out of the limitations of Ishmael, and I have become heir to the kingdom. Ishmael could not inherit anything, although his father was Abraham, or God. Ishmael did not have both parents of the godly; his mother was Hagar the bond-woman, and so he could not partake of his father's estate.

You are Abraham and Sarah, and contained within your own consciousness there is one waiting for recognition. In the Old Testament it is called Isaac, and in the New Testament it is called Jesus, and it is born without the aid of man.

No man can tell you that you are Christ Jesus, no man can tell you and convince you that you are God. You must toy with the idea and wonder what it would be like to be God.

No clear conception of the origin of phenomena is possible except that consciousness is all and all is consciousness. Nothing can be evolved from man that was not potentially involved in his nature. The ideal we serve and hope to attain could never be evolved from us were it not potentially involved in our nature.

234

Let me now retell and emphasize an experience of mine printed by me two years ago under the title, THE SEARCH. I think it will help you to understand this law of consciousness, and show you that you have no one to change but self, for you are incapable of seeing other than the contents of your own consciousness.

Once in an idle interval at sea, I meditated on "the perfect state," and wondered what I would be were I of too pure eyes to behold iniquity, if to me all things were pure and were I without condemnation. As I became lost in this fiery brooding, I found myself lifted above the dark environment of the senses. So intense was feeling I felt myself a being of fire dwelling in a body of air. Voices, as from a heavenly chorus, with the exaltation of those who had been conquerors in a conflict with death, were singing, "He is risen -He is risen," and intuitively I knew they meant me.

Then I seemed to be walking in the night. I soon came upon a scene that might have been the ancient Pool of Bethesda for in this place lay a great multitude of impotent folk -- blind, halt, withered - waiting not for the moving of the water as of tradition, but waiting for me.

As I came near, without thought or effort on my part, they were one after the other, molded as by the Magician of the Beautiful. Eyes, hands, feet -- all missing members -- were drawn from some invisible reservoir and molded in harmony with that perfection which I felt springing within me. When all were made perfect the chorus exulted, "It is finished."

I know this vision was the result of my intense meditation upon the idea of perfection, for my meditations invariably bring about union with the state contemplated. I had been so completely absorbed within the idea that for awhile I had become what I contemplated, and the high purpose with which I had for that moment identified myself drew the companionship of high things and fashioned the vision in harmony with my inner nature.

The ideal with which we are united works by association of ideas to awaken a thousand moods to create a drama in keeping with the central idea.

My mystical experiences have convinced me that there is no way to bring about the perfection we seek other than by the transformation of ourselves. As soon as we succeed in transforming ourselves, the world will melt magically before our eyes and reshape itself in harmony with that which our transformation affirms.

We fashion the world that surrounds us by the intensity of our imagination and feeling, and we illuminate or darken our lives by the concepts we hold of ourselves. Nothing is more important to us than our conception of ourselves, and especially is true of our concept of the deep, dimensionally greater One within us.

Those that help or hinder us, whether they know it or not, are the servants of that law which shapes outward circumstances in harmony with our inner nature. It is our conception of ourselves which frees or constrains us, though it may use material agencies to achieve its purpose.

Because life molds the outer world to reflect the inner arrangement of our minds, there is no way of bringing about the outer perfection we seek other than by the transformation of ourselves. No help cometh from without: the hills to which we lift our eyes are those of an inner range.

It is thus to our own consciousness that we must turn as to the only reality, the only foundation on which all phenomena can be explained. We can rely absolutely on the justice of this law to give us only that which is of the nature of ourselves.

To attempt to change the world before we change our concept of ourselves is to struggle against the nature of things. There can be no outer change until there is first an inner change.

As within, so without.

I am not advocating philosophical indifference when I suggest that we should imagine ourselves as already that which we want to be, living in a mental atmosphere of greatness, rather than using physical means and arguments to bring about the desired changes.

Everything we do, unaccompanied by a change of consciousness, is but futile readjustment of surfaces.

However we toil or struggle, we can receive no more than our concepts of Self affirm. To protest against anything which happens to us is to protest against the law of our being and our ruler ship over our own destiny.

The circumstances of my life are too closely related to my conception of myself not to have been formed by my own spirit from some dimensionally larger storehouse of my being. If there is pain to me in these happenings, I should look within myself for the cause, for I am moved here and there and made to live in a world in harmony with my concept of myself.

If we would become as emotionally aroused over our ideas as we become over our dislikes, we would ascend to the plane of our ideal as easily as we now descend to the level of our hates.

Love and hate have a magical transforming power, and we grow through their exercise into the likeness of what we contemplate. By intensity of hatred we create in ourselves the character we imagine in our enemies. Qualities die for want of attention, so the unlovely states might best be rubbed out by imagining '"beauty for ashes and joy for mourning" rather than by direct attacks on the state from which we would be free.

"Whatsoever things are lovely and of good report, think on these things," for we become that with which we are en rapport.

There is nothing to change but our concept of self. As soon as we succeed in transforming self, our world will dissolve and reshape itself in harmony with that which our change affirms.

I, by descent in consciousness, have brought about the imperfection that I see. In the divine economy nothing is lost. We cannot lose anything save by descent in consciousness from the sphere where the thing has its natural life.

"And now, O Faber, glorify thou me with thine own self with the glory which I had with thee before the world was."

John 17:5

As I ascend in consciousness the power and the glory that was mine return to me and I too will say "I have finished the work thou gavest me to do." The work is to return from my descent in consciousness, from the level wherein I believed that I was a son of man, to the sphere where I know that I am one with my Father and my Father is God.

I know beyond all doubt that there is nothing for man to do but to change his own concept of himself to assume greatness and sustain this assumption. If we walk as though we were already the ideal we serve, we will rise to the level of our assumption, and find a world in harmony with our assumption. We will not have to lift a finger to make it so, for it is already so. It was always so.

You and I have descended in consciousness to the level where we now find ourselves and we see imperfection because we have descended! When we begin to ascend while here in this three-dimensional world, we find that we move in an entirely different environment, we have entirely different circles of friends, and an entirely different world while still living here. We know the great mystery of the statement, "I am in the world but not of it."

Instead of changing things I would suggest to all to identify themselves with the ideal they contemplate. What would the feeling be like were you of too pure eyes to behold iniquity if to you all things were pure and you were without condemnation? Contemplate the ideal state and identify yourself with it and you will ascend to the sphere where you as Christ have your natural life.

You are still in that state where you were before the world was. The only thing that has fallen is your concept of self. You see the broken parts which really are not broken. You are seeing them through distorted eyes, as though you were in one of those peculiar amusement gallery's where a man walks before a mirror and he is elongated, yet he is the same man. Or he looks into another mirror and he is all big and fat. These things are seen today because man is what he is.

Toy with the idea of perfection. Ask no man to help you, but let the prayer of the 17th chapter of the Gospel of St. John be your prayer. Appropriate the state that was yours before the world was.

Know the truth of the statement, "None have I lost save the son of perdition." Nothing is lost in all my holy mountain. The only thing that you lose is the belief in loss or the son of perdition.

"And for their sake I sanctify myself, that they also might be sanctified through the truth."

John 17:19

There is no one to change but self. All you need do to make men and women holy in this world is to make yourself holy. You are incapable of seeing anything that is unlovely when you establish within your own mind's eye the fact that you are lovely.

It is far better to know this than to know anything else in the world. It takes courage, boundless courage, because many this night, after having heard this truth will still be inclined to blame others for their predicament. Man finds it so difficult to turn to himself, to his own consciousness as to the only reality. Listen to these words:

"No man can come to me, except the Father which hath sent me draw him."

John 6:44

"I and my Father are one."

John 10:30

"A man can receive nothing, except it be given him from heaven."

John 3:27

"Therefore doth my Father love me, because I lay down my life, that I might take it again."

"No man taketh it from me, but I lay it down of myself."

John 10:17, 18.

"You did not choose me, I have chosen you." My concept of myself molds a world in harmony with itself and draws men to tell me constantly by their behaviour who I am.

The most important thing in this world to you is your concept of self. When you dislike your environment, the circumstances of life and the behaviour of men, ask yourself, "Who am I?" It is your answer to this question hat is the cause of your dislikes.

If you do not condemn self there will be no man in your world to condemn you. If you are living in the consciousness of your ideal you will see nothing to condemn. "To the pure all things are pure."

Now I would like to spend a little time making as clear as I can what I personally do when I pray, what I do when I want to bring about changes in my world. You will find it interesting, and you will find that it works. No one here can tell me they cannot do it. It is so very simple all can do it. We are what we imagine we are.

This technique is not difficult to follow, but you must want to do it. You cannot approach it with the attitude of mind "Oh well I'll try it." You must want to do it, because the mainspring of action is desire.

Desire is the mainspring of all action. Now what do I want? I must define my objective. For example, suppose I wanted now to be elsewhere. This very moment I really desire to be elsewhere. I need not go through the door, I need not sit down. I need do nothing but stand just where I am and with my eyes closed, assume that I am actually standing where I desire to be. Then I remain in this state until it has the feeling of reality. Were I now elsewhere I could not see the world as I now see it from here. The world changes in its relationship to me as I change my position in space.

So I stand right here, close my eyes, and imagine I am seeing what I would see were I there. I remain in it long enough to feel it to be real. I cannot touch the walls of this room from here, but when you close your eyes and become still you can imagine and feel that you touch it. You can stand where you are and imagine you are putting your hand on that wall. To prove you really are, put it there and slide it up and feel the wood. You can imagine you are doing it without getting off your seat. You can do it and you will actually feel it if you become still enough and intense enough

I stand where I am and I allow the world that I want to see and to enter physically to come before me as though I were there now. In other words, I bring elsewhere here by assuming that I am there.

Is that clear? I let it come up, I do not make it come up. I simply imagine I am there and then let it happen.

If I want a physical presence, I imagine he is standing here, and I touch him All through the Bible I find these suggestions, "He placed his hands upon them. He touched them."

If you want to comfort someone, what is the automatic feeling? To put your hand on them, you cannot resist it. You meet a friend and the hand goes out automatically, you either shake hands or put your hand on his shoulder.

Suppose you were now to meet a friend that you have not seen for a year and he is a friend of whom you are very fond. What would you do? You would embrace him, wouldn't you? Or you would put your hand upon him.

In your imagination bring him close enough to put your hand upon him and feel him to be solidly real. Restrict the action to just that. You will be amazed at what happens. From then on things begin to move. Your dimensionally greater self will inspire, in all, the ideas and actions necessary to bring you into physical contact. It works that way.

Every day I put myself into the drowsy state; it is a very easy thing to do. But habit is a strange thing in man's world. It is not law, but habit acts as though it were the most compelling law in the world. We are creatures of habit.

If you create an interval every day into which you put yourself into the drowsy state, say at 3 o'clock in the afternoon do you know at that moment every day you will feel drowsy. You try it for one week and see if I am not right.

You sit down for the purpose of creating a state akin to sleep, as though you were sleepy, but do not push the drowsiness too far, just far enough to relax and leave you in control of the direction of your thoughts. You try it for one week, and every day at that hour, no matter what you are doing, you will hardly be able to keep your eyes open. If you know the hour when you will be free you can create it. I would not suggest that you do it lightly, because you will feel very, very sleepy and you may not want to.

I have another way of praying. In this case I always sit down and I find the most comfortable arm chair imaginable, or I lie flat on my back and relax completely. Make yourself comfortable. You must not be in any position where the body is distressed. Always put yourself into a position where you have the greatest ease. That is the first stage.

To know what you want is the start of prayer. Secondly you construct in your mind's eye one single little event which implies that you have realized your desire. I always let my mind roam on many things that could follow the answered prayer and I single out one that is most likely to follow the fulfillment of my desire. One simple little thing like the shaking of a hand, embracing a person, the receiving of a letter, the writing of a check, or whatever would imply the fulfillment of your desire.

After you have decided on the action which implies that your desire has been realized, then sit in your nice comfortable chair or lie flat on your back, close your eyes for the simple reason it helps to induce this state that borders on sleep.

The minute you feel this lovely drowsy state, or the feeling of gathered togetherness, wherein you feel- I could move if I wanted to, but I do not want to, I could open my eyes if I wanted to, but I do not want to. When you get that feeling you can be quite sure that you are in the perfect state to pray successfully.

In this feeling it is easy to touch anything in this world. You take the simple little restricted action which implies fulfillment of your prayer and you feel it or you enact it. Whatever it is, you enter into the action as though you were an actor in the part. You do not sit back and visualize yourself doing it. You do it.

With the body immobilized you imagine that the greater you inside the physical body is coming out of it and that you are actually performing the proposed action. If you are going to walk, you imagine that you are walking. Do not see yourself walk, FEEL that you are walking.

If you are going to climb stairs, FEEL that you are climbing the stairs. Do not visualize yourself doing it, feel yourself doing it. If you are going to shake a man's hand, do not visualize yourself shaking his hand, imagine your friend is standing before you and shake his hand. But leave your physical hands immobilized and imagine that your greater hand, which is your imaginary hand, is actually shaking his hand.

All you need do is to imagine that you are doing it. You are stretched out in time, and what you are doing, which seems to be a controlled day dream, is an actual act in the greater dimension of your being. You are actually encountering an event fourth-dimensionally before you encounter it here in the three-dimensions of space, and you do not have to raise a finger to bring that state to pass.

My third way of praying is simply to feel thankful. If I want something, either for myself or another, I immobilize the physical body, then I produce the state akin to sleep and in that state just feel happy, feel thankful, which thankfulness implies realization of what I want. I assume the feeling of the wish fulfilled and with my mind dominated by this single sensation I go to sleep. I need do nothing to make it so, because it is so. My feeling of the wish fulfilled implies it is done.

All these techniques you can use and change them to fit your temperament. But I must emphasize the necessity of inducing the drowsy state where you can become attentive without effort.

A single sensation dominates the mind, if you pray successfully.

What would I feel like, now, were I what I want to be? When I know what the feeling would be like I then close my eyes and lose myself in that single sensation and my dimensionally greater Self then builds a bridge of incident to lead me from this present moment to the fulfillment of my mood. That is all you need do. But people have a habit of slighting the importance of simple things.

We are creatures of habit and we are slowly learning to relinquish our previous concepts, but the things we formerly lived by still in some way influence our behaviour. Here is a story from the Bible that illustrates my point.

It is recorded that Jesus told his disciples to go to the crossroads and there they would find a colt, a young colt not yet ridden by a man. To bring the colt to him and if any man ask, "Why do you take this colt?" say, "The Lord has need of it."

They went to the crossroads and found the colt and did exactly as they were told. They brought the unbridled ass to Jesus and He rode it triumphantly into Jerusalem.

245

The story has nothing to do with a man riding on a little colt. You are Jesus of the story. The colt is the mood you are going to assume. That is the living animal not yet ridden by you. What would the feeling be like were you to realize your desire? A new feeling, like a young Colt, is a very difficult thing to ride unless you ride him with a disciplined mind. If I do not remain faithful to the mood the young colt throws me off. Every time you become conscious that you are not faithful to this mood, you have been thrown from the colt.

Discipline your mind that you may remain faithful to a high mood and ride it triumphantly into Jerusalem, which is fulfillment, or the city of peace.

This story precedes the feast of the Passover. If we would pass from our present state into that of our ideal, we must assume that we are already that which we desire to be and remain faithful to our assumption, for we must keep a high mood if we would walk with the highest.

A fixed attitude of mind, a feeling that it is done will make it so. If I walk as though it were, but every once in a while I look to see if it really is, then I fall off my mood or colt.

If I would suspend judgment like Peter I could walk on the water. Peter starts walking on the water, and then he begins to look unto his own understanding and he begins to go down. The voice said, "Look up, Peter." Peter looks up and he rises again and continues walking on the water.

Instead of looking down to see if this thing is really going to harden into fact, you simply know that it is already so, sustain that mood and you will ride the unbridled colt into the city of Jerusalem All of us must learn to ride the animal straight in to Jerusalem unassisted by a man. You do not need another to help you.

The strange thing is that as we keep the high mood and do not fall, others cushion the blows. They spread the palm leaves before me to cushion my journey. I do not have to be concerned. The shocks will be softened as I move into the fulfillment of my desire. My high mood awakens in others the ideas and actions which tend towards the embodiment of my mood. If you walk faithful to a high mood there will be no opposition and no competition.

The test of a teacher, or a teaching, is to be found in the faithfulness of the taught. I am leaving here on Sunday night. Do remain faithful to this instruction. If you look for causes outside the consciousness of man, then I have not convinced you of the reality of consciousness.

If you look for excuses for failure you will always find them, for you find what you seek. If you seek an excuse for failure, you will find it in the stars, in the numbers, in the tea cup, or most any place. The excuse will not be there but you will find it to justify your failure.

Successful business and professional men and women know that this law works. You will not find it in gossip groups, but you will find it in courageous hearts.

Man's eternal journey is for one purpose: to reveal the Father. He comes to make visible his Father. And his Father is made visible in all the lovely things of this world. All the things that are lovely, that are of good report, ride these things, and have no time for the unlovely in this world, regardless of what it is.

Remain faithful to the knowledge that your consciousness, your I AMness, your awareness of being aware of the only reality. It is the rock on which all phenomena can be explained. There is no explanation outside of that. I know of no clear conception of the origin of phenomena save that consciousness is all and all is consciousness.

That which you seek is already housed within you. Were it not now within you eternity could not evolve it. No time stretch would be long enough to evolve what is not potentially involved in you.

You simply let it into being by assuming that it is already visible in your world, and remaining faithful to your assumption. it will harden into fact. Your Father has unnumbered ways of revealing your assumption. Fix this in your mind and always remember, "An assumption, though false, if sustained will harden into fact."

You and your Father are one and your Father is everything that was, is and will be. Therefore that which you seek you already are, it can never be so far off as even to be near, for nearness implies separation.

The great Pascal said, "You never would have sought me had you not already found me." What you now desire you already have and you seek it only because you have already found it. You found it in the form of desire. It is just as real in the form of desire as it is going to be to your bodily organs.

You are already that which you seek and you have no one to change but Self in order to express it.

REMAIN FAITHFUL TO YOUR IDEA

(Lesson 5)

Tonight we have the fifth and last lesson in this course. First I shall give you a sort of summary of what has gone before. Then, since so many of you have asked me to elaborate further on Lesson 3, I shall give you a few more ideas on thinking fourth-dimensionally.

I know that when a man sees a thing clearly he can tell it, he can explain it. This past winter in Barbados a fisherman, whose vocabulary would not encompass a thousand words, told me more in five minutes about the behaviour of the dolphin than Shakespeare with his vast vocabulary could have told me, if he did not know the habits of the dolphin.

This fisherman told me how the dolphin loves to play on a piece of drift-wood, and in order to catch him, you throw the wood out and bait him as you would bait children, because he likes to pretend he is getting out of the water. As I said, this man's vocabulary was very limited, but he knew his fish, and he knew the sea. Because he knew his dolphin he could tell me all about their habits and how to catch them.

When you say you know a thing but you cannot explain it, I say you do not know it, for when you really know it you naturally express it.

If I should ask you now to define prayer, and say to you, "How would you, through prayer, go about realizing an objective, any objective?" If you can tell me, then you know it; but if you cannot tell me, then you do not know it. When you see it clearly in the mind's eye the greater you will inspire the words which are

249

necessary to clothe the idea and express it beautifully, and you will express the idea far better than a man with a vast vocabulary who does not see it as clearly as you do.

If you have listened carefully throughout the past four days, you know now that the Bible has no reference at all to any persons that ever existed, or to any events that ever occurred upon earth.

The authors of the Bible were not writing history, they were writing a great drama of the mind which they dressed up in the garb of history, and then adapted it to the limited capacity of the uncritical, unthinking masses.

You know that every story in the Bible is your story, that when the writers introduce dozens of characters in the same story they are trying to present you with different attributes of the mind that you may employ. You saw it as I took perhaps a dozen or more stories and interpreted them for you.

For instance, many people wonder how Jesus, the most gracious, the most loving man in the world, if he be man, could say to his mother, what he is supposed to have said to her as recorded in the second chapter of the Gospel of St. John. Jesus is made to say to his mother, "Woman, what have I to do with thee?" John 2:4.

You and I, who are not yet identified with the ideal we serve, would not make such a statement to our mother. Yet here was the embodiment of love saying to his mother, "Woman, what have I to do with thee?"

You are Jesus, and your mother is your own consciousness. For consciousness is the cause of all, therefore, it is the great father-mother of all phenomena.

You and I are creatures of habit. We get into the habit of accepting as final the evidence of our senses. Wine is needed for the guests and my senses tell me that there is no wine, and I through habit am about to accept this lack as final. When I remember that my consciousness is the one and only reality, therefore if I deny the evidence of my senses and assume the consciousness of having sufficient wine, I have in a sense rebuked my mother or the consciousness which suggested lack; and by assuming the consciousness of having what I desire for my guests, wine is produced in a way we do not know.

I have just read a note here from a dear friend of mine in the audience. Last Sunday he had an appointment at a church for a wedding; the clock told him he was late, everything told him he was late.

He was standing on a street corner waiting for a street car. There was none in sight. He imagined that, instead of being on the street corner, that he was in the church. At that moment a car stopped in front of him. My friend told the driver of his predicament and the driver said to him, "I am not going that way, but I will take you there." My friend got into the car and was at the church in time for the service. That is applying the law correctly, non-acceptance of the suggestion of lateness. Never accept the suggestion of lack.

In this case I say to myself, "What have I to do with thee?" What have I to do with the evidence of my senses? Bring me all the pots and fill them. In other words, I assume that I have wine and all that I desire. Then my dimensionally greater Self inspires in all, the thoughts and the actions which aid the embodiment of my assumption.

It is not a man saying to a mother, "Woman what have I to do with thee?" It is every man who knows this law who will say to himself, when his senses suggest lack, "what have I to do with thee. Get behind me." I will never again listen to a voice like that, because if I do, then I am impregnated by that suggestion and I will bear the fruit of lack.

We turn to another story in the Gospel of St. Mark where Jesus is hungry.

"And seeing a fig tree afar off having leaves, he came, if haply he might find anything thereon: and when he came to it, he found nothing but leaves; for the time of figs was not yet."

"And Jesus answered and said unto it, No man eat fruit of thee hereafter for ever. And his disciples heard it."

Mark 11:13, 14

"And in the morning, as they passed by, they saw the fig tree dried up from the roots."

Mark 11:20

What tree am I blasting? Not a tree on the outside. It is my own consciousness. "I am the vine." John 15:1. My consciousness, my I AMness is the great tree, and habit once more suggests emptiness, it suggests barrenness, it suggests four months before I can feast. But I cannot wait four months. I give myself this powerful suggestion that never again will I even for a moment relieve that it will take four months to realize my desire. The belief in lack must from this day on be barren and never again reproduce itself in my mind.

It is not a man blasting a tree. Everything in the Bible takes place in the mind of man: the tree, the city, the people, everything. There is not a statement made in the Bible that does not represent some attribute of the human mind. They are all personifications of the mind and not things within the world.

252

Consciousness is the one and only reality. There is no one to whom we can turn after we discover that our own awareness is God. For God is the cause of all and there is nothing but God. You cannot say that a devil causes some things and God others. Listen to these words.

"Thus saith the Lord to his anointed, to Cyrus, whose right hand I have holden, to subdue nations before him; and I will loose the loins of kings, to open before him the two leaved gates; and the gates shall not be shut."

"I will go before thee, and make the crooked places straight: I will break in pieces the gates of brass, and cut in sunder the bars of iron."

"And I will give thee the treasures of darkness, and hidden riches of secret places, that thou mayest know that I, the Lord, which call thee by thy name, am the God of Israel."

Isaiah 45: 1, 2, 3

"I form the light, and create darkness: I make peace, and create evil: I the Lord do all these things."

Isaiah 45:7.

"I have made the earth, and created man upon it: I, even my hands, have stretched out the heavens, and all their host have I commanded."

"I have raised him up in righteousness, and I will direct all his ways: he shall build my city, and he shall let go my captives, not for price nor reward, saith the Lord of hosts."

Isaiah 45:12, 13

"I AM the Lord, and there is none else, there is no God beside me."

Isaiah 45:5.

Read these words carefully. They are not my words, they are the inspired words of men who discovered that consciousness is the only reality. If I am hurt, I am self hurt. If there is darkness in my world, I created the darkness and the gloom and the depression. If there is light and joy, I created the light and the joy. There is no one but this I AMness that does all.

You cannot find a cause outside of your own consciousness. Your world is a grand mirror constantly telling you who you are. As you meet people, they tell you by their behaviour who you are.

Your prayers will not be less devout because you turn to your own consciousness for help. I do not think that any person in prayer feels more of the joy, the piety, and the feeling of adoration, than I do when I feel thankful, as I assume the feeling of my wish fulfilled, knowing at the same time it is to myself that I turned.

In prayer you are called upon to believe that you possess what your reason and your senses deny. When you pray believe that you have and you shall receive. The Bible states it this way:

"Therefore I say unto you, What things soever ye desire, when ye pray, believe that ye receive them, and ye shall have them.

"And when ye stand praying, forgive, if ye have ought against any: that your Father also which is in heaven may forgive you your trespasses."

"But if ye do not forgive, neither will your Father which is in heaven forgive your trespasses."

Mark 11:24, 25, 26

That is what we must do when we pray. If I hold some thing against another, be it a belief of sickness, poverty , or anything else, I must loose it and let it go, not by using words of denial but by believing him to be what he desires to be. In that way I completely forgive him. I changed my concept of him. I had ought against him and I forgave him. Complete forgetfulness is forgiveness. If I do not forget then I have not forgiven.

I only forgive something when I truly forget. I can say to you until the end of time, "I forgive you." But if every time I see you or think of you, I am reminded of what I held against you, I have not forgiven you at all. Forgiveness is complete forgetfulness. You go to a doctor and he gives you something for your sickness. He is trying to take it from you, so he gives you something in place of it.

Give yourself a new concept of self for the old concept. Give up the old concept completely.

A prayer granted implies that something is done in consequence of the prayer which otherwise would not have been done. Therefore, I myself am the spring of action, the directing mind and the one who grants the prayer.

Anyone who prays successfully turns within, and appropriates the state sought. You have no sacrifice to offer. Do not let anyone tell you that you must struggle and suffer. You need not struggle for the realization of your desire. Read what it says in the Bible.

"To what purpose is the multitude of your sacrifices unto me saith the Lord: I am full of the burnt offerings of rams, and the fat of fed beasts; and I delight not in the blood of bullocks, or of lambs, or of he goats."

"When ye come to appear before me, who hath required that at your hand, to tread my courts?"

"Bring no more vain oblations; incense is an abomination unto me; the new moons and Sabbaths, the calling of assemblies, I cannot endure iniquity and solemn assembly."

"Your new moons and your appointed feasts my soul hates: they have become a burden to me, I am weary of bearing them"

Isaiah 1:11-14

"Ye shall have a song as in the night when a holy solemnity is kept; and gladness of heart, as when one goeth with a pipe to come into the mountain of the Lord, to the mighty One of Israel."

Isaiah 30:29

"Sing unto the Lord a new song, and his praise from the end of the earth."

Isaiah 42: 10.

"Sing, O ye heavens; for the Lord hath done it: shout, ye lower parts of the earth: break forth into singing, ye mountains, O forest, and every tree therein: for the Lord hath redeemed Jacob, and glorified himself in Israel."

Isaiah 44:23

"Therefore the redeemed of the Lord shall return, and come with singing unto Zion; and everlasting joy shall be upon their head. They shall obtain gladness and joy; and sorrow and mourning shall flee away."

Isaiah 51:11

The only acceptable gift is a joyful heart. Come with singing and praise. That is the way to come before the Lord -- your own consciousness. Assume the feeling of your wish fulfilled, and you have brought the only acceptable gift. All states of mind other than that of the wish fulfilled are an abomination; they are superstition and mean nothing.

When you come before me, rejoice, because rejoicing implies that something has happened which you desired. Come before me singing, giving praise, and giving thanks, for these states of mind imply acceptance of the state sought. Put yourself in the proper mood and your own consciousness will embody it.

If I could define prayer for anyone and put it just as clearly as I could, I would simply say, "It is the feeling of the wish fulfilled." If you ask, "What do you mean by that?" I would say, "I would feel myself into the situation of the answered prayer and then I would live and act upon that conviction." I would try to sustain it without effort, that is, I would live and act as though it were already a fact, knowing that as I walk in this fixed attitude my assumption will harden into fact.

Time does not permit me to go any further into the argument that the Bible is not history. But if you have listened attentively to my message these past four nights, I do not think you want any more proof that the Bible is not history. Apply what you have heard and you will realize your desires.

****

"And now I have told you before it come to pass, that, when it is come to pass, ye might believe."

John 14:29

Many persons, myself included, have observed events before they occurred; that is, before they occurred in this world of three dimensions. Since man can observe an event before it occurs in the three dimensions of space, then life on earth proceeds according to plan; and this plan must exist elsewhere in another dimension and is slowly moving through our space.

If the occurring events were not in this world when they were observed, then to be perfectly logical they must have been out of this world. And whatever is THERE to be seen before it occurs HERE must be "pre-determined" from the point of view of man awake in a three-dimensional world. Yet the ancient teachers taught us that we could alter the future, and my own experience confirms the truth of their teaching.

Therefore, my object in giving this course is to indicate possibilities inherent in man, to show that man can alter his: future; but, thus altered, it forms again a deterministic sequence starting from the point of interference -- a future that will be consistent with the alteration.

The most remarkable feature of man's future is its flexibility. The future, although prepared in advance in every detail, has several outcomes. We have at every moment of our lives the choice before us which of several futures we will have.

There are two actual outlooks on the world possessed by everyone -- a natural focus and a spiritual focus. The ancient teachers called the one "the carnal mind," and the other "the mind of Christ." We may differentiate them as ordinary waking consciousness, governed by our senses, and a controlled imagination, governed by desire.

We recognize these two distinct centers of thought in the statement: "The natural man receiveth not the things of the Spirit of God: for they are foolishness unto him: neither can he know them, because they are spiritually discerned." I Cor. 2:14

The natural view confines reality to the moment called NOW. To the natural view, the past and future are purely imaginary. The spiritual view on the other hand sees the contents of time. The past and future are a present whole to the spiritual view. What is mental and subjective to the natural man is concrete and objective to the spiritual man.

The habit of seeing only that which our senses permit renders us totally blind to what, otherwise, we could see. To cultivate the faculty of seeing the invisible, we should often deliberately disentangle our minds from the evidence of the senses and focus our attention on an invisible state, mentally feeling it and sensing it until it has all the distinctness of reality.

Earnest, concentrated thought focused in a particular direction shuts out other sensations and causes them to disappear. We have only to concentrate on the state desired in order to see it.

The habit of withdrawing attention from the region of sensation and concentrating it on the invisible develops our spiritual outlook and enables us to penetrate beyond the world of sense and to see that which is invisible. "For the invisible things of him from the creation of the world are clearly seen." Rom. 1:20. This vision is completely independent of the natural faculties. Open it and quicken it!

A little practice will convince us that we can, by controlling our imagination, reshape our future in harmony with our desire. Desire is the mainspring of action. We could not move a single finger unless we had a desire to move it. No matter what we do, we follow the desire which at the moment dominates our minds. When we break a habit, our desire to break it is greater than our desire to continue the habit.

The desires which impel us to action are those which hold our attention. A desire is but an awareness of something we lack and need to make our life more enjoyable. Desires always have some personal gain in view, the greater the anticipated gain, the more intense is the desire. There is no absolutely unselfish desire. Where there is nothing to gain there is no desire, and consequently no action.

The spiritual man speaks to the natural man through the language of desire. The key to progress in life and to the fulfillment of dreams lies in ready obedience to its voice. Unhesitating obedience to its voice is an immediate assumption of the wish fulfilled. To desire a state is to have it. As Pascal has said, "You would not have sought me had you not already found me."

Man, by assuming the feeling of his wish fulfilled, and then living and acting on this conviction, alters the future in harmony with his assumption. Assumptions awaken what they affirm. As soon as man assumes the feeling of his wish fulfilled, his fourth-dimensional Self finds ways for the attainment of this end, discovers methods for its realization.

I know of no clearer definition of the means by which we realize our desires than to EXPERIENCE IN THE IMAGINATION WHAT WE WOULD EXPERIENCE IN THE FLESH WERE WE TO ACHIEVE OUR GOAL. This imaginary experience of the end with acceptance, wills the means. The fourth-dimensional Self then constructs with its larger outlook the means necessary to realize the accepted end.

The undisciplined mind finds it difficult to assume a state which is denied by the senses. But here is a technique that makes it easy to "call things which are not seen as though they were," that is, to encounter an event before it occurs. People have a habit of slighting the importance of simple things. But this simple formula for changing the future was discovered after years of searching and experimenting.

The first step in changing the future is DESIRE, that is, define your objective -- know definitely what you want.

Secondly, construct an event which you. believe you would encounter FOLLOWING the fulfillment of your desire -- an event which implies fulfillment of your desire -- something which will have the action of Self predominant.

Thirdly, immobilize the physical body, and induce a condition akin to sleep by imagining that you are sleepy. Lie on a bed, or relax in a chair. Then, with eyelids closed and your attention focused on the action you intend to experience in imagination, mentally feel yourself right into the proposed action; imagining all the while that you are actually performing the action here and. now.

You must always participate in the imaginary action; not merely stand back and look on, but feel that you are actually performing the action so that the imaginary sensation is real to you.

It is important always to remember that the proposed action must be one which FOLLOWS the fulfillment of your desire. Also you must feel yourself into the action until it has all the vividness and distinctness of reality.

For example, suppose you desire promotion in your office. Being congratulated would be an event you would encounter following the fulfillment of your desire. Having selected this action as the one you will experience in imagination, immobilize the physical body; and induce a state akin to sleep, a drowsy state, but one in which you are still able to control the direction of your thoughts, a state in which you are attentive without effort. Then visualize a friend standing before you. Put your imaginary hand into his. Feel it to be solid and real, and carry on an imaginary conversation with him in harmony with the action.

You do not visualize yourself at a distance in point of space and at a distance in point of time being congratulated on your good fortune. Instead, you make elsewhere HERE, and the future NOW. The future event is a reality NOW in a dimensionally larger world and oddly enough, now in a dimensionally larger world is equivalent to HERE in the ordinary three-dimensional space of everyday life.

The difference between FEELING yourself in action, here and now, and visualizing yourself in action, as though you were on a motion-picture screen, is the difference between success and failure. The difference will be appreciated if you will now visualize yourself climbing a ladder. Then, with eyelids closed imagine that a ladder is right in front of you and FEEL yourself actually climbing it.

Desire, physical immobility bordering on sleep, and imaginary action in which Sell feelingly predominates HERE AND NOW, are not only important factors in altering the future, but they are also essential conditions in consciously projecting the spiritual Self.

When the physical body is immobilized and we become possessed of the idea to do something -- if we imagine that we are doing it HERE AND NOW and keep the imaginary action feelingly going right up until sleep ensues -- we are likely to awaken out of the physical body to find ourselves in a dimensionally larger world with a dimensionally larger focus and actually doing what we desired and imagined we were doing in the flesh.

But whether we awaken there or not, we are actually performing the action in the fourth-dimensional world, and will in the future re-enact it here in the third-dimensional world.

Experience has taught me to restrict the imaginary action, to condense the idea which is to be the object of our meditation into a single act, and to re-enact it over and over again until it has the feeling of reality. Otherwise, the attention will wander off along an associational track, and hosts of associated images will be presented to our attention, and in a few seconds they will lead us hundreds of miles away from our objective in point of space, and years away in point of time.

If we decide to climb a particular flight of stairs, because that is the likely event to follow the realization of our desire, then we must restrict the action to climbing that particular flight of stairs. Should the attention wander off, bring it back to its task of climbing that flight of stairs, and keep on doing so until the imaginary action has all the solidity and distinctness of reality. The idea must be maintained in the field of presentation without any sensible effort on our part. We must, with the minimum of effort, permeate the mind with the feeling of the wish fulfilled.

Drowsiness facilitates change because it favours attention without effort, but it must not be pushed to the state of sleep, in which we shall no longer be able to control the movements of our attention, but a moderate degree of drowsiness in which we are still able to direct our thoughts.

A most effective way to embody a desire is to assume the feeling of the wish fulfilled and then, in a relaxed and sleepy state, repeat over and over again like a lullaby, any short phrase which implies fulfillment of your desire, such as, "Thank you, thank you, thank you, " until the single sensation of thankfulness dominates the mind. Speak these words as though you addressed a higher power for having done it for you.

If, however, we seek a conscious projection in a dimensionally larger world, then we must keep the action going right up until sleep ensues. Experience in imagination with all the distinctness of reality what would be experienced in the flesh were we to achieve our goal and we shall in time meet it in the flesh as we met it in our imagination.

Feed the mind with premises -- that is, assertions presumed to be true, because assumptions, though false, if persisted in until they have the feeling of reality, will harden into fact.

To an assumption, all means which promote its realization are good. It influences the behaviour of all, by inspiring in all the movements, the actions, and the words which tend towards its fulfillment.

To understand how man molds his future in harmony with his assumption -- by simply experiencing in his imagination what he would experience in reality were he to realize his goal - we must know what we mean by a dimensionally larger world, for it is to a dimensionally larger world that we go to alter our future.

The observation of an event before it occurs implies that the event is predetermined from the point of view of man in the three-dimensional world. Therefore to change the conditions here in the three dimensions of space we must first change them in the four dimensions of space.

Man does not know exactly what is meant by a dimensionally larger world, and would no doubt deny the existence of a dimensionally larger Self. He is quite familiar with the three dimensions of length, width and height, and he feels that, if there were a fourth-dimension, it should be just as obvious to him as the dimensions of length, width and height.

Now a dimension is not a line. It is any way in which a thing can be measured that is entirely different from all other ways. That is, to measure a solid fourth-dimensionally, we simply measure it in any direction except that of its length, width and height. Now, is there another way of measuring an object other than those of its length, width and height?

Time measures my life without employing the three dimensions of length, width and height. There is no such thing as an instantaneous object. Its appearance and disappearance are measurable. It endures for a definite length of time. We can measure its life span without using the dimensions of length, width and height. Time is definitely a fourth way of measuring an object.

The more dimensions an object has, the more substantial and real it becomes. A straight line, which lies entirely in one dimension, acquires shape, mass and substance by the addition of dimensions. What new quality would time, the fourth dimension give, which would make it just as vastly superior to solids, as solids are to surfaces and surfaces are to lines? Time is a medium for changes in experience, for all changes take time.

The new quality is changeability. Observe that, if we bisect a solid, its cross section will be a surface; by bisecting a surface, we obtain a line, and by bisecting a line, we get a point. This means that a point is but a cross section of a line; which is, in turn, but across section of a surface; which is, in turn, but a cross section of a solid; which is, in turn, if carried to its logical conclusion, but across section of a four-dimensional object.

We cannot avoid the inference that all three-dimensional objects are but cross sections of four-dimensional bodies. Which means: when I meet you, I meet a cross section of the four-dimensional you -- the four-dimensional Self that is not seen. To see the four-dimensional Self I must see every cross section or moment of your life from birth to death, and see them all as co-existing.

My focus should take in the entire array of sensory impressions which you have experienced on earth, plus those you might encounter. I should see them, not in the order in which they were experienced by you, but as a present whole. Because CHANGE is the characteristic of the fourth dimension, I should see them in a state of flux -- as a living, animated whole.

Now, if we have all this clearly fixed in our minds, what does it mean to us in this three-dimensional world? It means that, if we can move along times length, we can see the future and alter it if we so desire.

This world, which we think so solidly real, is a shadow out of which and beyond which we may at any time pass. It is an abstraction from a more fundamental and dimensionally larger world -- a more fundamental world abstracted from a still more fundamental and dimensionally larger world -- and so on to infinity. For the absolute is unattainable by any means or analysis, no matter how many dimensions we add to the world.

Man can prove the existence of a dimensionally larger world by simply focusing his attention on an invisible state and imagining that he sees and feels it. If he remains concentrated in this state, his present environment will pass away, and he will awaken in a dimensionally larger world where the object of his contemplation will be seen as a concrete objective reality.

I feel intuitively that, were he to abstract his thoughts from this dimensionally larger world and retreat still farther within his mind, he would again bring about an externalization of time. He would discover that, every time he retreats into his inner mind and brings about an externalization of time, space becomes dimensionally larger. And he would therefore conclude that both time and space are serial, and that the drama of life is but the climbing of a multitudinous dimensional time block.

Scientists will one day explain WHY there is a Serial Universe. But in practice HOW we use this Serial Universe to change the future is more important. To change the future, we need only concern ourselves with two worlds in the infinite series; the world we know by reason of our bodily organs, and the world we perceive independently of our bodily organs.

I have stated that man has at every moment of time the choice before him which of several futures he will have. But the question arises: "How is this possible when the experiences of man, awake in the three-dimensional world, are predetermined?" as his observation of an event before it occurs implies.

This ability to change the future will be seen if we liken the experiences of life on earth to this printed page. Man experiences events on earth singly and successively in the same way that you are now experiencing the words of this page.

Imagine that every word on this page represents a single sensory impression. To get the context, to understand my meaning, you focus your vision on the first word in the upper left-hand corner and then move your focus across the page from left to right, letting it fall on the words singly and successively. By the time your eyes reach the last word on this page you have extracted my meaning.

But suppose on looking at the page, with all the printed words thereon equally present, you decided to rearrange them. You could, by rearranging them, tell an entirely different story, in fact you could tell many different stories.

A dream is nothing more than uncontrolled four-dimensional thinking, or the rearrangement of both past and future sensory impressions. Man seldom dreams of events in the order in which he experiences them when awake. He usually dreams of two or more events which are separated in time fused into a single sensory impression; or else he so completely rearranges his single waking sensory impressions that he does not recognize them when he encounters them in his waking state.

For example, I dreamed that I delivered a package to the restaurant in my apartment building. The hostess said to me, "You can't leave that there," whereupon, the elevator operator gave me a few letters and as I thanked him for them he, in turn, thanked me. At this point, the night elevator operator appeared and waved a greeting to me.

The following day, as I left my apartment, I picked up a few letters which had been placed at my door. On my way down I gave the day elevator operator a tip and thanked him for taking care of my mail, whereupon, he thanked me for the tip.

On my return home that day I overheard a doorman say to a delivery man, "You can't leave that there." As I was about to take the elevator up to my apartment, I was attracted by a familiar face in the restaurant, and as I looked in the hostess greeted me with a smile. That night I escorted my dinner guests to the elevator and as I said good-bye to them, the night operator waved good-night to me.

By simply rearranging a few of the single sensory impressions I was destined to encounter, and by fusing two or more of them into single sensory impressions, I constructed a dream which differed quite a bit from my waking experience.

When we have learned to control the movements of our attention in the four-dimensional world, we shall be able to consciously create circumstances in the three-dimensional world. We learn this control through the waking dream, where our attention can be maintained without effort, for attention minus effort is indispensable to changing the future. We can, in a controlled waking dream, consciously construct an event which we desire to experience in the three-dimensional world.

The sensory impressions we use to construct our waking dream are present realities displaced in time or the four-dimensional world. All that we do in constructing the waking dream is to select from the vast array of sensory impressions those, which, when they are properly arranged, imply that we have realized our desire.

With the dream clearly defined we relax in a chair and induce a state of consciousness akin to sleep. A state which, although bordering on sleep, leaves us in conscious control of the movements of our attention. Then we experience in imagination what we would experience in reality were this waking dream an objective fact.

In applying this technique to change the future it is important always to remember that the only thing which occupies the mind during the waking dream is THE WAKING DREAM, the predetermined action and sensation which implies the fulfillment of our desire. How the waking dream becomes physical fact is not our concern. Our acceptance of the waking dream as physical reality wills the means for its fulfillment.

Let me again lay the foundation of prayer, which is nothing more than a controlled waking dream:

1. Define your objective, know definitely what you want.

2. Construct an event which you believe you will encounter FOLLOWING the fulfillment of your desire -- something which will

have the action of Self predominant -- an event which implies the fulfillment of your desire.

3. Immobilize the physical body and induce a state of consciousness akin to sleep. Then, mentally feel yourself right into the proposed action, until the single sensation of fulfillment dominates the mind; imagining all the while that you are actually performing the action HERE AND NOW so that you experience in imagination what you would experience in the flesh were you now to realize your goal. Experience has convinced me that this is the easiest way to achieve our goal.

However, my own many failures would convict me were I to imply that I have completely mastered the movements of my attention. But I can, with the ancient teacher, say:

"This one thing I do, forgetting those things which are behind, and reaching forth unto those things which are before, I press toward the mark for the prize."

Phil. 3:13, 14

'*'**************

Again I want to remind you that the responsibility to make what you have done real in this world is not on your shoulders. Do not be concerned with the HOW, you have assumed that it is done, the assumption has its own way of objectifying itself. All responsibility to make it so is removed from you.

There is a little statement in the book of Exodus which bears this out. Millions of people who have read it, or have had it mentioned to them throughout the centuries have completely misunderstood it. It is said, "Steep not a kid in its mothers milk." (King James version, "Thou shalt not seethe a kid in his mothers milk." Exodus 23:19).

270

Unnumbered millions of people, misunderstanding this statement, to this very day in the enlightened age of 1948, will not eat any dairy products with a meat dish. It just is not done.

They think the Bible is history, and when it says, "Steep not a kid in its mother's milk," milk and the products of milk, butter and cheese, they will not take at the same time they take the kid or any kind of meat. In fact they even have separate dishes with which to cook their meat.

But you are now about to apply it psychologically. You have done your meditation and you have assumed that you are what you want to be. Consciousness is God, your attention is like the very stream of life or milk itself that nurses and makes alive that which holds your attention. In other words, what holds your attention has your life.

Throughout the centuries a kid has been used as the symbol of sacrifice. You have given birth to everything in your world. But there are things that you no longer wish to keep alive, although you have mothered and fathered them. You are a jealous father that can easily consume, like Cronus, his children. It is your right to consume what formerly you expressed when you did not know better.

Now you are detached in consciousness from that former state. It was your kid, it was your child, you embodied and expressed it in your world. But now that you have assumed that you are what you want to be, do not look back on your former state and wonder HOW it will disappear from your world. For if you look back and give attention to it, you are steeping once more that kid in its mother's milk.

Do not say to yourself, 'I wonder if I am really detached from that state," or "I wonder if so and so is true." Give all your attention to the assumption that the thing is so, because all responsibility to make it so is completely removed from your shoulders. You do not have to make it so, it IS so. You appropriate what is already fact, and you walk in the assumption that it is, and in a way that you do not know, I do not know, no man knows, it becomes objectified in your world.

Do not be concerned with the how, and do not look back on your former state. "No man, having put his hand to the plow, and looking back, is fit for the kingdom of God." Luke 9:62

Simply assume that it is done and suspend reason, suspend all the arguments of the conscious three-dimensional mind. Your desire is outside of the reach of the three-dimensional mind.

Assume you are that which you wish to be; walk as though you were it; and as you remain faithful to your assumption -- it will harden into fact.

QUESTIONS AND ANSWERS

1. Question: What is the meaning of the insignia on your book covers?

Answer: It is an eye imposed upon a heart which, in turn is imposed upon a tree laden with fruit, meaning that what you are conscious of, and accept as true, you are going to realize. As a man thinketh in his heart, so he is.

* * * * * * * * *

2. Question: I would like to be married, but have not found the right man. How do I imagine a husband? Answer: Forever in love with ideals, it is the ideal state that captures the mind. Do not confine the state of marriage to a certain man, but a full, rich and

overflowing life. You desire to experience the joy of marriage. Do not modify your dream, but enhance it by making it lovelier. Then condense your desire into a single sensation, or act which implies its fulfillment.

In this western world a woman wears a wedding ring on the third finger of her left hand. Motherhood need not imply marriage; intimacy need not imply marriage, but a wedding ring does.

Relax in a comfortable arm chair, or lie flat on your back and induce a state akin to sleep. Then assume the feeling of being married. Imagine a wedding band on your finger. Touch it. Turn it around the finger. Pull it off over the knuckle. Keep the action going until the ring has the distinctness and feeling of reality. Become so lost in feeling the ring on your finger that when you open your eyes, you will be surprised that it is not there.

If you are a man who does not wear a ring, you could assume greater responsibility. How would you feel if you had a wife to care for? Assume the feeling of being a happily married man right now.

* * * * * * * * * *

3. Question: What must I do to inspire creative thoughts such as those needed for writing?

Answer: What must you do? Assume the story has already been written and accepted by a great publishing house. Reduce the idea of being a writer to the sensation of satisfaction.

Repeat the phrase, "Isn't it wonderful!" or "Thank you, thank you, thank you," over and over again until you feel successful. Or, imagine a friend congratulating you. There are unnumbered ways of implying success, but always go to the end. Your acceptance of the end wills its fulfillment. Do not think about getting in the mood to write, but live and act as though you are now the author you desire to be. Assume you have the talent for writing. Think of the pattern you want displayed on the outside. If you write a book and no one is willing to buy it, there is no satisfaction. Act as though people are hungry for your work. Live as though you cannot produce stories, or books fast enough to meet the demand. Persist in this assumption and all that is necessary to achieve your goal will quickly burst into bloom and you will express it.

* * * * * * * *

4. Question: How do I imagine larger audiences for my talks?

Answer: I can answer you best by sharing the technique used by a very able teacher I know. When this man first came to this country he began speaking in a small hall in New York City. Although only fifty or sixty people attended his Sunday morning meeting, and they sat in front, this teacher would stand at the podium and imagine a vast audience. Then he would say to the empty space, "Can you hear me back there?"

Today this man is speaking in Carnegie Hall in New York City to approximately 2500 people every Sunday morning and Wednesday evening. He wanted to speak to crowds. He was not modest. He did not try to fool himself but built a crowd in his own consciousness, and crowds come. Stand before a large audience. Address this audience in your imagination. Feel you are on that stage and your feeling will provide the means.

* * * * * * * * *

5. Question: Is it possible to imagine several things at the same time, or should I confine my imagining to one desire?

Answer: Personally I like to confine my imaginal act to a single thought, but that does not mean I will stop there. During the course of a day I may imagine many things, but instead of imagining lots of small things, I would suggest that you imagine something so big it includes all the little things. Instead of imagining wealth, health and friends, imagine being ecstatic. You could not be ecstatic and be in pain. You could not be ecstatic and be threatened with a dispossession notice. You could not be ecstatic if you were not enjoying a full measure of friendship and love.

What would the feeling be like were you ecstatic without knowing what had happened to produce your ecstasy? Reduce the idea of ecstasy to the single sensation, "Isn't it wonderful!" Do not allow the conscious, reasoning mind to ask why, because if it does it will start to look for visible causes, and then the sensation will be lost. Rather, repeat over and over again, "Isn't it wonderful!" Suspend judgment as to what is wonderful. Catch the one sensation of the wonder of it all and things will happen to bear witness to the truth of this sensation. And I promise you, it will include all the little things.

****

6. Question: How often should I perform the imaginal act, a few days or several weeks?

Answer: In the Book of Genesis the story is told of Jacob wrestling with an angel. This story gives us the clue we are looking for; that when satisfaction is reached, impotence follows.

When the feeling of reality is yours, for the moment at least, you are mentally impotent. The desire to repeat the act of prayer is lost, having been replaced by the feeling of accomplishment. You cannot persist in wanting what you already have. If you assume you are what you desire to be to the point of ecstasy, you no longer want it.

275

Your imaginal act is as much a creative act as a physical one wherein man halts, shrinks and is blessed, for as man creates his own likeness, so does your imaginal act transform itself into the likeness of your assumption. If, however, you do not reach the point of satisfaction, repeat the action over and over again until you feel as though you touched it and virtue went out of you.

* * * * * * * * *

7. Question: I have been taught not to ask for earthly things, only for spiritual growth, yet money and things are what I need.

Answer: You must be honest with yourself. All through scripture the question is asked, "What do you want of me?" Some wanted to see, others to eat, and still others wanted to be made straight, or "That my child live."

Your dimensionally larger self speaks to you through the language of desire. Do not deceive yourself. Knowing what you want, claim you already have it, for it is your Father's good pleasure to give it to you and remember, what you desire, that you have.

* * * * * * * * *

8. Question: When you have as assumed your desire, do you keep in mind the ever presence of this greater one protecting and giving you your assumption?

Answer: The acceptance of the end wills the means. Assume the feeling of your wish fulfilled and your dimensionally greater self will determine the means. When you appropriate a state as though you had it, the activity of the day will divert your mind from all anxious thoughts so that you do not look for signs. You do not have to carry the feeling that some presence is going to do it for you, rather you know it is already done. Knowing it is already a fact,

276

walk as though it were, and things will happen to make it so. You do not have to be concerned about some presence doing anything for you. The deeper, dimensionally greater you has already done it. All you do is move to the place where you encounter it.

Remember the story of the man who left the master and was on his way home when he met his servant who said, "Your son lives." And when he asked at what hour it was done the servant replied, "The seventh hour." The self-same hour that he assumed his desire, it was done for him, for it was at the seventh hour that the master said, "Your son lives." Your desire is already granted. Walk as though it were and, although time beats slowly in this dimension of your being, it will nevertheless bring you confirmation of your assumption. I ask you not to be impatient, though. If there is one thing you really have need of, it is patience.

* * * * * * * * *

9. Question: Isn't there a law that says you cannot get something for nothing? Must we not earn what we desire?

Answer: Creation is finished! It is your Father's good pleasure to give you the kingdom. The parable of the prodigal son is your answer. In spite of man's waste, when he comes to his senses and remembers who he is, he feeds on the fatted calf of abundance and wears the robe and ring of authority. There is nothing to earn. Creation was finished in the foundation of time. You, as man, are God made visible for the purpose of displaying what is, not what is to be. Do not think you must work out your salvation by the sweat of your brow. It is not four months until the harvest, the fields are already white, simply thrust in the sickle.

* * * * * * * * *

10. Question: Does not the thought that creation is finished rob one of his initiative?

Answer: If you observe an event before it occurs, then the occurring event must be predetermined from the point of view of being awake in this three-dimensional world. Yet, you do not have to encounter what you observe. You can, by changing your concept of self, interfere with your future and mold it in harmony with your changed concept of self.

* * * * * * * * *

11. Question: Does not this ability to change the future deny that creation is finished?

Answer: No. You, by changing your concept of self, change your relationship to things. If you rearrange the words of a play to write a different one, you have not created new words, but simply had the joy of rearranging them. Your concept of self determines the order of events you encounter. They are in the foundation of the world, but not their order of arrangement.

* * * * * * * * *

12. Question: Why should one who works hard in metaphysics always seem to lack?

Answer: Because he has not really applied metaphysics. I am not speaking of a mamby-pamby approach to life, but a daily application of the law of consciousness. When you appropriate your good, there is no need for a man, or state, to act as a medium through which your good will come.

Living in a world of men, money is needed in my every day life. If I invite you to lunch tomorrow, I must pick up the check. When I leave the hotel, I must pay the bill. In order to take the train back to

New York my railway fare must be paid. I need money and it has to be there. I am not going to say, "God knows best, and He knows I need money." Rather, I will appropriate the money as though it were!

We must live boldly! We must go through life as though we possessed what we want to possess. Do not think that because you helped another, someone outside of you saw your good works and will give you something to ease your burden. There is no one to do it for you. You, yourself must go boldly on appropriating what your Father has already given you.

****

13. Question: Can an uneducated person educate himself by assuming the feeling of being educated?

Answer: Yes. An aroused interest is awarded information from every side. You must sincerely desire to be well schooled. The desire to be well read, followed by the assumption that you are, makes you selective in your reading. As you progress in your education, you automatically become more selective, more discriminating in all that you do.

* * * * * * * * *

14. Question: My husband and I are taking the class together. Should we discuss our desires with each other?

Answer: There are two spiritual sayings which permeate the Bible. One is, "Go tell no man," and the other is " I have told you before it comes to pass that when it does come to pass you may believe." It takes spiritual boldness to tell another that your desire is fulfilled before it is seen on the outside. If you do not have that kind of boldness, then you had better keep quiet.

I personally enjoy telling my plans to my wife, because we both get such a thrill when they come into being. The first person a man wants to prove this law to is his wife. It is said that Mohammad is everlastingly great because his first disciple was his wife.

****

15. Question: Should my husband and I work on the same project or on separate ones?

Answer: That is entirely up to you. My wife and I have different interests, yet we have much in common. Do you recall the story I told of our return to the United States this spring? I felt it was my duty as a husband to get passage back to America, so I appropriated that to myself. I feel there are certain things that are on my wife's side of the contract, such as maintaining a clean, lovely home and finding the appropriate school for our daughter, so she takes care of those.

Quite often my wife will ask me to imagine for her, as though she has greater faith in my ability to do it than in her own. That flatters me because every man worthy of the name wants to feel that his family has faith in him. But I see nothing wrong in the communion between two who love one another.

* * * * * * * * *

16. Question: I would think that if you get too much into the sleepy state there would be a lack of feeling.

Answer: When I speak of feeling I do not mean emotion, but acceptance of the fact that the desire is fulfilled. Feeling grateful, fulfilled, or thankful, it is easy to say, "Thank You," "Isn't it wonderful!" or "It is finished." When you get into the state of thankfulness, you can either awaken knowing it is done, or fall asleep in the feeling of the wish fulfilled.

* * * * * * * * * * *

17. Question: Is love a product of your own consciousness?

Answer: All things exist in your consciousness, be they love or hate. Nothing comes from without. The hills to which you look for help are those of an inner range. Your feelings of love, hate or indifference all spring from your own consciousness. You are infinitely greater than you could ever conceive yourself to be. Never, in eternity will you reach the ultimate you. That is how wonderful you are. Love is not a product of you, you are love, for that is what God is and God's name is I am, the very name you call yourself before you make the claim as to the state you are now in.

* * * * * * * * * *

18. Question: Suppose my wants cannot materialize for six months to a year, do I wait to imagine them?

Answer: When the desire is upon you, that is the time to accept your wish in its fullness. Perhaps there are reasons why the urge is given you at this time. Your three-dimensional being may think it cannot be now, but your fourth dimensional mind knows it already is, so the desire should be accepted by you as a physical fact now.

Suppose you wanted to build a house. The urge to have it is now, but it is going to take time for the trees to grow and the carpenter to build the house. Although the urge seems big, do not wait to adjust to it. Claim possession now and let it objectify itself in its own strange way. Do not say it will take six months or a year. The minute the desire comes upon you, assume it is already a fact! You and you alone have given your desire a time interval and time is relative when it comes to this world. Do not wait for anything to come to pass, accept it now as though it were and see what happens.

When you have a desire, the deeper you, who men call God, is speaking. He urges you, through the language of desire, to accept that which is not that which is to be! Desire is simply his communion with you, telling you that your desire is yours, now! Your acceptance of this fact is proved by your complete adjustment to it as though it were true.

****

19. Question: Why do some of us die young?

Answer: Our lives are not, in retrospect, measured by years but by the content of those years.

****

20. Question: What would you consider a full life?

Answer: A variety of experiences. The more varied they are, the richer is your life. At death you function in a dimensionally larger world, and play your part on a keyboard made up of a life time of human experiences. Therefore, the more varied your experiences, the finer is your instrument and the richer is your life.

* * * * * * * * *

21. Question: What about a child who dies at birth?

Answer: The child who is born, lives forever, as nothing dies. It may appear that the child who dies at birth has no keyboard of human experience but, as a poet once said:

"He drew a circle that shut me out, Infidel, scoundrel, a thing to flout. But Love and I had the wit to win! We drew a circle that took him in."

The loved one has access to the sensory experiences of the lover. God is love; therefore, ultimately everyone has an instrument, the keyboard of which is the sensory impressions of all men.

****

22. Question: What is your technique of prayer?

Answer: It starts with desire, for desire is the mainspring of action. You must know and define your objective, then condense it into a sensation which implies fulfillment. When your desire is clearly defined, immobilize your physical body and experience, in your imagination, the action which implies its fulfillment. Repeat this act over and over again until it has the vividness and feeling of reality.

Or, condense your desire into a single phrase that implies fulfillment such as, "Thank you Father," "Isn't it wonderful," or "It is finished." Repeat that condensed phrase, or action in your imagination over and over again. Then either awaken from that state, or slip off into the deep. It does not matter, for the act is done when you completely accept it as being finished in that sleepy, drowsy state.

****

23. Question: Two people want the same position. One has it. The other had it and now wants it back.

Answer: Your Father (the dimensionally greater you) has ways and means you know not of. Accept his wisdom. Feel your desire is fulfilled, then allow your Father to give it to you. The present one

283

may be promoted to a higher position, or marry a man of great wealth and give up her job. She may come into a great deal of money, or choose to move to another state.

Many people say they want to work, but I question that seriously. They want security and condition security on a job. But I really do not think the average girl truly wants to get up in the morning and go to work.

* * * * * * * * *

24. Question: What is the cause of disease and pain?

Answer: The physical body is an emotional filter. Many human ailments, hitherto considered purely physical, are now recognized as rooted in emotional disturbances.

Pain comes from lack of relaxation. When you sleep there is no pain. If you are under an anesthetic, there is no pain because you are relaxed, as it were. If you have pain it is because you are tense and trying to force something. You cannot force an idea into embodiment, you simply appropriate it. It is attention minus effort. Only practice will bring you to that point where you can be attentive and still be relaxed.

Attention is tension toward an end, and relaxation is just the opposite. Here are two completely opposite ideas that you must blend until you learn, through practice, how to be attentive, but not tense. The word "contention" means "attention minus effort." In the state of contention you are held by the idea without tension.

****

25. Question: No matter how much I try to be happy, underneath, I have a melancholy feeling of being left out. Why?

Answer: Because you feel you are not wanted. Were I you, I would assume I am wanted. You know the technique. The assumption that you are wanted may seem false when first assumed, but if you will feel wanted and respected, and persist in that assumption, you will be amazed how others will seek you out. They will begin to see qualities in you they had never seen before. I promise you. If you will but assume you are wanted, you will be.

****

26. Question: If security came to me through the death of a loved one, did I bring about that death?

Answer: Do not think for one second that you brought about a death by assuming security. The greater you is not going to injure any one. It sees all and, knowing the length of life of all, it can inspire the other to give you that which can fulfill your assumption.

You did not kill the person who named you in his will. If, a few days after your complete acceptance of the idea of security, Uncle John made his exit from this three-dimensional plane and left you his estate, it is only because it was time for Uncle John to go. He did not die one second before his time, however. The greater you saw the life span of John and used him as the way to bring about the fulfillment of your feeling of security.

The acceptance of the end wills the means toward the fulfillment of that end. Do not be concerned with anything save the end. Always bear in mind that the responsibility to make it so is completely removed from your shoulders. It is yours because you accept it as so!

* * * * * * * * *

27. Question: I have more than one objective. Would it be ineffective to concentrate on different objectives at different periods of concentration?

Answer: I like to take one consuming ambition, restrict it to a single short phrase, or act that implies fulfillment, but I do not limit my ambition. I only know that my real objective will include all the little ones.

****

28. Question: I find it difficult to change my concept of self. Why?

Answer: Because your desire to change has not been aroused. If you would fall in love with what you really want to be, you would become it. It takes an intense hunger to bring about a transformation of self.

"As the hart panteth after the waterbrooks, so panteth my soul after thee, O Lord." If you would become as thirsty for perfection as the little hart is for water that it braves the anger of the tiger in the forest, you would become perfect.

****

29. Question: I am contemplating a business venture. It means a great deal to me, but I cannot imagine how it can come into being.

Answer: You are relieved of that responsibility. You do not have to make it a reality, it already is! Although your concept of self seems so far removed from the venture you now contemplate, it exists now as a reality within you. Ask yourself how you would feel and what you would be doing if your business venture were a great success. Become identified with that character and feeling and you will be amazed how quickly you will realize your dream.

The only sacrifice you are called upon to make, is to give up your present concept of self and appropriate the desire you want to express.

* * * * * * * * *

30. Question: As a metaphysical student I have been taught to believe that race beliefs and universal assumptions affect me. Do you mean that only to the degree I give these universal beliefs power over me, am I influenced by them?

Answer: Yes. It is only your individual viewpoint, as your world is forever bearing witness to your present concept of self. If someone offends you, change your concept of self. That is the only way others change. Tonight's paper may be read by any six people in this room and no two will interpret the same story in the same way. One will be elated, the other depressed, another indifferent, and so on, yet it is the same story.

Universal assumptions, race beliefs, call them what you will, they are not important to you. What is important is your concept, not of another, but of yourself, for the concept you hold of yourself determines the concept you hold of others. Leave others alone. What are they to you? Follow your own desires.

The law is always in operation, always absolute. Your consciousness is the rock upon which all structures rest. Watch what you are aware of. You need not concern yourself with others because you are sustained by the absoluteness of this law. No man comes to you of his own accord, be he good, bad or indifferent. He did not choose you! You chose him! He was drawn to you because of what you are.

You cannot destroy the state another represents through force. Rather, leave him alone. What is he to you? Rise to a higher level of consciousness and you will find a new world awaiting you, and as you sanctify yourself, others are sanctified.

* * * * * * * * *

31. Question: Who wrote the Bible?

Answer: The Bible was written by intelligent men who used solar and phallic myths to reveal psychological truths. But we have mistaken their allegory for history and, therefore, have failed to see their true message.

It is strange, but when the Bible was launched upon the world, and acceptance seemed to be in sight, the great Alexandria Library was burnt to the ground, leaving no record as to how the Bible came into being. Few people can read other languages, so they cannot compare their beliefs with others. Our churches do not encourage us to compare. How many of the millions who accept the Bible as fact, ever question it? Believing it is the word of God, they blindly accept the words and thus lose the essence they contain. Having accepted the vehicle, they do not understand what the vehicle conveys.

* * * * * * * * *

32. Question: Do you use the Apocrypha?

Answer: Not in my teaching. I have several volumes of them at home. They are no greater than the sixty-six books of our present Bible. They are simply telling the same truth in a different way. For instance, the story is told of Jesus, as a young boy, watching children make birds out of mud. Holding the birds in their hands, they pretend the birds are flying. Jesus approaches and knocks the birds out of their hands. As they begin to cry, he picks up one of the broken birds and re-molds it. Holding it high, he breaths upon it and the bird takes wing.

Here is a story of one who came to break the idols in the minds of men, then show them how to use the same substance and re-mold it into a beautiful form and give it life. That is what this story is trying to convey. "I come, not to bring peace, but a sword." Truth slays all the little mud hens of the mind; slays illusions and then re-molds them into a new pattern which sets man free.

****

33. Question: If Jesus was a fictional character created by Biblical writers for the purpose of illustrating certain psychological dramas, how do you account for the fact that he and his philosophy are mentioned in the nonreligious and non-Christian history of those times? Were not Pontius Pilate and Herod real flesh and blood Roman officials in those days?

Answer: The story of Jesus is the identical story as that of the Hindu savior, Krishna. They are the same psychological characters. Both were supposed to have been born of virgin mothers. The rulers of the time sought to destroy them when they were children. Both healed the sick, resurrected the dead, taught the gospel of love and died a martyr's death for mankind. Hindus and Christians alike believe their savior to be God made man.

Today people quote Socrates, yet the only proof that Socrates ever existed is in the works of Plato. It is said that Socrates drank hemlock, but I ask you, who is Socrates? I once quoted a line from Shakespeare and a lady said to me, "But Hamlet said that." Hamlet never said it, Shakespeare wrote the lines and put the words in the mouth of a character he created and named Hamlet. St. Augustine once said, "That which is now called the Christian religion existed among the ancients. They began to call Christianity the true religion, yet it never existed."

* * * * * * * * *

34. Question: Do you use affirmations and denials?

Answer: Let us leave these schools of thought that use affirmations and denials. The best affirmation, and the only effective one is an assumption which, in itself implies denial of the former state.

The best denial is total indifference. Things wither and die through indifference. They are kept alive through attention. You do not deny a thing by saying it does not exist. Rather you put feeling into it by recognizing it, and what you recognize as true, is true to you, be it good, bad or indifferent.

* * * * * * * * *

35. Question: Is it possible for one to appear dead and still not be dead?

Answer: General Lee was supposed to have been born two years after his mother, believed to be dead, was buried alive. Lucky for her she was not embalmed or buried in the earth, but in a vault where someone heard her cry and released her. Two years later Mrs. Lee bore a son who became General Lee. That is part of this country's history.

* * * * * * * * *

36. Question: How could one who was deprived in his youth become a success in life?

Answer: We are creatures of habit, forming patterns of the mind which repeat themselves over and over again. Although habit acts like a compelling law which drives one to repeat the patterns, it is not a law, for you and I can change the patterns. Many successful men such as Henry Ford, Rockefeller and Carnegie were deprived in their youth. Many of the great names in this country came from poor families, yet they left behind them great accomplishments in the political, artistic and financial world.

One evening a friend of mine attended a meeting for young advertising executives. The speaker of the evening said to these young men: "I have but one thing to say to you tonight,and that is to make yourself big and you cannot fail."

Taking an ordinary fish bowl, he filled it with two bags, one of English walnuts and the other of small beans. Mixing them with his hand, he began to shake the bowl and said, "This bowl is life. You cannot stop its shaking as life is a constant pulsing, living rhythm, but watch." And as they watched the big walnuts came to the top of the bowl as the little beans fell to the bottom.

Looking into the bowl the man asked, "Which one of you is complaining, asking why?" Then added, "Isn't it strange, the sound is coming from the bowl and not the outside. A bean is complaining that if he had had the same environment as the walnut he, too would do big things, but he never had the chance." Then he took a little bean from the bottom of the bowl and placed him on top saying, "I can move the bean through sheer force, but I cannot stop the bowl of life from shaking," and as he shook the bowl, the little bean once again slid to the bottom.

Hearing another voice of complaint he asked, "What's that I hear? You are saying that I should take one of those big fellows who thinks he is so big and put him on the bottom and see what happens to him? You believe he will be just as limited as you because he will be robbed of the opportunity of big things just as you are? Let's see."

Then the speaker took one of the big walnuts and pushed him right down to the bottom of the bowl saying, "I still can't stop the bowl from shaking," and as the men watched the big walnut came to the top again. Then the speaker added:

"Gentlemen, if you really want to be successful in life, make yourself big."

My friend took this message to heart and began to assume he was a successful businessman. Today he is truly a big man if you judge success by dollars. He now employs over a thousand people in the city of New York. Each one of you can do what he did. Assume you are what you want to be. Walk in that assumption and it will harden into fact.

Neville (1970)

QUESTIONS AND ANSWERS

QUESTION ASKED FOLLOWING LECTURE, 15 July 1970

Question: Do you believe in the theory of evolution?

Neville: No, I do not believe in evolution as to the creative power of God. I believe in evolution only in the affairs of men. Instead of digging the field with my hands,

I now use a tractor. That's evolution. Instead of walking across the country, I can now take a flight and be there in a few hours. Instead of going across the ocean and large bodies of water on a raft, I go now propelled by atomic power. So, this is evo- lution in the affairs of men, but not in the creation of God.

God's plan was "before that the world was." This is not any *emergency* thinking. The whole thing is done, and to this day, we have no evidence whatsoever to support the theory of evolution – none whatsoever! It is still a marvelous, glorious, exciting theory, but it remains a theory. There is no evidence to support the fact that a fish became an animal and the animal became man – none whatsoever.

So, they speak of a "missing link." Well that justifies anything – beautifully written, exciting, and then it is compulsory reading in all the universities and schools of the world, and man has accepted the theory. Yet we cannot read in our schools God's Word! Call that a theory, too, but they never read it, because you read the other theory. They say you can't produce any evidence for the historicity of Jesus – and we can't. All right, read it anyway as theory.

If we are compelled to read as fact what has no fact to support it, then why can't we read this and then call it theory?

But I do not, for one moment, accept the theory of evolution as fact. It's not fact. But I do accept evolution in the affairs of man. But don't tell me that the little tool that is called a hoe in some strange way changed itself and became a tractor. Man changed it from the hoe to a plow drawn by a horse or drawn by an ox, and then he changed that to something even better. Then he changed his way of sailing a boat. He still sails a boat, but the boat didn't suddenly go through a metamorphosis in itself and become a steamship. No, man's imagination conceived this strange thing for himself, and we call that "evolution."

When you stand in the presence of the Risen Lord, you see man, and he's Infinite Love – Infinite Love. And you will never exercise Infinite Power until you first are incorporated into the body of Infinite Love, because to have such power without love, you could ruin the universe! So, you will never come into such power until you are incorporated into the body of Love and become one with the body of Love. For, he who is united with the Spirit becomes one Spirit with It, and, therefore, you exercise the power through love.

But evolution – let them have it! I would let every man have everything he wants in this world. Let him have it. He has an imagination, and you can't stop him from using it. Today there are people who love war – the excitement of war. A war correspondent – he wants war. A professional soldier, especially if he is an officer – why, the most boring thing in the world for the professional soldier who is an officer is peacetime! Why, he's an ambitious man. He wants more things on his shoulder. You can't get them in peacetime. These fellows live for a long time, unless they die off or resign, or disappear. You can't promote them. They can have only so many of one rank and another rank. You can't have numberless five-star Generals! So, they either die off or have another war, or get killed off or something.

So, a man, if he's ambitious, he wants to transcend whatever he is. If he is in business, he wants to expand beyond what he is. You can't blame him; that's what he wants. If he has made a million this year – turned over a million, he wants to turn over two next year. That is part of business. When he turns over two, he isn't satisfied with that; he wants to turn over four. It is perfectly all right.

Well, the same thing is true if you are trained, not in business, but trained as a professional soldier. When you come out of an academy, you come out as a Lieutenant. You don't want to remain a Lieutenant. You are either going to quit the service and go into some other thing, or, if you remain in the service, you don't want to die a Lieutenant! You can't afford a wife.

But if war breaks suddenly, our President who was a five-star General – Mr. Eisenhower – when the war broke, I think he was a Major. He quickly, in three years, rose to be General of all the Armies of Europe, and then, with that popularity, he couldn't fail to carry the country when we were all aroused, and then we gave the victory to the one who led the Army. So, who could defeat him running for office? So, he rose from Major to the top rank in the Army, and then from that to the highest position in our country, and he was loved to the very end. He was dearly loved. Everyone loved him, even those who were on the other side of the political picture – they loved him. But from Major to that in a few short years!

So, in peacetime, the most horrible thing for a professional soldier – well, if he's ambitious – you see, all these things happen in God's world. You use your mind – your imagination, and have a noble goal, a lovely goal.

And don't let anybody tell you that you aren't entitled to it. Why aren't you entitled to it? If you are not born to wealth, why can't you earn it? There is no reason why you can't earn it. Some are born to it, and some earn it and there's no reason in the world – you have the same talent. He gave you a *talent* and that talent is your own wonderful human imagination.

But have faith in God. If you have faith in God, you have confidence in yourself, for God and man – the true Man – are one!

QUESTION ASKED FOLLOWING LECTURE, 15 July 1970

Verne Hanson: In one of your books, Neville – I think it is "Feeling Is the Secret" – you say that you have to have a change in conception to have a change in feeling, but from the lecture platform you tell us that when we hear others tell us they can't do this because – and so forth, we should use our imagination to help them.

Neville: Why, certainly. I will repeat that.

Verne Hanson: My question is this: If that person will not change his conception, how can we change it for him?

Neville: If you realize that the great confession of the Jewish faith is, "Hear, O Israel, the Lord our God, the Lord is One," you look out upon the world, and there seem to be billions of people, but one day you'll discover it's only your own being fragmented. There is no *other*. The whole vast world is yourself "pushed out."

So, if my daughter fell down the stairs, as she did as a child, I don't scold her. I rush down and pick her up and bring her back and comfort her. I don't say, "It serves you right. Let her learn her lesson."

I told her one day, "You want a dog. All right, you'll have a dog, but you will take the dog out and air it," and she didn't want to go down sixteen flights – we lived on the top floor – to the street and walk up the sidewalk to air it, so she was allowed to take it on the outside of the apartment. We had a lovely little garden on the outside, about 30-square with lovely plants. I said, "You may take the dog out and air the dog there, but you have to clean up the mess." And after about four days it wasn't clean, so I said to her, "You know, Vicki, I told you, you can have your dog, but that little place has to be clean."

Well, at the moment it didn't suit her, but she had to clean it, so she went outside with her broom and her pail, and she was cleaning like mad. We have three long French doors, all glass, and in her anger she struck the glass and broke it. I didn't complain. I said, "You see what temper does. Learn your lesson. You simply smashed the door. I'll put it back. But learn your lesson now. Your anger – your emotion – caused this thing to happen. Yet, you are supposed to clean this place. You know that. We gave you the dog; we allowed you to have a dog. All right, but you have to do what we said was your condition on owning the dog." She understood it. She has never forgotten it.

So, in her case, if she is injured, I don't blame her. As her father who loves her, I don't blame her; I paint a mental picture of her as I would like her to be, and persuade myself that she is what I believe and want her to be.

So, help everyone in the world. Tell them the story, that they may stand upon their own feet, but in the end, you are God, and God is One, and the whole vast world is yourself "pushed out." This is just fragmented Being, the whole vast world. But you do it by starting with yourself just where you are, and then you push out your circle. You start with your family. My wife and my daughter are dearer to me because they are right at my home – my responsibility. But I can't just limit it to that. I have friends, and then from friends

297

to other friends, and others and others, and then finally it pushes itself out to the whole vast world, taking in races and nations, because I can't limit it just to one. But you do start with the circle where you are. And it should be in your case, or anyone's case who has a wife – it should be right where the wife comes. Or if it is a woman, where the husband comes. If an offspring is there, then naturally the children, and then you start spreading it out. If one cannot help himself, I would not say, "All right, it serves you right." You step in, and you do it. It is yourself pushed out."

As I brought out the first night, if this hand itches, or the back of it and I say, "All right, you are itching, but this hand isn't itching, so it serves you right." Well, all right, if I let it itch and this other one can come to its assistance but I won't let it, then who is suffering? I am! I am suffering, so instead of suffering because I am stupid about it, I compel this hand to go right over and scratch it, for the whole vast world is myself "pushed out," and if I cannot, at this moment, do it, then I call upon this to do it. But know a principle. This is a principle of which I speak tonight.

And, so, there are always two within a man, and they are in conflict. The rational mind is always in conflict with imagination.

That letter which you wrote me, which I got the other night and read with great, great interest, for all your things are perfectly wonderful and your interpretations are marvelous, but the quote that you gave of Paul Brunton I thought was perfectly stupid. Here is a man who tells us that the credulous mind is a weak mind. But if you aren't credulous, what on earth could you ever do in this world? I could not go to the moon if I could not be credulous and believe it. I wouldn't dare to cut a piece of cloth and believe I could put it into a dress if I wasn't credulous. So, what on earth does he mean? That's why I said earlier, 99 percent of the stuff that finds its way into print isn't worth my eyesight. I can't read it.

Now, he has a name, and he has written all kinds of things and he speaks of an Oversoul. In quest of something outside of himself, he'll look forever, and he will never in eternity find it other than himself. But he has books, and they sell because it's highly publicized. Well, when you quoted that, I said, "My lord!" You quoted it at the very beginning of your letter, but I love you, so I went through your entire letter and loved all that you said about your personal experiences. But that quote at the beginning annoyed me; I would have closed the whole thing up if that was the preface. If that simply determined what followed, I would have closed the whole thing up, but I didn't in your case because I like you.

QUESTION ASKED FOLLOWING LECTURE, 15 July 1970

A Lady: I am exposed to so many young people right now. How can I correct the way they dress without telling them right to their face? [This question was not very clear on the tape.]

Neville: Well, first of all, I do not know what they have done to displease you. I know many of them dress unlike the way we dress, but I can't blame you. I mean, if that is their choice of dress, all well and good. I only have to go back a few centuries to find in the western world they all looked that way. If they go back and take the pictures of the western world three or four hundred years ago, they all had beards and long hair, and they never bathed – never bathed! A little bit of perfume here and a little bit of perfume there, and that was the last of it. But they didn't clean themselves.

I can't say they are not moving back like a circle into that same state. I, for one, like a daily shower. When I was running a temperature of 104 and 105 last year with that silly flu that I got, I still took my shower every day. I took it unknown by my wife and other members of the family because they would have protested, but I didn't feel clean until I took my shower. Well, I am not going to say that I am the criterion of what others should do. Who am I to be the criterion? I would not allow anyone to set himself up as the criterion for me, therefore, I would not set myself up as the criterion for another. I like to shave every day. I like to have my hair cut short. But why should I say you should do the same thing?

But when these kids come and they force strange things on you – well, then, be a lady and tell them of the difference between your thinking and their thinking.

I was waiting for the bus in L.A., and these two kids came up, 18 years of age, thumbing their way and no car was stopping for them. They were going by like mad, but buses were running every 20 minutes. So, I at least thought of them for thirteen minutes anyway. Then one fellow said to me, "Could you loan me a dime?"

I said, "I do not know who you are. You have no collateral. I do not know where you live. And you want a loan! If you want a loan, you must prove that you are capable of paying it back. You don't want a loan; you are asking me to give you a dime. Why didn't you say that?"

He said, "Well, I've got to go back to school and study the English language."

I said, "You'd better do that. Now here is a quarter" and I gave him a quarter. He said, "Man, man! You are a gentle man." And the other one, he said to me, "Man, man, man! You're a gentle man." That's all he could say. Everything was, "Man, man, man, man." I said, "You'd better go back to school if you ever went to school, and then come out so you can actually tell me what you want. You want a loan – a loan of a dime, and without collateral!"

QUESTION ASKED FOLLOWING LECTURE 16 July 1970

Question: Neville, would you talk a little on the 40 days and 40 nights?

Neville: Well, you see, in the Bible, numbers have their symbolical meaning. They have multiple meanings. *Forty* is the 13th letter of the Hebrew alphabet. The letter is "MEM." Its symbol is the womb of a woman, that which gives birth.

So, here he goes into the period of creativity. Will he accept the test? He accepts the test, but he plays only Scripture in defiance of his own temptation. It's not a being outside of himself tempting him. The whole story unfolds within the mind of the individual. Will I believe what I have heard tonight? Then the test starts. Will I accept what I've heard tonight and bring forth from it, or will I simply go back?

So, he said, "If you are the Son of God" – do this, that, and the other. You should not test the Lord. If I believe it, will I accept the tests?

In New York City, I was on a midnight panel that went through the night, and a professor of philosophy from an eastern college said to me, "If what you say is true, that imagining creates reality, then turn this pencil – "It was a yellow pencil." "Turn it into red." I said to him, on radio – and all his students were listening in because he told them he was going to get the better of me. I said, "Get behind me, Satan. You are a scoffer, and I'm told that the scoffers come in the last days who will deny and say, 'Where is he who is to come?' But ever since the world was made, things have gone on just as they did in the beginning of time."

He blushed and blushed and blushed. I said, "You want me to turn this – I would not turn it into any other color than it is. If you want to turn it into any other color, go and paint it! That's simple enough. If you want the yellow to turn to red, go and paint it."

301

Don't take the challenge of anyone in the world. It's all within you. The challenge comes from within you. Do you believe it, or don't you believe it? Don't let anyone else challenge you. But they will, only when – within you – there is still that little question mark. But don't accept it.

If I have a cold – so I have a cold. And many will say, "Why should you have a cold?" I am in the world of Caesar, and the body decays, as all bodies here decay. So, I get a cold, as anyone else here gets a cold. And I have demonstrated –

People are always demonstrating something. We came from New York City through Chicago on our way to San Francisco, years ago, and a lady ran ahead of us and knocked my little girl down – she was only three – knocked her down on her way to get a table in the dining room. I picked my little Vicki up and walked quietly forward and sat down at a table. There were lots of seats. And she was a Christian Science practitioner on her way to some convention in Chicago, and she had *demonstrated* a table. She had demonstrated a seat by almost killing my daughter. Well, I don't call that *demonstration*. She was a lovely practitioner, and I learned from the conversation that she would go to the convention and tell them how she had demonstrated a seat in the diner. Lovely, isn't it?

Well, I don't go for that. Let them all pass by – there will be a seat there for me, and, if not now, I will wait until they get up. I don't call this "applying the principle."

She must live in constant confusion demonstrating. And if she gets a cold, she'll remain at home where no one will know, and swear by all the bibles in the world she never had one, because they didn't see it. If she has a headache, she will take a couple of aspirin. No one knows that, you see. No one will ever know she took two aspirin to simply ease the pain, and, so, when she really can't see,

302

she will go to the oculist, and he will give her good glasses, and she will see with nice glasses. When she has a pain in her mouth and the dentist says, "You know, this has to come out," no one knows she is going to the dentist, but she will have it out, and get a good tooth put in that God gave the dentist the intelligence to make for her.

So, why try any of these stupid things? I *wear* this body. It is almost 66 now, and it's wearing out. It used to be very, very strong – unusually strong, but when it reaches its peak, then it starts going, and it is moving towards complete disintegration.

Well, what am I trying to do? Compete with the young boys of 20? I have no desire to compete with these handsome young fellows in their 30's and 40's. I've had that!

Then came that day when the energy that went down into generation is turned around and moves up into regeneration, when the serpent within me turned up as a fiery being right back into my skull from which it came. What a joy now!

Just imagine to be able to say, with complete honesty, "If you unveiled the entire world of three and a half billion men and women and put them all before me, they would leave me cold and completely unmoved." I could not always say that. So, when the attitude is turned down into generation, you don't have to unveil it all – just one would be enough. But, then, suddenly it turns up, and it is completely turned around from generation into regeneration. Now, unveil the whole vast world before me – it would mean nothing to me. I remain completely unmoved, for the energies have been turned up, where before, they were turned down. They were all turned down – that fiery being, and we simply went berserk, exercising that power in a thousand and one different ways.

All of a sudden came that bolt of lightning that split me in two, and there at the base, the blood of God! And I fused with it, and then

I became it, and like a fiery serpent went right up into the interior of my own being; and, from then on, the whole vast thing that formerly disturbed me ceased to be. That's *peace* – the only kind of peace in the world.

QUESTION ASKED FOLLOWING LECTURE, 17 JULY 1970

Question By A Man In The Audience: What is the meaning of the statement, "Down with the bluebloods"?

Neville: What does the statement, "Down with the bluebloods," mean? *Blueblood* in Scripture is church protocol, external worship, ceremony; anything that is external is the *blueblood*. Down with all such worship! No matter how they justify it or tell you that it was in order. I was commanded to clear from my own mind's eye all external worship. I don't care how beautiful it appears to be in pageantry, it is not in order. It does nothing for the soul. You go to church and a man prays audibly, and you can't get into the Silence. "Let us pray," in a very solemn, solemn voice, he says; and then repeats all these words. That's not what you want. You went to church to hear about God. And if you are going to pray, you pray for a friend's recovery or a friend's good fortune or your own recovery and your own good fortune, and you want something very tangible and right down here. And he's leading with all this pompous, pompous stuff, and is crossing himself and crossing this, and genuflecting that, and you see all the pageantry. He said, "Down with the bluebloods." Down with all ceremony, all external rites whatsoever! That's what I heard.

The word "blueblood" has nothing to do with the social order. If you read the Scripture, he never once tried to change the social structure. Not once will you find in any part of Scripture where there was any attempt on the part of the central figure of Scripture to change the social order. There were slaves in those days. There was no statement as to changes in structure. He only brought the message of Salvation, the message of redemption. And man has missed the thought and built all kinds of peculiar things round about it.

I know, when I was a child in the Episcopal Church, why, the pageantry! All the little boys coming round with their collars, all the little ruffs and the red tunics, oh, undoubtedly they looked very pretty to the mothers who saw them. I recall vividly when someone told my Mother that her boys should be in the choir, so she was persuaded by this very serious and interfering neighbor who was always giving advice to my Mother – she had two children. She couldn't raise them well, but she thought she could tell my Mother how to raise her ten! So, my Mother said, "All right, you've got to go and try out for the choir."

Well, we didn't want the choir; we wanted to go and play football or cricket – play all the games, go swimming, fishing; but we had to go and try out for the choir! Well, I was determined I was not going to have a voice, and my brothers, I shared my knowledge with them. I was the fourth one. There were four of us, and so we all agreed that we were going to pretend that we had never heard singing before. So, when he struck a note on the organ, he struck C. We struck everything in the world but a C. He said, "Don't you have any ear? Try again. We tried this one, that one, the other one – you never heard such caterwauling in your life! He said, "You go back and tell your Mother that I've tried my best, and you just don't have it. That's all there is to it."

Well, I thought, Now this is really fun! I am going to have a little fun before I go, too. Now, my eldest brother, Cecil – and so I said to Mr. Taggert, who was the organist; just as we were about to leave, I said to Mr. Taggert, "Oh, Mr. Taggert, my brother Cecil can whistle."

305

Well, he could have killed me! We all "broke up," and Cecil couldn't whistle unless he started laughing, so Mr. Taggert knew it was a joke, and dismissed us. But when we got out, he really could have killed me! I said, "He can whistle."

To see myself all dressed in this robe coming down on Sunday mornings – well, I wanted to get out and start whistling. So, we just beat that little neighbor at her own little game.

But I was told in no uncertain terms, "Down with the bluebloods!" And it hasn't a thing to do with any so-called *blueblood* in the world. If you want to feel that you are a blueblood, feel it. There are those in every walk of life who feel that they are in the highest of the social stratus. It's perfectly all right. I wouldn't change it at all. Leave it alone. I personally have never felt inferior to anyone I've ever met. I have never in my life felt inferior to anyone. I admire them if they have money – much more than I have. I have little, and they have much, but that doesn't mean that I am impressed. Also, there are those who come into the world, and they have all the lovely things in the world. I admire them – go to their homes and admire all the beauty that they can afford, and lovely pieces, but it doesn't make me feel inferior to them. I feel one with it all!

My maid comes and cleans for me once a week. I like to look upon Doris as a friend. She's a friend. I talk with her just as I would with a friend. She cleans for me and does all the lovely things that I wouldn't do for myself, so I treat her as a friend. I can't see that, because she works for me, she must be below me. On the other hand, I can't see, because someone has a billion dollars, that I should think him important.

As someone said, I think it was Lloyd George – he tried to put through the House of Commons a bill making some kind of a

306

change in the land ownership of England, and he said to the entire House – he said, "You know, if you are all honest with yourselves, you all know that any Englishman can prove ownership to his land by tracing his ancestry back to the first one who stole it!"

Well, that is just about what you will find in all kinds of fabulous things, but I don't envy them. I'm all for it! If I have a dollar when I die, I want my wife, if she survives me, to have it. And if I had a million, I'd still want her to have it. If she goes before I do, I want my children to have it. If they inherit it, what's wrong with that? I see not a thing wrong in that, because it comes within the code of that wonderful law, where it says, "Do unto others as you would have them do unto you." Wouldn't you like to receive a million dollars? Or, would you give it back? All right, I wouldn't give it back. I would take it. Well, the same thing is true of all inheritance laws. My father gave us all that he could; he gave the ten of us his entire estate. None of us gave it to the government, although they took much of it without asking.

QUESTION ASKED FOLLOWING LECTURE, 20 JULY 1970

Question By A Man In The Audience: Will you elaborate on the technique of arresting the action?

Neville: Can I elaborate on the technique of arresting the motion within man? Sir, I can only tell you the first time that it happened in me. I came upon a scene that seemed to be about a hundred and fifty years ago in the New England states. I could tell from the dress of the people that it was about a hundred and fifty years prior to that moment in time that it happened to me.

It seemed to be a Sunday afternoon when they were dining, – I would say about 2:00 o'clock in the afternoon. But I could tell from their dress that it was about a hundred and fifty years prior to that moment in time, which was about twenty-odd years ago, when it first happened.

I came into a restaurant, and there were four people seated at a table, two sons in their early 20's and their parents, the father and mother. One boy was bringing the food to his mouth to eat it, and the waitress came through a little door, and she was all dressed in the same kind of a dress she would have a hundred and fifty years ago – very stiffly starched; her collar was starched, her sleeves were starched, and she was animated.

Through the huge, big bay window I could see leaves falling. It was the Fall of the year, and I could see the leaves coming down slowly. I could see a bird in motion, and I could see the wind blowing the grass. Here was an animated restaurant.

At that moment I knew intuitively that if I could arrest that activity that I felt within me that everything would stand still. And, strangely enough, I knew how to arrest it. Now, you want to know how to do it.

I can only say, at that moment when you come upon such a scene and you know – you will know how to do it. I simply stilled an activity in my own brain, as it were. Yet, I was in Spirit. Here my body was on the bed. I felt something in me stand still, yet my consciousness was alive and completely alert. I knew what I'm doing. But at that moment the boy bringing his food to his mouth couldn't bring it. The waitress walking, walked not. The bird flying, flew not. The grass waving, waved not. The leaves falling, fell not. Everything stood still. I examined them, and they were all as though they were made of clay. Then I released – in me – the activity, and the bird continued to fly, the waitress continued her intentions to serve the food, and the boy eating the food brought it to his mouth, and everything moved on as it had intended.

308

That was my first experience of life-in-me. Prior to that moment, I did not understand that statement in Scripture that says, "As the Father has life in Himself, so He has granted the Son also to have life in himself."

Then I knew what it meant to have life in myself. The whole vast world, believe it or not, is the individual "pushed out"; and he has animated it, but he doesn't know how to stop it or change it. He can only change it without stopping it.

You can change it now by bringing into your mind's eye an individual in your world and changing him for the good. You can change it for the worse if you want to, but don't. Change him for the good, because "he is yourself "pushed out," and then let him conceive in his world a change in motivation.

But the day will come that you can still the entire, vast world, and change it, motivationally, and it will be changed. But you do it all within you. You feel it in your head. Everything is felt in the head. It's a peculiar thing, but I can tell you how to stop it here, but the day will come, you will taste of the power of the Age to come, as told us in the book of Hebrews. He has "tasted of the power of the age to come." (Hebrews 6:5, RSV[1])

And when you are completely "born from above" – because unless man is "born from above," he cannot enter the Kingdom of Heaven, and the Kingdom of Heaven is made up of those whose bodies are in complete control by the individual who wears it. And that body has life in itself. That is, it stops and starts anything in the world. It has no fear, because everything is itself "pushed out." How can it be hurt by its own being pushed out and still be in control of its pushed-out self?

---

[1] Revised Standard Version

It is in complete control, but you will never completely harness this power unless you are first incorporated into the Body of Love. God, truly, is Love, because to use this power without love, you would wreck the universe. But no one would actually be given the power until he is first called by the Risen Lord and incorporated into the Body of Love. So, you will always be guided by Love.

QUESTION ASKED FOLLOWING LECTURE, 22 July 1970

Question By A Lady: Neville, in the restoration you say everybody is the same. I have never heard you say there were births from the womb of woman in the restoration. [Question was not altogether audible on the tape.]

Neville: The Bible teaches that if you are not resurrected in this section of time, then all the things that you now do in this section of time you will continue doing. That is stated so clearly in the book of Luke when 'the wise men of the day, the Sadducees, ask the very simple question, "Whose wife will this woman be in the Resurrection?" (Luke 20:33) because she married seven brothers and they left no offspring. And the answer is quite clearly stated, that "the children of this age marry and are given in marriage, but those who are accounted worthy to obtain to That Age, they neither marry nor are they given in marriage, for they are sons of the Resurrection. Being sons of God, they die no more," (Luke 20:35-36) which would imply that all they do here they will do there unless resurrected.

So, if they die here, they find themselves restored to life there in that section of time into which they go. But they will age there too, as they age here. But they do not start there from the womb of woman; they start there from the grave. But you don't go to any grave; you are already in the grave when you are here. These bodies are our *graves*.

310

The Lady: Well, this being the lowest form – [not audible].

Neville: This is the most important one. It's the limit of contraction. This is the complete limit of contraction, the limit of opacity. Here is contraction. Men die. And you and I watch them die. We see them die. We cremate the body. It's all dust. And, yet, that Being never *died* – not to himself, not to herself. They are restored instantly; and many of them do not even know that they have departed this world, because to them they haven't died.

How can you think of a person who is very much alive – you talk with him, he talks with you – and you tell him that he is dead? I don't tell them they are dead. I will tell them – "You *died* at a certain point in time and I went to your funeral, and what you *wore* when I first knew you is now buried or cremated," depending on what I know of it. They will deny it because they aren't dead, and they cannot associate what I am saying with anything that they are experiencing, because they never experienced death.

The only ones who ever experience *death* are those who watch them *die*. I can watch a man *die*, and bury him or cremate him. I experience his departure and call it *death*, but he who went through that state – he didn't die! When he is restored, he does not know a thing about having *died*. So, no one ever really experiences *death*, except those who watch the other one depart, and many of them don't even know they are gone. They are amazed at me when I say, "I went to your funeral." They think, Why, he's insane.

But, you know in Scripture, "The man is mad." "He has a spirit." "He has a demon." (See John 10:20) And there are areas in which all visionary men are accounted *mad* men, but this is not new to me. I've been all over that. When I first started, I came to a book store where they had my books displayed, and two ladies, looking at the picture in the window and my books – a few of my books – one said to the other, "You know who he is?"

She said, "No."

"Well, he is the mad mystic of 38th Street. You must go and hear him. He's as mad as a hatter," she said. She didn't know I was standing right next to her. She said, "You should hear that man. He is mad, but he isn't violent." It's perfectly all right. So, I have been called *mad*, and having a demon from the time that I started in with this work, because it is mad if I deny the evidence of my senses and say I will not accept the dictates of my senses. I will not accept reason; it is in conflict with what I want. I will accept my senses if they are confirming what I want in this world, but if they don't confirm it, I ignore them and assume a state where I want to know all my senses do confirm. And I turn to the Knower, which is my imagination. So, a man who denies his senses, certainly he is a little bit *touched*.

So, they said of him, "This man, we know his father, we know his mother;" (See John 6:42) we know his brothers and we know his sisters, and he tells us he came from heaven, and he tells us God was his father, and that he and God the Father are one. Well, the man is insane, and he doesn't know it. Read it in the book of John. It is clearly stated.

QUESTION ASKED FOLLOWING LECTURE, 23 July 1970

Question By A Lady [inaudible on my tape] concerning restoration to life in different time segments.

Neville: You see, we think that death ends something and birth begins something, but time is bigger than the little, small spectrum we call "threescore and ten." It's the same world, just like this, and is this world.

The Year Three Thousand exists now, and the Year One Thousand did not pass away. It still exists now. I have gone into sections of time that the world thinks have ceased to be and others the world thinks do not yet exist. But, read the book of Ecclesiastes, "Is there a thing of which it is said, See, this is new? It has been already in ages past. But there is no remembrance of former things, nor shall there be any remembrance of things to come after among those who will come later." (Ecclesiastes 1:10, 11)

In other words, it has already come. The "Play" is over. The whole thing is finished and has been brought to a climax.

And, so – we came, and come, into human history in that strange, mysterious being we call "Jesus Christ." And in the end, there will only be Jesus, and you are He.

We think, now, this is 1970, and we are looking forward to the Year Two Thousand, and wouldn't it be wonderful if you lived in the Year 2000, and celebrated the turn of the century? But it is now!

You may depart here, say, in the year 1990. I have no desire to reach any 1990. As far as I am concerned, it could come tonight. But I have no desire, honestly, to go far beyond this moment in time – none whatsoever.

I know, in my own case, I will not be restored to life. I am entering the New Age, clothed in that body with which I am very familiar, which is a perfect body, where – in its presence – nothing will remain imperfect – nothing. You are in need of nothing in that body, and everything is made perfect, because you are clothed in that body of the Risen Lord. But everyone who has not had the experience will be restored, and need not find themselves, if they go tonight, in the year 1970 a day later. They could find themselves in the Year One Thousand, as the environment best suited for the work yet to be done in them, because it can be done better in that environment than it can in the year 1971.

The whole thing is the most glorious, wonderful play, and in the end everyone is perfect. And because "there is only one body, one spirit... one lord... one God and Father of all," (Ephesians 4:4-6) we can't brag and beg to be placed one above the other.

And I tell you that your face will be like yours, but raised to the nth degree of beauty. Imagine it, a character that you would never dream of possessing in this world! You will have the human face, as you have. You will have the human voice. You will have human hands. Don't ask beyond that. I couldn't describe the form. It is light, fire; it has nothing to resist it. It is, in itself, the life of everything round about you. You give life to it. Nothing remains dead in your presence. A Petrified Forest would burst into flower if you entered the forest. A barren desert would erupt into glorious bloom because of your presence. You are life.

But the body itself – well, you can't describe it. But it will have a human face, human voice, and human hands.

QUESTION ASKED FOLLOWING LECTURE, 23 July 1970

Question By A Lady In The Audience: Will you please interpret the Scripture, "My God, my God, why hast thou forsaken me?"

Neville: "My God, my God, why hast thou forsaken me?" (Matthew 27:46 and Mark 15:34) It appears only in the books of Matthew and Mark; it doesn't appear in the other two Gospels. Well, it is in the 22nd Psalm. (Psalm 22:1) In other words, God is not pretending that He is you. If He knew that He is God and playing the part that is your part, then He could not be a Savior. He had to completely empty Himself of His entire wisdom and His power and everything to become you!

314

So, He can't pretend; He's not an actor playing the part. He is The Only Actor, but He is so much the part that He ceases to be an actor knowing that He is playing a part. He became you in the most literal form.

So, that's the cry. But Luke does not use the 22nd Psalm. Luke uses the 31st Psalm; only the whole verse is not quoted. Luke says, "Into thy hands I commit my spirit. Thou hast redeemed me, O Lord, faithful God." (

So, he cried out, knowing that he is already redeemed because he has had the experience of redemption, but the Crucifixion is the first act. It took place in the beginning. It doesn't come at the end of the drama, as we are told in the story. We are told in Scripture, "We have been united with Him in a death like His; therefore we shall be united with Him in a resurrection like His." (Romans 6:5, RSV) In other words, see the change in tense. We have been united with Him in a Crucifixion like His; we shall be united with Him in a Resurrection like His.

So, the Crucifixion is over. The Resurrection is taking place. So, he warns Timothy of those who teach that the resurrection is over and past, that they are misleading the people and turning the people from the true faith. He says, Anathema to them for the teaching of the resurrection as already finished.

No, it is taking place in one after the other. But the Crucifixion is over, because that was the beginning of the drama, when God literally became Humanity – not just you individually, but Humanity. He is crucified on the Cross of Man, and individual man is redeemed. Because he was once crucified with The One, he is now redeemed in The One. One after the other, he is drawn back into "the one Body, the one spirit... the one lord... the one God and Father of all." (Ephesians 4:4-6)

315

So, that cry is a wonderful cry, and it should not be removed from Scripture, but it is only in Matthew and Mark. Of the seven cries on the cross, Matthew and Mark only considered one, and this is the one. John considered three, and Luke considered three, and Mark and Matthew considered the same words on the Cross.

We speak of the "seven last words" – "words" being not a single word, but a sentence, a thought. They considered one thought which is the prayer that God actually, literally became man to the point where He had to forget He was God, and suffered total amnesia, for if He remained aware that He is God, He couldn't play the part – a complete and total giving of Self.

As Blake said it so beautifully, "Unless I die, thou canst not live; but if I die, I shall arise again, and thou with me." [From "Jerusalem"]

He will rise, and you will rise as Him. But He has to die just as a seed. Unless it fall into the ground and *die*, it remains alone, but if it dies, it bears much fruit. So, He actually became you, and then He rises in you, and He cries out on the cross of you – for you are the cross that He wears.

I must confess, there isn't a person in the world that could actually say to me honestly, until he has the resurrection, that he knows he is the Lord Jesus Christ. Therefore, he is totally unaware of his true identity, and he is crying out to a god outside of himself. Therefore, he is actually saying, "My God, my God, why hast thou forsaken me?" Because he doesn't know He is God until the Resurrection. And when He breaks the bonds of the tomb, He knows Who He is. Until then, He too is saying, without the use of words, "My God, my God, why hast thou forsaken me?"

Every mother who says good-bye to a little child at the gate of death wonders why God did not answer her prayer. You say

316

goodbye to your mother, your father, your brother, your friend, and you wonder, Why God, why –calling to another god. Therefore, that is the cry on the Cross – because this [referring to the physical body] is the Cross. And I will wear this Cross – until the very end, and then, during the wearing of the Cross; I am resurrected from it.

And I tell the story. Some believe it; some disbelieve it, but I will continue to tell the story until He takes it off for the final time, and then I'm clothed in the Divine Body.

QUESTIONS ASKED FOLLOWING LECTURE, 24 JULY 1970

Question By A Lady: When you say "coming down," descending," "below," what do you mean?

Neville: Well, these are just figures of speech. Certainly not from heaven, because heaven is within you, as we are told in the 17th chapter of the book of Luke, "The Kingdom of Heaven is within you." (Luke 17:21)

In Scripture, "above" and "within" are the same, and "below" and "without" are the same. If I point there [indicating], that's without, and that is, in Scripture, "below." He said, "I am from above" – therefore I am within you – "you are from below," (John 3:23) therefore, you are "without."

So, wherever I point in the world outside, that is below where He stands. He stands "within." God is within you. His name forever and forever is "I AM."

When I speak of "coming down," I mean descending in consciousness to lower and lower and lower levels of awareness to the level called, in Scripture, "death"; because God is infinite in power and can overcome even death. And to become man, the limit of contraction, God assumes the grave to prove the Infinite power that is God, because there is no limit to His expansion. He set a limit to His contraction, to his opacity, but no limit to His expansion or translucency. So, when you reach the limit of contraction, then you start to expand.

If God could not expand beyond what He is, there would be eternal failure, but God is forever expanding, and in His own plan. He creates the plan, fulfills His own plan, and expands. That's the joy of creation. God is a Creator.

So, I do not mean "coming down" in the sense of coming from the stars – for all the stars, infinite as they are, and trillions of light years away – they are still "without," therefore, they are "below." God is "within."

Question By A Lady [inaudible on the tape, but having to do with the "linen clothes."]

Neville: The "linen clothes" are the physical body in Scripture. He ran away and he was still naked. He had not yet been clothed with the Divine Body of the Lord Jesus Christ. They can take from you your body, and you will be naked as far as that world goes. You must be clothed. To be really clothed in the "wedding garment" in order to enter the Kingdom of Heaven; you must be clothed with the Body of the Lord Jesus Christ. In the end, there is only "one body, one spirit... one Lord... one God and Father of all." (Ephesians 4:4-6)

So, today many people suffer for the Word of God, and they will take from them their physical bodies, like many of our missionaries who have been martyred. They took from them the "linen clothes" that the mother wove for them, and left them, in a way, naked, because they are not yet clothed with the Body of Jesus Christ, but they will be. They will be.

Question [inaudible on my tape, but referring to the angels, witnesses, et cetera, present at the birth of the Christ Child]

Neville: This is all beautiful imagery. When I rose from the skull and came out from the "linen clothes" – and when I came out, the three brothers appeared, and there were the angels; they came from afar. If you took it literally, they were five thousand miles from here.

If you took the story literally in the Bible, it would be almost impossible for the shepherds to have made the journey in the short interval between the appearance of the angel and the discovery of the child, so they came "in spirit," as told in the 2nd chapter of the book of Luke when Simeon "came in the Spirit to the temple," (Luke 2:27) for it all takes place in the Temple of God. You are the Temple of God, because all things exist in the human imagination. So, they came – humanly – "from afar," but they are always in you anyway.

When the drama is ready to erupt within you, they will come, and the story will reenact itself within you. So, do not give credit to this one or that one or the other; the whole story is within you.

Question By A Lady [inaudible on the tape] about Repentance.

Neville: My Dear, you are invited in Scripture – the very first word put into the mouth of the Lord Jesus Christ in the earliest Gospel, which is the book of Mark. In the canonical setup, Matthew comes first, but in the actual, chronological order,

Mark is the earliest of the Gospels. So, the first word put into the mouth of Jesus in the book of Mark is, "Repent." The Kingdom of Heaven is at hand.

"The time is fulfilled, the kingdom of heaven is at hand. Repent, and believe the gospel."

319

(Mark 1:15)

Well, the word "repent" does not mean to feel remorseful. It hasn't a thing to do with regret. The word is "metanoia," which means, by literal translation, a radical, radical change of attitude; a radical change of mind, which tests the individual's ability to enter into the very opposite of what he sees with his senses.

Now, do it, for you are invited. The very first words of the Lord are to get the individual to use the talent which is in himself, which is his imagination, therefore, use your imagination to bring about a radical change of attitude towards effects – towards the world in which you live. And to the degree that you are successful in changing this attitude of mind, the world will change to confirm it.

That is "repentance" as known by the mystics. It has not a thing to do with regret or remorse. He never demands penance of anyone. The whole secret of Christ is forgiveness. That is repentance. He conquers by repentance. He conquers by forgiveness. That is the secret of Christianity.

You see someone and they are not well. You don't blame them. You don't bawl them out because of a former state, which has resulted now in their illness. You simply represent them to yourself in your mind's eye, as you would like them to be. Suppose that individual who is now a total stranger were your mother, you wouldn't criticize her, because you love your mother, and you would do for your mother what maybe you would not do for a stranger. Well, learn to do for the stranger what you would do for your mother.

If Mother asked anything of me, she would not ask anything that would not come within the Golden Rule – she wouldn't! Why, she couldn't conceive of asking of her son that she loved to do anything that would embarrass her, or in some way bring shame to the name.

So, it would always come within the Golden Rule, "Do unto others as you would have them do unto you." Well, then, is it a stranger or your mother? Do it, and to the degree that you are self-persuaded of the reality of what you've done in your imagination, to that degree they are changed, and the environment in which they live will be changed to conform to the change in them. You do it, and you will bring it about by your imagination and faith.

Faith is the subjective appropriation of the objective hope. What do I want? What do I hope for, for my mother? Well, then, let me subjectively appropriate it, and that is practicing "repentance." He tells the whole vast world, "Repent," but believe the story – the Good News, which is called the Gospel. Believe the good news of salvation, for it has come to the world, "The time is fulfilled, and the kingdom of heaven is at hand." (Mark 1:15)

So, the climax has been reached. You can forget what the world is talking about. The climax – redemption – is upon us. It has been done, God has completed the act of redemption, and therefore there is no possibility of failure for anyone in the world, because He became all.

Question By A Lady [mostly inaudible on tape] – I want very much to do whatever is necessary for my son to overcome his___.

Neville: Well, my Dear, causation is mental. People do not realize it. He teaches that causation is mental. Listen to His words; it is the Sermon on the Mount, "You have heard it said by men of old" – He's telling you what came down through the ages – "You have heard it said by men of old, You shall not commit adultery." You have heard that – "But I say unto you" – this is something entirely different now. He now speaks with authority – this is the Lord speaking, "But I say unto you, Any man who looks [concupiscently] lustfully upon a woman has already committed the act of adultery in his heart with her." (Matthew 5:27, 28, RSV) He puts the whole thing on an entirely different level. It's mental.

I may not have the courage to go forward and perform the act that I long to do. I may have many reasons for not doing it; I may contemplate the consequences along with the act, and restrain the impulse, but He tells me restraining the impulse isn't good enough. I am told it isn't good enough if I restrain the impulse because I am a coward, or restrain the impulse because I am afraid of the consequences that would bring shame to my family or to myself. Well, then, that is still not good enough, if I look lustfully on another.

Therefore all men have committed sin. There isn't a man in this world who can tell me he is not guilty of that act, but we are told in the 11th chapter of Romans: "God has consigned all men to disobedience, that He may have mercy upon all." (Romans 11:32, RSV) God is merciful. He has consigned all men to disobedience, that He may have mercy; therefore, no one earns the Kingdom. It is Grace – Grace – Grace, and still more Grace! Our fitness for the Kingdom is the consequence, and not the condition, of this choice of ours.

So, I know, as a man – I've been married twice; I have two children (one 46, one 28) and I know as a man that I am not unique. I am guilty of that act. If a man stood before me and told me that he is not guilty of that, I wouldn't even argue with him. Why call him a liar? It's such an obvious fact that he is a liar – stupid! And by "man," I mean generic man. I mean, "Male female made he them, and called their name Man," (Genesis 5:2) as told us in the 5th chapter of Genesis, so I mean generic man.

So, "He has consigned all men to disobedience, that He may have mercy upon all." (Romans 11:32, RSV)

"For Mercy, Pity, Peace and Love

Is God, our Father dear,

And Mercy, Pity, Peace and Love

Is Man, his child and care."

– Wm. Blake, from "The Divine Image"

Question By A Lady: One more thing, when you say this is your last night, I hope you are planning to return to this City.

Neville: Well, my Dear, thank you. I say it is the last night for this year. But do you know, no one knows when the Father will call him. I feel, really, I have finished the work that my Father gave me to do. I have accomplished the story. He did it in me. I take no credit, because He gave me Himself. He who started a good work in me has brought it to completion, (See Philippians 1:6, RSV) and therefore He could call me now; the work has been completed in me.

Now, if I am needed to still tell it to others who are coming who must hear it before I depart from me, then I will be here until they come. I will not go one second before or one second later. But, as I said last night, it would make no difference to me if I went now.

I felt, when I had a little child, uneducated, that I had unfinished business, because she wanted college. Well, now, she has had her college training. She has gone to a lovely college, graduated, and has a lovely job, and she is well equipped for life. I feel that I have left my wife provided for in the world of Caesar. That was my one concern. So, I know today I have left her a sufficient investment in the world of Caesar to live graciously without having to go out and ask for alms. Well, now, that has comforted me, for that was my only concern. My son pulls his own weight. My daughter pulls her own weight. And when my wife eventually goes – I left it all to her;

then I have left a condition upon my will that she cannot dispose of it, save to give it to my two children.

So, I feel satisfied that I am qualified to go now. I am not saying I want to. I am enjoying life; I'm enjoying every moment of time. But if tonight was my moment to go – and I am not going to make a conscious effort to go, but if I slept tonight and did not wake here, I know that I will awake in the Body of the Lord Jesus Christ, for I have finished the work. I will not be restored to continue the journey. I will awake in the One Body, with the one Lord, with the one Spirit. That I know, therefore, what could concern me?

But to come back to your question, if it is in the sphere of my Father's wish that I be here to tell it once more to those who are not now hearing me, I will be here. For, He has used me under compulsion, and yet, He and I are one.

Question By A Lady [largely inaudible on the tape] about some people having more imagination than others.

Neville: Well, first of all, "God is One." We may not exercise our imagination, but, may I tell you, when we think that one has more imagination than another, it could not be, because "God is One" (Deuteronomy 6:1) – undivided. But one misuses imagination. Who knows if someone tonight in a dungeon feeling themselves wrongfully confined could be using that imagination to start a world conflict?

If you know the power of imagination, it could be some woman treading the wine press who starts the conflict in men's minds. If a man does not use his own imagination, it may be used for him by someone else. And if I confine my imagination to my senses and only what reason allows – well, I would never exercise it.

Someone quoted from a book the other night from some very prominent speaker, who also has written many books, and they are all popular books and very successful books, and he said, "The credulous mind is a weak mind that must be strengthened." Of all the nonsense in the world!

In almost every particular is the world about us different from what we think. Why, then, should we be thought incredulous? Life calls upon us to believe, not less, but more. The most incredulous story in the world is the Christian story. It's the most incredulous thing in the world, the story of Christ. And may I tell you from experience, it is the only really true story! All the others are "played," and that will be forever and forever. It is forever extant in the depths of the soul of man.

Neville (July 1951)

BE WHAT YOU WISH;

BE WHAT YOU BELIEVE

Radio Talk, Station KECA, Los Angeles

A newspaperman related to me that our great scientist, Robert Millikan, once told him that he had set a goal for himself at an early age when he was still very poor and unproven in the great work he was to do in the future. He condensed his dream of greatness and security into a simple statement, which statement, implied that his dream of greatness and security was already realized. Then he repeated the statement over and over again to himself until the idea of greatness and security filled his mind and crowded all other ideas out of his consciousness. These may not have been the words of Dr. Millikan but they are those given to me and I quote, "I have a lavish, steady, dependable income, consistent with integrity and mutual benefit." As I have said repeatedly, everything depends upon our attitude towards ourselves. That which we will not affirm as true of ourselves cannot develop in our life. Dr. Millikan wrote his dream of greatness and security in the first person, present tense. He did not say, "I will be great; I will be secure," for that would have implied that he was not great and secure. Instead, he made his future dream a present fact. "I have," said he, "a lavish, steady, dependable income, consistent with integrity and mutual benefit."

The future dream must become a present fact in the mind of him who seeks to realize it. We must experience in imagination what we would experience in reality in the event we achieved our goal, for the soul imagining itself into a situation takes on the results of that imaginary act. If it does not imagine itself into a situation, it is ever free of the result.

It is the purpose of this teaching to lift us to a higher state of consciousness, to stir the highest in us to confidence and self-assertion, for that which stirs the highest in us is our teacher and healer. The very first word of correction or cure is always, "Arise." If we are to understand the reason for this constant command of the Bible to "arise," we must recognize that the universe understood internally is an infinite series of levels and man is what he is according to where he is in that series. As we are lifted up in consciousness, our world reshapes itself in harmony with the level to which we are lifted. He who rises from his prayer a better man, his prayer has been granted.

To change the present state we, like Dr. Millikan, must rise to a higher level of consciousness. This rise is accomplished by affirming that we are already that which we want to be; by assuming the feeling of the wish fulfilled. The drama of life is a psychological one which we bring to pass by our attitudes rather than by our acts. There is no escape from our present predicament except by a radical psychological transformation. Everything depends upon our attitude towards ourselves. That which we will not affirm as true of ourselves will not develop in our lives.

We hear much of the humble man, the meek man – but what is meant by a meek man? He is not poor and groveling, the proverbial doormat, as he is generally conceived to be. Men who make themselves as worms in their own sight have lost the vision of that life – into the likeness of which it is the true purpose of the spirit to transform this life. Men should take their measurements not from life as they see it but from men like Dr. Millkan, who, while poor and unproven, dared to assume, "I have a lavish, steady, dependable income, consistent with integrity and mutual benefit." Such men are the meek of the Gospels, the men who inherit the earth. Any concept of self less than the best robs us of the earth. The promise is, "Blessed are the meek, for they shall inherit the earth." In the original text, the word translated as meek is the opposite of the words – resentful – angry. It has the meaning of becoming "tamed" as a wild animal is tamed. After the mind is tamed, it may be likened to a vine, of which it may be said, "Behold this vine. I found it a wild tree whose wanton strength had swollen into irregular twigs. But I pruned the plant, and it grew temperate in its vain expense of useless leaves, and knotted as you see into these clean, full clusters to repay the hand that wisely wounded it."

A meek man is a self-disciplined man. He is so disciplined he sees only the finest, he thinks only the best. He is the one who fulfills the suggestion, "Brethren, whatsoever things are true, whatsoever things are honest, whatsoever things are just, whatsoever things are pure, whatsoever things are lovely, whatsoever things are of good report; if there be any virtue and if there be any praise, think on these things."

We rise to a higher level of consciousness, not because we have curbed our passions, but because we have cultivated our virtues. In truth, a meek man is a man in complete control of his moods, and his moods are the highest, for he knows he must keep a high mood if he would walk with the highest.

It is my belief that all men can, like Dr. Millikan, change the course of their lives. I believe that Dr. Millikan's technique of making his desire a present fact to himself is of great importance to any seeker after the "truth." It is also his high purpose to be of "mutual benefit" that is inevitably the goal of us all. It is much easier to imagine the good of all than to be purely selfish in our imagining. By our imagination, by our affirmations, we can change our world, we can change our future. To the man of high purpose, to the disciplined man, this is a natural measure, so let us all become disciplined men. Next Sunday morning, July 15th, I am speaking as the guest of Dr. Bailes at 10:30 at the Fox-Wilshire Theater on

Wilshire Boulevard, near La Cienega. My subject for next Sunday is "Changing Your Future." It is a subject near to the hearts of us all. I hope you will all come on Sunday to learn how to be the disciplined man, the meek man, who "changes his future" to the benefit of his fellow man. If you are observant, you will notice the swift echo or response to your every mood in this message and you will be able to key it to the circumstances of your daily life. When we are certain of the relationship of mood to circumstance in our lives, we welcome what befalls us. We know that all we meet is part of ourselves. In the creation of a new life we must begin at the beginning, with a change of mood. Every high mood of man is the opening of the door to a higher level for him. Let us mould our lives about a high mood or a community of high moods. Individuals, as well as communities, grow spiritually in proportion as they rise to a higher ideal. If their ideal is lowered, they sink to its depths; if their ideal is exalted, they are elevated to heights unimagined. We must keep the high mood if we would walk with the highest; the heights, also, were meant for habitation. All forms of the creative imagination imply elements of feeling. Feeling is the ferment without which no creation is possible. There is nothing wrong with our desire to transcend our present state. There would be no progress in this world were it not for man's dissatisfaction with himself. It is natural for us to seek a more beautiful personal life; it is right that we wish for greater understanding, greater health, greater security. It is stated in the sixteenth chapter of the Gospel of St. John, "Heretofore have ye asked for nothing in my name; ask and ye shall receive, that your joy may be full."

A spiritual revival is needed for mankind, but by spiritual revival I mean a true religious attitude, one in which each individual, himself, accepts the challenge of embodying a new and higher value of himself as Dr. Millikan did. A nation can exhibit no greater wisdom in the mass than it generates in its units. For this reason, I have always preached self-help, knowing that if we strive passionately after this kind of self-help, that is, to embody a new and higher concept of ourselves, then all other kinds of help will be at our service.

The ideal we serve and hope to achieve is ready for a new incarnation; but unless we offer it human parentage it is incapable of birth. We must affirm that we are already that which we hope to be and live as though we were, knowing like Dr. Millikan, that our assumption, though false to the outer world, if persisted in, will harden into fact.

The perfect man judges not after appearances; he judges righteously. He sees himself and others as he desires himself and them to be. He hears what he wants to hear. He sees and hears only the good. He knows the truth, and the truth sets him free and leads him to good. The truth shall set all mankind free. This is our spiritual revival. Character is largely the result of the direction and persistence of voluntary attention.

"Think truly, and thy thoughts shall the world's famine feed;

Speak truly, and each word of thine shall be a fruitful seed;

Live truly, and thy life shall be a great and noble creed."

Neville (July 1951)

BY IMAGINATION WE BECOME

Radio Talk, Station KECA, Los Angeles

How many times have we heard someone say, "Oh, it's only his imagination?" Only his imagination - man's imagination is the man himself. No man has too little imagination, but few men have disciplined their imagination. Imagination is itself indestructible. Therein lies the horror of its misuse. Daily, we pass some stranger on the street and observe him muttering to himself, carrying on an imaginary argument with one not present. He is arguing with vehemence, with fear or with hatred, not realizing that he is setting in motion, by his imagination, an unpleasant event which he will presently encounter.

The world, as imagination sees it, is the real world. Not facts, but figments of the imagination, shape our daily lives. It is the exact and literal minded who live in a fictitious world. Only imagination can restore the Eden from which experience has driven us out. Imagination is the sense by which we perceived the above, the power by which we resolve vision into being. Every stage of man's progress is made by the exercise of the imagination. It is only because men do not perfectly imagine and believe that their results are sometimes uncertain when they might always be perfectly certain. Determined imagination is the beginning of all successful operation. The imagination, alone, is the means of fulfilling the intention. The man who, at will, can call up whatever image he pleases is, by virtue of the power of his imagination, least of all subject to caprice. The solitary or captive can, by intensity of imagination and feeling, affect myriads so that he can act through many men and speak through many voices. "We should never be certain," wrote William Butler Yeats in his IDAS OF GOOD AND

EVIL, "that it was not some woman treading in the wine-press who began that subtle change in men's minds, or that the passion did not begin in the mind of some shepherd boy, lighting up his eyes for a moment before it ran upon its way."

Let me tell you the story of a very dear friend of mine, at the time the costume designer of the Music Hall in New York. She told me, one day, of her difficulty in working with one of the producers who invariably criticized and rejected her best work unjustly; that he was often rude and seemed deliberately unfair to her. Upon hearing her story, I reminded her, as I am reminding you, that men can only echo to us that which we whisper to them in secret. I had no doubt but that she silently argued with the producer, not in the flesh, but in quiet moments to herself. She confessed that she did just that each morning as she walked to work. I asked her to change her attitude toward him, to assume that he was congratulating her on her fine designs and she, in turn, was thanking him for his praise and kindness. This young designer took my advice and as she walked to the theater, she imagined a perfect relationship of the producer praising her work and she, in turn, responding with gratitude for his appreciation. This she did morning after morning and in a very short while, she discovered for herself that her own attitude determined the scenery of her existence. The behavior of the producer completely reversed itself. He became the most pleasant professional employer she had encountered. His behavior merely echoed the changes that she had whispered within herself. What she did was by the power of imagination. Her fantasy led his; and she, herself, dictated to him the discourse they eventually had together at the time she was seemingly walking alone.

Let us set ourselves, here and now, a daily exercise of controlling and disciplining our imagination. What finer beginning than to imagine better than the best we know for a friend. There is no coal of character so dead that it will not glow and flame if but slightly turned. Don't blame; only resolve. Life, like music, can by a new setting turn all its discords into harmonies. Represent your friend to yourself as already expressing that which he desires to be. Let us know that with whatever attitude we approach another, a similar attitude approaches us.

How can we do this? Do what my friend did. To establish rapport, call your friend mentally. Focus your attention on him and mentally call his name just as you would to attract his attention were you to see him on the street. Imagine that he has answered, mentally hear his voice – imagine that he is telling you of the great good you have desired for him. You, in turn, tell him of your joy in witnessing his good fortune. Having mentally heard that which you wanted to hear, having thrilled to the news heard, go about your daily task. Your imagined conversation must awaken what it affirmed; the acceptance of the end wills the means. And the wisest reflection could not devise more effective means than those which are willed by the acceptance of the end.

However, your conversation with your friend must be in a manner which does not express the slightest doubt as to the truth of what you imagine that you hear and say. If you do not control your imagination, you will find that you are hearing and saying all that you formerly heard and said. We are creatures of habit; and habit, though not law, acts like the most compelling law in the world. With this knowledge of the power of imagination, be as the disciplined man and transform your world by imagining and feeling only what is lovely and of good report. The beautiful idea you awaken in yourself shall not fail to arouse its affinity in others. Do not wait four months for the harvest. Today is the day to practice the control and discipline of your imagination. Man is only limited by weakness of attention and poverty of imagination. The great secret is a controlled imagination and a well sustained attention, firmly and repeatedly focused on the object to be accomplished.

"Now is the acceptable time to give beauty for ashes, joy for mourning, praise for the spirit of heaviness; that they might be called trees of righteousness, the planting of the Lord that He might be glorified."

Now is the time to control our imagination and attention. By control, I do not mean restraint by will power but rather cultivation through love and compassion. With so much of the world in discord we cannot possibly emphasize too strongly the power of imaginative love. Imaginative Love, that is my subject next Sunday morning when I shall speak for Dr. Bailes while he is on his holiday. The services will be held as always at the Fox Wilshire Theater on Wilshire Boulevard, near La Cienega at 10:30. "As the world is, so is the individual," should be changed to, "As the individual is so is the world." And I hope to be able to bring to each of you present the true meaning of the words of Zechariah, "Speak ye every man the truth to his neighbor and let none of you imagine evil in your hearts against his neighbor." What a wonderful challenge to you and to me. "As a man thinketh in his heart so is he." As a man imagines so is he. Hold fast to love in your imagination. By creating an ideal within your mental sphere you can approximate yourself to this "ideal image" till you become one and the same with it, thereby transforming yourself into it, or rather, absorbing its qualities into the very core of your being. Never, never, lose sight of the power that is within you. Imaginative love lifts the invisible into sight and gives us water in the desert. It builds for the soul its only fit abiding place. Beauty, love and all of good report are the garden, but imaginative love is the way into the garden.

Sow an imaginary conversation, you reap an act;

Sow an act, you reap a habit;

Sow a habit, you reap a character;

336

Sow a character, you reap your destiny.

By imagination, we are all reaping our destinies, whether they be good, bad, or indifferent. Imagination has full power of objective realization and every stage of man's progress or regression is made by the exercise of imagination. I believe with William Blake, "What seems to be, is, to those to whom it seems to be, and is productive of the most dreadful consequences to those to whom it seems to be, even of torments, despair, and eternal death. By imagination and desire we become what we desire to be. Let us affirm to ourselves that we are what we imagine. If we persist in the assumption that we are what we wish to be, we will become transformed into that which we have imagined ourselves to be. We were born by a natural miracle of love and for a brief space of time our needs were all another's care. In that simple truth lies the secret of life. Except by love, we cannot truly live at all. Our parents in their separate individualities have no power to transmit life. So, back we come to the basic truth that life is the offspring of love. Therefore, no love, no life. Thus, it is rational to say that, "God is Love."

Love is our birthright. Love is the fundamental necessity of our life. "Do not go seeking for that which you are. Those who go seeking for love only make manifest their own lovelessness and the loveless never find love. Only the loving find love and they never have to seek for it."

Neville (July 1951)

ANSWERED PRAYER

Radio Talk – Station KECA, Los Angeles

Have you ever had a prayer answered? What wouldn't men give just to feel certain that when they pray, something definite would happen. For this reason, I would like to take a little time to see why it is that some prayers are answered and some apparently fall on dry ground. "When ye pray, believe that ye receive, and ye shall receive." Believe that ye receive – is the condition imposed upon man. Unless we believe that we receive, our prayer will not be answered. A prayer – granted – implies that something is done in consequence of the prayer which otherwise would not have been done. Therefore, the one who prays is the spring of action – the directing mind – and the one who grants the prayer. Such responsibility man refuses to assume, for responsibility it seems, is mankind's invisible nightmare.

The whole natural world is built on law. Yet, between prayer and its answer we see no such relation. We feel that God may answer or ignore our prayer, that our prayer may hit the mark or may miss it. The mind is still unwilling to admit that God subjects Himself to His own laws. How many people believe that there is, between prayer and its answer, a relation of cause and effect?

Let us take a look at the means employed to heal the ten lepers as related in the seventeenth chapter of the Gospel of St. Luke. The thing that strikes us in this story is the method that was used to raise their faith to the needful intensity. We are told that the ten lepers appealed to Jesus to "have mercy" on them – that is – to heal them. Jesus ordered them to go and show themselves to the priests, and "as they went, they were cleansed." The Mosaic Law demanded that

339

when a leper recovered from his disease he must show himself to the priest to obtain a certificate of restored health. Jesus imposed a test upon the lepers' faith and supplied a means by which their faith could be raised to its full potency. If the lepers refused to go – they had no faith – and, therefore, could not be healed. But, if they obeyed Him, the full realization of what their journey implied would break upon their minds as they went and this dynamic thought would heal them. So, we read, "As they went, they were cleansed."

You, no doubt, often have heard the words of that inspiring old hymn – "Oh, what peace we often forfeit; oh, what needless pain we bear, all because we do not carry everything to God in prayer." I, myself, came to this conviction through experience, being led to brood upon the nature of prayer. I believe in the practice and philosophy of what men call prayer, but not everything that receives that name is really prayer.

Prayer is the elevation of the mind to that which we seek. The very first word of correction is always "arise." Always lift the mind to that which we seek. This is easily done by assuming the feeling of the wish fulfilled. How would you feel if your prayer were answered? Well, assume that feeling until you experience in imagination what you would experience in reality if your prayer were answered. Prayer means getting into action mentally. It means holding the attention upon the idea of the wish fulfilled until it fills the mind and crowds all other ideas out of the consciousness. This statement that prayer means getting into action mentally and holding the attention upon the idea of the wish fulfilled until it fills the mind and crowds all other ideas out of the consciousness, does not mean that prayer is a mental effort – an act of will. On the contrary, prayer is to be contrasted with an act of will. Prayer is a surrender. It means abandoning oneself to the feeling of the wish fulfilled. If prayer brings no response – there is something wrong with the prayer and the fault lies generally in too much effort. Serious confusion arises insofar as men identify the state of prayer with an act of will, instead of contrasting it with an act of will. The sovereign rule is to make no effort, and if this is observed, you will intuitively fall into the right attitude.

Creativeness is not an act of will, but a deeper receptiveness – a keener susceptibility. The acceptance of the end – the acceptance of the answered prayer – finds the means for its realization. Feel yourself into the state of the answered prayer until the state fills the mind and crowds all other states out of your consciousness. What we must work for is not the development of the will, but the education of the imagination and the steadying of attention. Prayer succeeds by avoiding conflict. Prayer is, above all things, easy. Its greatest enemy is effort. The mighty surrenders itself fully only to that which is most gentle. The wealth of Heaven may not be seized by a strong will, but surrenders itself, a free gift, to the God-spent moment. Along the lines of least resistance travel spiritual as well as physical forces.

We must act on the assumption that we already possess that which we desire, for all that we desire is already present within us. It only waits to be claimed. That it must be claimed is a necessary condition by which we realize our desires. Our prayers are answered if we assume the feeling of the wish fulfilled and continue in that assumption. One of the loveliest examples of an answered prayer I witnessed in my own living room. A very charming lady from out of town came to see me concerning prayer. As she had no one with whom to leave her eight-year old son, she brought him with her the time of our interview. Seemingly, he was engrossed in playing with a toy truck, but at the end of the interview with his mother he said, "Mr. Neville, I know how to pray now. I know what I want – a collie puppy – and I can imagine I am hugging him every night on my bed." His mother explained to him and to me the impossibilities of his prayer, the cost of the puppy, their confined home, even his inability to care for the dog properly. The boy looked into his mother's eyes and simply said, "But, Mother, I know how to pray now." And he did. Two months later during a "Kindness to Animals Week" in his city, all the school children were required to write an essay on how they would love and care for a pet. You have guessed the answer. His essay, out of the five thousand submitted, won the prize, and that prize, presented by the mayor of the city to the lad – was a collie puppy. The boy truly assumed the feeling of his wish fulfilled, hugging and loving his puppy every night.

Prayer is an act of Imaginative Love which is to be the subject of my message next Sunday morning at 10:30 at the Fox Wilshire Theater on Wilshire Boulevard near La Cienega. It is my desire, next Sunday, that I may explain to you, how you, like the young boy; can yield yourselves to the lovely images of your desires and persist in your prayer even though you, like the lad, are told that your desires are impossible.

The necessity of persistence in prayer is shown us in the Bible. "Which of you," asked Jesus, "shall go unto him at midnight, and say unto him: Friend, lend me three loaves; for a friend of mine is come to me from a journey, and I have nothing to set before him; and he from within shall answer and say, 'Trouble me not; the door is now shut and my children are with me in bed; I cannot rise and give thee.' I say unto you, though he will not rise and give him because he is his friend, yet because of his importunity he will arise and give as many as he needeth." Luke 2. The word translated as "importunity" means, literally, shameless impudence. We must persist until we succeed in imagining ourselves into the situation of the answered prayer. The secret of success is found in the word "perseverance." The soul imagining itself into the act, takes on the results of the act. Not imagining itself into the act, it is ever free from the result. Experience in imagination what you would experience in reality were you already what you want to be, and you will take on the result of that act. Do not experience in imagination what you want to experience in reality and you will ever be free of the result. "When ye pray, believe that ye receive, and ye shall receive." One must persist until he reaches his friend on a higher level of consciousness. He must persist until his feeling of the wish fulfilled has all the sensory vividness of reality.

Prayer is a controlled waking dream. If we are to pray successfully, we must steady our attention to observe the world as it would be seen by us were our prayer answered.

Steadying attention makes no call upon any special faculty, but it does demand control of imagination. We must extend our senses – observe our changed relationship to our world and trust this observation. The new world is not there to grasp, but to sense, to touch. The best way to observe it is to be intensely aware of it. In other words, we can, by listening as through we heard and by looking as though we saw, actually hear voices and see scenes from within ourselves that are otherwise not audible or visible. With our attention focused on the state desired, the outer world crumbles and then the world – like music – by a new setting, turns all its discords into harmonies. Life is not a struggle but a surrender. Our prayers are answered by the powers we invoke not by those we exert. So long as the eyes take notice, the soul is blind -- for the world that moves us is the one we imagine, not the world round about us. We must yield our whole being to the feeling of being the noble one we want to be. If anything is kept back, the prayer is vain. We often are deprived of our high goal by our effort to possess it. We are called upon to act on the assumption that we already are the man we would be. If we do this without effort – experiencing in imagination what we would experience in the flesh had we realized our goal, we shall find that we do, indeed, possess it. The healing touch is in our attitude. We need change nothing but our attitude towards it. Assume a virtue if you have it not, assume the feeling of your wish fulfilled. "Pray for my soul; more things are wrought by prayer than this world dreams of."

Neville (July 1951)

MEDITATION

Radio Talk, Station KECA, Los Angeles

Many people tell me they cannot meditate. This seems to me a bit like saying they cannot play the piano after one attempt. Meditation, as in every art or expression, requires constant practice for perfect results. A truly great pianist, for instance, would feel he could not play his best if he missed one day of practice. If he missed a week or a month of practice he would know that even his most uninitiated audience would recognize his defects. So it is with meditation. If we practice daily with joy in this daily habit, we perfect it as an art. I find that those who complain of the difficulty in meditation do not make it a daily practice, but rather, wait until something pressing appears in their world and then, through an act of will, try to fix their attention on the desired state. But they do not know that meditation is the education of the will, for when will and imagination are in conflict, imagination invariably wins.

The dictionaries define meditation as fixing one's attention upon; as planning in the mind; as devising and looking forward; engaging in continuous and contemplative thought. A lot of nonsense has been written about meditation. Most books on the subject get the reader nowhere, for they do not explain the process of meditation. All that meditation amounts to is a controlled imagination and a well sustained attention. Simply hold the attention on a certain idea until it fills the mind and crowds all other ideas out of consciousness. The power of attention shows itself the sure guarantee of an inner force. We must concentrate on the idea to be realized, without permitting any distraction. This is the great secret of action. Should the attention wander, bring it back to the idea you wish to realize and do so again and again, until the attention becomes immobilized and undergoes an effortless fixation upon the idea presented to it. The idea must hold the attention – must fascinate it – so to speak. All meditation ends at last with the thinker, and he finds he is what he, himself, has conceived. The undisciplined man's attention is the servant of his vision rather than its master. It is captured by the pressing rather than the important.

In the act of meditation, as in the act of adoration, silence is our highest praise. Let us keep our silent sanctuaries, for in them the eternal perspectives are preserved. Day by day, week by week, year by year, at times where none through love or lesser intentions were allowed to interfere, I set myself to attain mastery over my attention and imagination. I sought out ways to make more securely my own, those magical lights that dawned and faded within me. I wished to evoke them at will and to be the master of my vision.

I would strive to hold my attention on the activities of the day in unwavering concentration so that, not for one moment, would the concentration slacken. This is an exercise – a training for higher adventures of the soul. It is no light labor. The ploughman's labor, working in the fields is easier by far.

Empires do not send legions so swiftly to obstruct revolt as all that is alive in us hurries along the nerve highways of the body to frustrate our meditative mood. The beautiful face of one we love glows before us to enchant us from our task. Old enmities and fears beleaguer us. If we are tempted down these vistas, we find, after an hour of musing, that we have been lured away. We have deserted our task and forgotten that fixity of attention we set out to achieve. What man is there who has complete control of his imagination and attention. A controlled imagination and steadied attention, firmly and repeatedly focused on the idea to be realized, is the beginning of all magical operations. If he persists through weeks and months, sooner or later, through meditation, he creates in himself a center of

346

power. He will enter a path all may travel but on which few do journey. It is a path within himself where the feet first falter in shadow and darkness, but which later is made brilliant by an inner light. There is no need for special gifts or genius. It is not bestowed on any individual but won by persistence and practice of meditation. If he persists, the dark caverns of his brain will grow luminous and he will set out day after day for the hour of meditation as if to keep an appointment with a lover. When it comes, he rises within himself as a diver, too long under water, rises to breathe the air and see the light. In this meditative mood he experiences in imagination what he would experience in reality had he realized his goal, that he may in time become transformed into the image of his imagined state.

The only test of religion worth making is whether it is trueborn; whether it springs from the deepest consciousness of the individual; whether it is the fruit of experience; or whether it is anything else whatever. This is my reason for speaking to you on my last Sunday in Los Angeles about The True Religious Attitude. What is your religious attitude? What is my religious attitude? I shall speak on this subject next Sunday morning at 10:30 as Dr. Bailes' guest. The service will be held at the Fox Wilshire Theater on Wilshire Boulevard near La Cienega. I shall endeavor to show you that the methods of mental and spiritual knowledge are entirely different. For we know a thing mentally by looking at it from the outside, by comparing it with other things, by analyzing and defining it; whereas we can know a thing spiritually only by becoming it. We must be the thing itself and not merely talk about it or look at it. We must be in love if we are to know what love is. We must be God-like if we are to know what God is.

Meditation, like sleep, is an entrance into the subconscious. "When you pray, enter into your closet, and when you have shut your door, pray to your Father which is in secret and your Father which is in secret shall reward you openlhy." Meditation is an illusion of sleep which diminishes the impression of the outer world and renders the mind more receptive to suggestion from within. The mind in meditation is in a state of relaxation akin to the feeling attained just before dropping off to sleep. This state is beautifully described by the poet, Keats, in his ODE TO A NIGHTINGALE. It is said that as the poet sat in the garden and listened to the nightingale, he fell into a state which he described as "A drowsy numbness pains my senses as though of hemlock I had drunk." Then after singing his ode to the nightingale, Keats asked himself this question, "Was it a vision or a waking dream? Fled is the music; do I wake or sleep?" Those are the words of one who has seen something with such vividness or reality that he wonders whether the evidence of his physical eyes can now be believed.

Any kind of meditation in which we withdraw into ourselves without making too much effort to think is an outcropping of the subconscious. Think of the subconscious as a tide which ebbs and flows. In sleep, it is a flood tide, while at moments of full wakefulness, the tide is at its lowest ebb. Between these two extremes are any number of intermediary levels. When we are drowsy, dreamy, lulled in gentle reverie, the tide is high. The more wakeful and alert we become, the lower the tide sinks. The highest tide compatible with the conscious direction of our thoughts occurs just before we fall asleep and just after we wake. An easy way to create this passive state is to relax in a comfortable chair or on a bed. Close your eyes and imagine that you are sleepy, so sleepy, so very sleepy. Act precisely as though you were going to take a siesta. In so doing, you allow the subconscious tide to rise to sufficient height to make your particular assumption effective.

When you first attempt this, you may find that all sorts of counter-thoughts try to distract you, but if you persist, you will achieve a passive state. When this passive state is reached, think only on "things of good report" -- imagine that you are now

348

expressing your highest ideal, not how you will express it, but simply feel HERE AND NOW that you are the noble one you desire to be. You are it now. Call your high ideal into being by imagining and feeling you are it now.

I think all happiness depends on the energy to assume the feeling of the wish fulfilled, to assume the mask of some other more perfect life. If we cannot imagine ourselves different from what we are and try to assume that second more desirable self, we cannot impose a discipline upon ourselves though we may accept discipline from others.

Meditation is an activity of the soul; it is an active virtue; and an active virtue, as distinguished from passive acceptance of a code is theatrical. It is dramatic; it is the wearing of a mask. As your goal is accepted, you become totally indifferent to possible failure, for acceptance of the end wills the means to the end. When you emerge from the moment of meditation it is as though you were shown the happy end of a play in which you are the principal actor. Having witnessed the end in your meditation, regardless of any anti-climatic state you encounter, you remain calm and secure in the knowledge that the end has been perfectly defined.

Creation is finished and what we call creativeness is really only a deeper receptiveness or keener susceptibility on our part, and this receptiveness is "Not by might, nor by power, but by my spirit, saith the Lord of Hosts." Through meditation, we awaken within ourselves a center of light, which will be to us a pillar of cloud by day and a pillar of fire by night.

Neville (July 1951)

THE LAW OF ASSUMPTION

Radio Talk, Station KECA, Los Angeles

The great mystic, William Blake, wrote almost two hundred years ago, "What seems to be, is, to those to whom it seems to be and is productive of the most dreadful consequences to those to whom it seems to be." Now, at first, this mystical gem seems a bit involved, or at best to be a play on words; but it is nothing of the kind. Listen to it carefully. "What seems to be, is, to those to whom it seems to be." That is certainly clear enough. It is a simple truth about the law of assumption, and a warning of the consequences of its misuse. The author of the Epistle to the Romans declared in the fourteenth chapter, "I know, and am persuaded by the Lord Jesus, that there is nothing unclean of itself; but to him that esteemeth anything to be unclean, to him it is unclearn."

We see by this that it is not superior insight but purblindness that reads into the greatness of men some littleness with which it chances to be familiar, for what seems to be, is, to those to whom it seems to be.

Experiments recently conducted at two of our leading universities revealed this great truth about the law of assumption. They stated in their releases to the newspapers, that after two thousand experiments they came to the conclusion that, 'What you see when you look at something depends not so much on what is there as on the assumption you make when you look. What you believe to be the real physical world is actually only an assumptive world." In other words, you would not define your husband in the same way that you mother would. Yet, you are both defining the same person. Your particular relationship to a thing influences your feelings with respect to that thing and makes you see in it an element which is not there. If your feeling in the matter is a self-element; it can be cast out. If it is a permanent distinction in the state considered, it cannot be cast out. The thing to do is to try. If you can change your opinion of another, then what you now believe of him cannot be absolutely true, but relatively true.

Men believe in the reality of the external world because they do not know how to focus and condense their powers to penetrate its thin crust. Strangely enough, it is not difficult to penetrate this view of the senses. To remove the veil of the senses, we do not employ great effort; the objective world vanishes as we turn our attention from it. We have only to concentrate on the state desired to mentally see it; but to give reality to it so that it will become an objective fact, we must focus our attention upon the desired state until it has all the sensory vividness and feeling of reality. When, through concentrated attention, our desire appears to possess the distinctness and feeling of reality; when the form of thought is as vivid as the form of nature, we have given it the right to become a visible fact in our lives. Each man must find the means best suited to his nature to control his attention and concentrate it on the desired state. I find for myself the best state to be one of meditation, a relaxed state akin to sleep, but a state in which I am still consciously in control of my imagination and capable of fixing my attention on a mental object.

If it is difficult to control the direction of your attention while in this state akin to sleep, you may find gazing fixedly into an object very helpful. Do not look at its surface, but rather into and beyond any plain object such as a wall, a carpet or any object which possesses depth. Arrange it to return as little reflection as possible. Imagine, then, that in this depth you are seeing and hearing what you want to see and hear until your attention is exclusively occupied by the imagined state.

At the end of your meditation, when you awake from your controlled waking dream you feel as though you had returned from a great distance. The visible world which you had shut out returns to consciousness and, by its very presence, informs you that you have been self-deceived into believing that the object of your contemplation was real; but if you remain faithful to your vision this sustained mental attitude will give reality to your visions and they will become visible concrete facts in your world.

Define your highest ideal and concentrate your attention upon this ideal until you identify yourself with it. Assume the feeling of being it – the feeling that would be yours were you now embodying it in your world. This assumption, though now denied by your senses, "if persisted in" – will become a fact in your world. You will know when you have succeeded in fixing the desired state in consciousness simply by looking mentally at the people you know. This is a wonderful check on yourself as your mental conversations are more revealing than your physical conversations are. If, in your mental conversations with others, you talk with them as you formerly did, then you have not changed your concept of self, for all changes of concepts of self result in a changed relationship to the world. Remember what was said earlier, "What you see when you look at something depends not so much on what is there as on the assumption you make when you look." Therefore, the assumption of the wish fulfilled should make you see the world mentally as you would physically were your assumption a physical fact. The spiritual man speaks to the natural man through the language of desire. The key to progress in life and to the fulfillment of dreams lies in the ready obedience to the voice. Unhesitating obedience to its voice is an immediate assumption of the wish fulfilled. To desire a state is to have it. As Pascal said, "You would not have sought me had you not already found me." Man, by assuming the feeling of the wish fulfilled and then living and acting on this conviction changes his future in harmony with his assumption. To "change his future" is the inalienable right of freedom loving individuals. There would be no progress in the world were it not for the divine discontent in man which urges him on to higher and higher levels of consciousness. I have chosen this subject so close to the hearts of us all – "Changing Your Future" -- for my message next Sunday morning. I am to have the great joy of speaking for Dr. Bailes while he is vacationing. The service will be held at 10:30 at the Fox Wilshire Theater on Wilshire Boulevard near La Cienega Boulevard.

Since the right to change our future is our birthright as sons of God, let us accept its challenge and learn just how to do it. Again today, speaking of changing your future, I wish to stress the importance of a real transformation of self – not merely a slight alteration of circumstances which, in a matter of moments, will permit us to slip back into the old dissatisfied man. In your meditation, allow others to see you as they would see you were this new concept of self a concrete fact. You always seem to others the embodiment of the ideal you inspire. Therefore, in meditation, when you contemplate others, you must be seen by them mentally as you would be seen by them physically were your conception of yourself an objective fact. That is, in meditation, you imagine that they see you expressing this nobler man you desire to be. If you assume that you are what you want to be, your desire is fulfilled and, in fulfillment, all longing "to be" is neutralized. This, also, is an excellent check on yourself as to whether or not you have actually succeeded in changing self. You cannot continue desiring what has been realized. Rather, you are in a mood to give thanks for a gift received. Your desire is not something you labor to fulfill, it is recognizing something you already possess. It is assuming the feeling of being that which you desire to be.

Believing and being are one. The conceiver and his conception are one. Therefore, that which you conceive yourself to be can never

354

be so far off as even to be near, for nearness implies separation. "If thou canst believe, all things are possible to him that believeth." Faith is the substance of things hoped for, the evidence of things not yet seen. If you assume that you are that finer, nobler one you wish to be, you will see others as they are related to your high assumption. All enlightened men wish for the good of others. If it is the good of another you seek, you must use the same controlled contemplation. In meditation, you must represent the other to yourself as already being or having the greatness you desire for him. As for yourself, your desire for another must be an intense one. It is through desire that you rise above your present sphere and the road from longing to fulfillment is shortened as you experience in imagination all that you would experience in the flesh were you or your friend the embodiment of the desire you have for yourself or him. Experience has taught me that this is the perfect way to achieve my great goals for others as well as for myself. However, my own failures would convict me were I to imply that I have completely mastered the control of my attention. I can, however, with the ancient teacher say: "This one thing I do, forgetting those things which are behind, and reaching forth unto those things which are before – I press towards the mark for the prize."

Neville (July 1951)

TRUTH

Radio Talk, Station KECA, Los Angeles

I wish to ask each one of you listening to me today a question – a question which must be close to the hearts of us all concerning truth. If a man known to you as a murderer broke into your home and asked the whereabouts of your mother, would you tell him where she was? Would you tell him the truth? Would you? I venture not – I hope not. In the most mystical of the Gospels – in the Gospel of St. John we read, "Ye shall know the truth, and the truth shall make you free." Therein lies a challenge to us all, "The truth shall make you free." If you told the truth concerning your mother, would you set her free? Again, in John we read, "Sanctify them by the truth." If you gave your mother up to a murderer, would you "sanctify her?" What, then, is the truth of which the Bible so constantly speaks? The truth of the Bible is always coupled with love. The truth of the Bible is that spiritual realization of conscious life in God towards which the human soul evolves through all eternity.

Truth is an ever-increasing illumination. No one who seeks sincerely for truth need fear the outcome for every raising erstwhile truth brings into view some larger truth which it had hidden. The true seeker after truth is not a smug, critical, holier than thou person. Rather, the true seeker after truth knows the words of Zechariah to be true. "Speak ye every man the truth to his neighbor and let none of you imagine evil in your hearts against his neighbor." The seeker after truth does not judge from appearances – he sees the good, the truth in all he observes. He knows that a true judgment need not conform to the external reality to which it relates. Never are we so blind to the truth as when we see things as they seem to be. Only

357

pictures that idealize really depict the truth. It is never superior insight but rather, purblindness that reads into the greatness of another some littleness with which it happens to be familiar.

We all know at least one petty gossip who not only imagines evil against his neighbor, but also insists upon spreading that evil far and wide. His cruel accusations are always accompanied by the statement, "It's a fact," or "I know it's the truth." How far from the truth he is. Even if it were the truth as he knows the truth, it is better not to voice it for "A truth told with bad intent beats all the lies you can invent." Such a man is not a seeker after the truth as revealed in the Bible. He seeks not truth so much as support for his own point of view. By his prejudices, he opens a door by which his enemies enter and make their own the secret places of his heart. Let us seek sincerely for the truth as Robert Browning expresses it:

"Truth is within ourselves; it take no rise

From outward things, whate'er you may believe.

There is an immortal center in us all

Where truth abides in fullness."

The truth that is within us is governed by imaginative love. Knowing this great truth, we can no longer imagine evil against any neighbor. We will imagine the best of our neighbor.

It is my belief that wherever man's attitude towards life is governed by imaginative love, there it is religious – there he worships – there he perceives the truth. I am going to speak on this subject next Sunday morning when my title will be, "Imaginative Love." At that time, I am to have the pleasure and the privilege of taking Dr. Frederick Bailes' service at the Fox Wilshire Theater on

Wilshire Boulevard near La Cienega. The service will be held as Dr. Bailes always conducts it at 10:30 Sunday morning.

It is an intuitive desire of all mankind to be a finer, nobler being, to do the loving thing. But we can do the loving thing only when all we imagine is full of love for our neighbor. Then we know the truth, the truth that sets all mankind free. I believe this is a message that will aid us all in the art of living a better and finer life. Infinite love in unthinkable origin was called God, the Father. Infinite love in creative expression was called God, the Son. Infinite love in universal interpenetration, in Infinite Immanence, and in Eternal procession, was called God, the Holy Ghost. We must learn to know ourselves as Infinite Love, as good rather than evil. This is not something that we have to become; it is, rather, for us to recognize something that we are already.

The original birthplace of imagination is in love. Love is its lifeblood. Insofar as imagination retains its own life's blood, its visions are images of truth. Then it mirrors the living identity of the thing it beholds. But if imagination should deny the very power that has brought it to birth then the direst sort of horror will begin. Instead of rendering back living images of the truth, imagination will fly to love's opposite – fear and its visions will then be perverted and contorted reflections cast upon a screen of frightful fantasy. Instead of being the supremely creative power, it will become the active agent of destruction. Wherever man's attitude to life is truly imaginative, there man and God are merged in creative unity. Remember that Love is always creative, causative in every sphere from the highest to the very lowest. There never has existed thought, word or deed that was not caused by love, or by its opposite – fear of some kind, even if it were only a desire of a not very worthy aim. Love and fear are the mainspring of our mental machinery. Everything is a thought before it becomes a thing. I suggest the pursuit of a high ideal to make a fact of being become a fact of consciousness and to do this by training the imagination to realize that the only atmosphere in which we truly live and move and have our being is Infinite Love. God is Love. Love never faileth. Infinite Creative Spirit is Love. The urge that caused Infinite unconditioned consciousness to condition Itself into millions of sensitive forms is Love.

Love regarded as an abstraction – apart from an object – is unthinkable. Love is not love if there is no beloved. Love only becomes thinkable in relation, in process in act. Let us recognize with Blake that, "He who will not live by love must be subdued by fear," and set ourselves the highest of ideals to love and to live by. But our highest ideals do not bless unless they come down and take on flesh. We must make results and accomplishments the crucial test of our imagination and our love, for incarnation is the only true realization. Our faithfulness must be to the sum of all the truth we know and it must be absolute. Otherwise, that truth lacks a vehicle and cannot be incarnated in us.

Our concept of ourselves determines the scenery of our lives. We are ever our own jailers. The prison doors that we thought closed are truly ajar – waiting for us to see the truth. "Man ever surrounds himself with the true image of himself," said Emerson. "Every spirit builds itself a house and beyond its house, a world, and beyond its world, a heaven. Know then the world exists for you, for you the phenomenon is perfect. What we are that only can we see. All that Adam had, all the Caesar could, you have and can do."

Adam called his house heaven and earth. Caesar called his house, Rome. You perhaps call yours a cobbler's trade, or a hundred acres of land, or a scholar's garret. Yet line for line, and point for point, your dominion is as great as theirs, though without such fine names. Build, therefore, your own world and as fast as you conform your life to the pure idea in your mind, that will unfold its great proportions.

The truth is our secret inward reality, the cause, the meaning, the relation of our lives to all things. Let the truth carry us heavenwards, expanding our conceptions, increasing our understanding until we know the "Truth" and are made "Free."

Neville (July 1951)

STONE, WATER OR WINE?

Radio Talk, Station KECA, Los Angeles

It has been my privilege and pleasure to address Dr. Frederick Bailes' Sunday audiences in the past few years. Today, I am to extend the privilege in speaking to you, his unseen audience of the radio. This will be a very practical series of talks for my subjects will be drawn largely from the Bible, the most spiritual of all books. And I am firmly convinced that whatever is most profoundly spiritual is, in reality, most directly practical. All mistakes made in Biblical interpretation come from referring statements of which the intention is spiritual and mystical, and implying principles or states to times, persons or places. In one sense, not one work of Scripture is true <u>according to the letter</u>. Yet, I say that every word <u>is</u> true; but the Scriptures are true only as He intended them that spoke them; they are true as God meant them, not as man will have them. A spiritual and symbolical interpretation alone yields truth, whilst a literal acceptation profits nothing. The Bible contains historical elements, but these are always used as picture language of great ideas.

The Gospel narrative is to be studied in order that we may know. It does not convey knowledge immediately. Getting to know is a gradual process – a progressive inner experience. God reveals Himself within us as we are able to receive Him. The deep meanings have always been recognized partially by a few, as will be found by consulting the writings of the seers of all past ages.

In assigning to the Bible its proper meaning, it is necessary to remember that as mystical Scriptures it deals primarily, not with material things or persons, but with spiritual significations. The

Bible is addressed not to the outer sense or reason, but to the soul. Its object is not to give an historical account of physical life, but to exhibit the spiritual possibilities of humanity, at large, for religion is not in its nature historical and dependent upon actual sensible events, but consists in processes such as Faith and Redemption. These, being interior to all men, subsist irrespective of what any particular man has at any time done. The perennial value of the Bible is its symbolic value. There are great controversies as to what is and what is not historical in the Bible, but let us remember that if we could settle all the historical questions tomorrow, that would not give us religion, nor would it give the Bible a biding value. Everything depends upon our finding the symbolical value of the facts. A fact of past history has nothing in it for present day religion unless it stands forth as a symbol of a Reality behind itself.

The Bible is a revelation of Truth expressed in Divine symbolism. From the literal point of view, the wording may sometimes be confusing; it is the symbolism, alone, which is precious and worthy of our best efforts to elucidate. All Scripture was written from the inward mystery and not with a mystical sense put into it. The stories conceal an underlying meaning, and the task of scripture interpretation is to discover these psychological truths which are expressed in this symbolism. We, here, are not concerned with the surface meaning of the Scripture, whether it be reasonable or absurd, for in no case does it constitute the inner truth we are seeking. Throughout the centuries we have mistakenly taken personification for persons, allegory for history, the vehicle that conveyed the instruction for the instruction itself and the gross first sense for the ultimate sense intended. In most of the little things of life, this confusion is of trivial consequence. But the error which arises when you carry the confusion into questions of greater moment, such as religion, assumes gigantic proportions. For centuries, men have sought eagerly for bits of evidence which might be related to the happenings described in the Bible. While most people believe that its characters lived, no proof of their lives on earth has ever been found and may never be found. This is unimportant for the ancient teachers were not writing history, but an allegorical picture lesson of certain basic principles, which they clothed in the garb of history. The form of the various stories of the Bible is as distinct from its substance as the form of a grain of wheat is distinct from the life germ within it. As the assimilative organs of the body discriminate between food that can be built into the physical system and food that must be cast off, so do the awakened intuitive faculties discover, beneath allegory and parable, the psychological life germ, and feeding on this, they cast off the fiction which conveyed it. The Bible is the largest selling book in this country. It is probably the least read and certainly the least understood. Throughout the Bible, the symbols of stone, water and wine are used. The stones of the Bible are its literal truths. The Ten Commandments, we are told, were written on stone. The water of the Bible is the psychological meaning hidden in these literal truths of stone. "I give you living waters," that is, the inner knowledge that can make these stories a living reality in your life. The wine you must make for yourself through the wise use of this living water or psychological truth. This is an absolute necessity to the truly religious man. This is what Sir Walter Scott meant when he said, "Man's greatest education is that which he gives to himself."

On Sunday morning, I shall speak on, "Are You Stone, Water or Wine?" I shall be taking Dr. Bailes' service at 10:30 at the Fox Wilshire Theater on Wilshire Boulevard near La Cienega. When you hear this message, you may ask yourselves, "Are you stone, water or wine?" You may judge whether your understanding of the Bible is merely literal, psychological, or truly spiritual and, therefore, profoundly practical.

The Bible is, from beginning to end, all about transcending the violence which characterizes mankind's present level of being. It affirms the possibility of a development of another level of being surmounting violence. The point of view taken is that the goal of man is this inner development, which is the only real psychology. To take the Bible away from its central idea of rebirth, which means an inner evolution and implies the existence of a higher level, is to understand nothing of its real meaning. The Word of God, that is, the psychological teaching in the Bible, is to make a man different, first in thought and then in being, so that he becomes a new man or is born again.

Whenever an entirely new attitude enters into a person's life, psychological rebirth to some extent has occurred. Man wants to be better, not different. The Bible speaks, not of being better, but of another man, a man reborn. "Except a man be born again, he cannot see the Kingdom of God... Except a man be born of water and the spirit, he cannot enter into the Kingdom of God. Marvel not that I said unto thee, ye must be born again." (John 3.) The Ten Commandments were written on tablets of stone for those incapable of seeing any deeper meaning. Stone represents the most external and literal form of spiritual truth, and water refers to another way of understanding the same truth. Wine or spirit is the highest form of understanding it.

"Such as men themselves are, such will God appear to them to be," wrote John Smith, the Cambridge Platonist. "The God of the moralist is before all things a great judge and schoolmaster; the God of Science is impersonal and inflexible Vital Law; the God of the savage is the kind of chief he would be himself if he had the opportunity." No man's conduct will be higher than his conception of God, and his conception of God is determined by the kind of man he, himself, is. "For such as men themselves are, such will God appear to them to be," and what is true of man's concept of God is equally true of man's concept of God's Word, the Bible. It will be to him what he is to himself.

"God is God from the creation,

Truth alone is man's salvation;

But the God that now you worship

Soon shall be your God no more

For the soul in its unfolding

Evermore its thoughts remolding,

Learns more truly in its progress

How to love and to adore."

Neville (July 1951)

FEELING IS THE SECRET

Radio Talk, Station KECA, Los Angeles

Recently, I asked a very successful businessman his formula for success. He laughed and was a little embarrassed. Then he replied, "I guess it's just because I can't conceive of failure. It's nothing that I think about much. It's more a <u>feeling</u> that I have." His statement coincided completely with my own beliefs and experiments. We can think about something forever and never see it in our world, but once let us <u>feel</u> its reality, and we are bound to encounter it. The more intensely we feel, the sooner we will encounter it. We all regard feelings far too much as effects, and not sufficiently as causes of the events of the day. Feeling is not only the result of our conditions of life, it is also the creator of those conditions. We say we are happy because we are well, not realizing that the process will work equally well in the reverse direction. We are well because we are happy. We are all far too undisciplined in our feelings. To be joyful for another is to bless ourselves as well as him. To be angry with another is to punish ourselves for his fault. The distressed mind stays at home though the body travels to the ends of the earth, while the happy mind travels though the body remains at home.

Feeling <u>is</u> the secret of successful prayer, for in prayer, we feel ourselves into the situation of the answered prayer and, then, we live and act upon that conviction. Feeling after Him, as the Bible suggests, is a gradual unfolding of the soul's hidden capacities. Feeling yields in importance to no other. It is the ferment without which no creation is possible. All forms of creative imagination imply elements of feeling. All emotional dispositions whatever may influence the creative imagination. Feeling after Him has no finality. It is an acquisition, increasing in proportion to receptivity, which has not and never will have finality. An idea which is only an idea produces nothing and does nothing. It acts only if it is felt, if it is accompanied by effective feeling. Somewhere within the soul there is a mood which, if found, means wealth, health, happiness to us. The creative desire is innate in man. His whole happiness is involved in this impulse to create. Because men do not perfectly "feel," the results of their prayers are unsure, when they might be perfectly sure. We read in Proverbs, "A merry heart doeth good like a medicine but a broken spirit drieth the bones." Orchestral hearts burn in the oil of the lamp of the king. The spirit sings unto the Lord a new song. All true prayer wears a glad countenance; the good are anointed with the oil of gladness above their fellows. Let us, then, watch our feelings, our reactions to the day's events. And let us guard our feelings even more zealously in the act of prayer, for prayer is the true creative state. Dignity indicates that man hears the greater music of life, and moves to the tempo of its deeper meaning. If we did nothing but imagine and feel the lovely, the world's reform would, at once, be accomplished. Many of the stories of the Bible deal exclusively with the power of imagination and feeling. "Feeling after Him" is the cry of the truth seeker. Only imagination and feeling can restore the Eden from which experience has driven us. Feeling and imagination are the senses by which we perceive the beyond. Where knowledge ends, they begin. Every noble feeling of man is the opening for him of some door to the divine world. Let us measure men, not by the height of their cities, but by the magnificence of their imaginations and feelings. Let us turn our thought up to Heaven and mix our imagination with the angels. The world that moves us is the one we imagine, not the world that surrounds us. In the imagination lie the unexplored continents, and man's great future adventure. This consciousness of non-finality in "feeling after God" has been the experience of all earnest God-ward feelers. They realize that their conception of the Infinite has constantly deepened and expanded with experience. Those who endeavor to think out the meaning of the experience and to coordinate it with the rest of our knowledge, are the philosophic mystics; those who try to develop the faculty in themselves, and to deepen the experience are the practical or experimental mystics. Some, and among them the greatest, have tried to do both. Religion begins in subjective experience. Religion is what a man does with his solitude, for in solitude we are compelled to subjective experience.

It is of the Religious Attitude that I shall speak next Sunday morning. This will be the last Sunday morning I shall take the service for Dr. Bailes this season. The service is held at 10:30 at the Fox Wilshire Theater on Wilshire Boulevard, near La Cienega. A True Religious Attitude is man's salvation. God never changes; it is we who are changing; our spiritual eyes are ever getting keener; and this enlargement of truth will bring us an ever-increasing inner peace.

The best defense against the deceptive assault upon our mental and moral eyesight is the spiritual eye or the Eye of God. In other words, a spiritual ideal that cannot be changed by circumstance, a code of personal honor and integrity in ourselves and good will and love to others. "Not what thou art, nor what thou hast been, beholdeth God with his merciful eyes, but that thou wouldst be." Through the veins of the humblest man on earth runs the royal blood of being. Therefore, let us look at man through the eyes of imaginative love which is really seeing with the Eye of God. Under the influence of the Eye of God, the ideal rises up out of the actual as water is etherialized by the sun into the imagery cloudland. Things altogether distant are present to the spiritual eye. The Eye of God makes the future dream a present fact. Not four months to harvest – look again, If we persist in this seeing, one day we will arise with the distance in our eyes, and all the staying, stagnant nearby will suddenly be of no importance. We will brush it aside as we pass on to our far-seen objective. The man who really finds himself cannot do otherwise than let himself be guided by love. He is of too pure eyes to behold iniquity. Our ability to help others will be in proportion to our ability to control and help ourselves. The day a man achieves victory over himself, history will discover that to have been a victory over his enemy. The healing touch is in an attitude, and one day man will discover that one governs souls only with serenity. The mighty surrenders itself fully only to the most gentle.

Recognizing the power of feeling, let us pay strict attention to our moods and attitudes. Every stage of man's progress is made through the exercise of his imagination and feeling. By creating an "ideal" within our mental sphere we can feel ourselves into this "ideal image" till we become one and the same with it, absorbing its qualities into the very core of our being. The solitary or captive can, by the intensity of his imagination and feeling, effect myriads so that he can act through many men and speak through many voices. Extend your feelers, trust your touch, participate in all flights of your imaginations and be not afraid of your own sensitivities. The best way to feel another's good is to be more intensely aware of it. Be like my friend and have "more of a feeling" for the health, the wealth, the happiness you desire. Ideas do not bless unless they descend from Heaven and take flesh. Make results or accomplishments the crucial test of true imagination. As you observe these results, you will determine to fill your images with love and to walk in a high and noble mood for you will know with the poet:

"That which ye sow ye reap.

See yonder fields

The sesamum was sesamum, the corn

Was corn. The Silence and the Darkness knew

So is man's fate born."

Neville (July 1951)

AFFIRM THE REALITY OF OUR OWN GREATNESS

Radio Talk, Station KECA, Los Angeles

In the creation of a new way of life, we must begin at the beginning, with our own individual regeneration. The formation of organizations, political bodies, religious bodies, social bodies is not enough. The trouble we see goes deeper than we perceive. The essential revolution must happen within ourselves. Everything depends on our attitude towards ourself – that which we will not affirm within ourself can never develop in our world. This is the religion by which we live, for religion begins in subjective experience, like charity, it begins at home. "Be ye transformed by the renewing of your mind" is the ancient formula and there is no other. Everything depends upon man's attitude toward himself. That which he cannot or will not claim as true of himself can never evolve in his world. Man is constantly looking about his world and asking, "What's to be done? What will happen?" when he should ask himself "Who am I? What is my concept of myself?" If we wish to see the world a finer, greater place, we must affirm the reality of a finer, greater being within ourselves. It is the ultimate purpose of my teaching to point the road to this consummation. I am trying to show you how the inner man must readjust himself – what must be the new premise of his life, in order that he may lose his soul on the level he now knows and find it again on the high level he seeks.

It is impossible for man to see other than the contents of his own consciousness, for nothing has existence for us save through the consciousness we have of it. The ideal man is always seeking a new incarnation but unless we, ourselves, offer him human parentage, he is incapable of birth. We are the means whereby the redemption of nature from the law of cruelty is to be effected. The great purpose of consciousness is to effect this redemption. If we decline the burden and point to natural law as giving us conclusive proof that redemption of the world by imaginative love is something that can never come about, we simply nullify the purpose of our lives through want of faith. We reject the means, the only means, whereby this process of redemption must be effected.

The only test of religion worth making is whether it is trueborn – whether it springs from the deepest conviction of the individual, whether it is the fruit of inner experience. No religion is worthy of a man unless it gives him a deep and abiding sense that all is well, quite irrespective of what happens to him personally. The methods of mental and of spiritual knowledge are entirely different, for we know a thing mentally by looking at it from the outside, by comparing it with other things by analyzing and defining it. Whitehead has defined religion as that which a man does with his solitude. I should like to add, I believe it is what a man is in his solitude. In our solitude we are driven to subjective experience. It is, then, that we should imagine ourselves to be the ideal man we desire to see embodied in the world. If, in our solitude, we experience in our imagination what we would experience in reality had we achieved our goal, we will in time, become transformed into the image of our ideal. "Be renewed in the spirit of your mind – put on the new man – speak every man truth with his neighbor." The process of making a "Fact of being a fact of consciousness" is by the "renewing of our mind." We are told to change our thinking. But we can't change our thought unless we change our ideas. Our thoughts are the natural outpouring of our ideas, and our innermost ideas are the man himself. The end of longing is always to be – not to do. Be still and know "I am that which I desire." Strive always after being. External reforms are useless if your heart is not reformed. Heaven is entered not by curbing our passions; but rather, by cultivating our virtues. An old idea is not fickly forgotten, it is crowded out by new ideas. It disappears when a wholly new and absorbing idea occupies our attention. Old habits of thinking and feeling – like dead oak leaves – hang on till they are pushed off by new ones. Creativeness is basically a deeper receptiveness, a keener susceptibility. The future dream must become a present fact in the mind of anyone who would alter his life. Every great out-picturing is preceded by a period of profound absorption. When that absorption is filled with our highest ideal, -- when we become that ideal – then we see it manifest in our world and we realize that the present does not recede into the past, but advances into the future. This is essentially how we change our future. A "now" which is "elsewhere" has for us no absolute meaning. We only recognize "now" when it is at the same time "here." When we feel ourselves into the desired state "here" and "now" we have truly changed our future. It is this "Changing Your Future" which I hope to explain to you fully next Sunday morning when I am speaking for Dr. Bailes at 10:30 at the Fox Wilshire Theater on Wilshire Boulevard near La Cienega. It is my purpose to stir you to a higher concept of yourself and to explain so clearly the method by which you can achieve this concept that each one of you will leave the service on Sunday morning a transformed being.

Discouraged people are sorely in need of the inspiration of great principles. We must get back to first principles if we are to speak with a voice that will kindle the imagination and rouse the spirit. Again, I must repeat, in the creation of a new way of life, we must begin at the very beginning with our own individual regeneration. Man's chief delusion is his conviction that he can do anything. Everyone thinks he can do – everyone wants to do and all ask, "What to do?" What to do? It is impossible to do anything. One must be. It is hard for us to accept the fact that "We, of ourselves, do nothing." It is especially difficult because it is the truth and the truth is always difficult for man to accept. But, actually, nobody can do anything. Everything happens – all that befalls man – all that is done by him – all that comes from him – all this happens, and it happens in exactly the same way that rain falls -- as a result of a change in the temperature in the higher regions of the atmosphere. This is a challenge to us all. What concept are we holding of ourselves in the higher regions of our soul?

Everything depends upon man's attitude towards himself. That which he will not affirm as true within himself can never develop in his world. A change of concept of self is the right adjustment – the new relationship between the surface and the depth of man. Deepening is, in principle, always possible, for the ultimate depth lives in everyone, and it is only a question of becoming conscious of it. Life demands of us the willingness to die and to be born again. This is not meant that we die in the flesh. We die in the spirit of the old man to become the new man, then we see the new man in the flesh. "Subjection to the will of God" is an old phrase for it and there is, I believe, no new one that is better. In that self-committal to the ideal we desire to express, all conflict is dispersed and we are transformed into the image of the ideal in whom we rest. We are told that the man without a wedding garment reaches the Kingdom by cleverly pretending. He does not believe internally what he practices externally. He appears good, kind, charitable. He uses the right words, but inwardly he believes nothing. Coming into the strong light of those far more conscious than himself, he ceases to deceive. A wedding garment signifies a desire for union. He has no desire to unite with what he teaches, even if what he teaches is the truth. Therefore, he has no wedding garment. When we are united with the truth, then we will put off the old nature and be renewed in the spirit of our mind.

Truth will strip the clever pretenders of their false aristocracy. Truth, in its turn, will be conquered and governed by the aristocracy of goodness, the only unconquerable thing in the world.

VOLUME I

A Divine Event

A Lesson in Scripture

A Movement of Mind

A Movement Within GOD

A Parabolic Revelation

A Prophecy

A Riddle

A State Called Moses

All-Powerful Human Words

All That Is Divine

All That You Behold

All Things Are Possible (1967)

All Things Are Possible (1969)

All Things Exist

An Assured Understanding

An Inner Conviction

Arise

At Your Command

Awake, O Sleeper (January 1968)

Awake, O Sleeper (July 1968)

Awakened Imagination

Barabbas or Jesus

Be Imitators of GOD

Bear Ye One Another's Burdens

Before Abraham, Was I AM

VOLUME II

VOLUME III

VOLUME IV

God Speaks to Man

God's Almighty Power

God's Creative Power

God's Dwelling Place

God's Plan of Redemption (1969)

God's Plan of Redemption (1970)

God's Promise to Man

God's Wisest Creature

God's Word

Good Friday – Easter

Grace vs. Law

Have You Found Him?

He Dreams in Me

He Is Dreaming Now (1970)

He Is My Resurrection

He Wakes in Me

He Is Dreaming Now (no date)

His Name

His Purpose

His to Give; Yours to Receive

I Am in You

I Am the Cause

I Am the Lord

I Remember When

If Any Two Agree …

VOLUME V

If You Can Really Believe

Imagination Fulfills Its Self

Imagination Plus Faith

Imagination

Imagining Creates

Infinite Power

Infinite States

Is Christ Your Imagination

Jeremiah's Discovery

Jesus Christ

Judas the Revealer

Live in the End

Live the Answer Now

Love Endureth

Many Mansions

Moses – Elijah – Jesus

My Word

Neville's Purpose Revealed

No Other Foundation (I)

No Other Foundation (II)

No Other God

No Other Gods

North of the Strip

One Thousand Two Hundred Sixty Days

Order – Then Wait

VOLUME VI

Order Your Conversations Aright

Paul's Autobiography

Paul's Prayer Interpreted

Perception

Persistent Assumption (March1968)

Persistent Assumption (June1968)

Power and Wisdom

Power Called "The Law"

Power

Predestined Glory

Pre-Existence

Proof, the Law Works

Prophetic Blueprints

Prophetic Sketches (1967)

Prophetic Sketches (1968)

The Pure in Heart

Reconciliation

Redemption

Release Barabbas And Crucify Jesus

Revealed Truth

Revelation of Purpose

Salvation History – Not Secular

Salvation History

Secret of Imagination

Seedtime and Harvest

VOLUME VII

VOLUME VIII

VOLUME IX

The Last Days

The Law

The Light of the World

The Living Word

The Lord, Our Potter

The Man Within

The Miraculous Child

The Morning Star

The Most Precious Gift

The Mystery Called Christ

The Mystery of Baptism

The Mystery of Inspiration

The Mystery of Life

The Nature of God

The New Christology

The Only Christianity

The Pattern Man (no date)

The Pattern Man (1968)

The Pattern of Scripture Is Real

The Perfect Image

The Perfect Law of Liberty

The Potter's House

The Power and the Wisdom

The Power of Awareness

The Promise Explained

VOLUME X

The Promise Fulfilled

The Pruning Shears of Revision

The Revealer

The Rock

The Role of the Book

The Second Vision

The Secret of Causation

The Secret of Imagining

The Secret of Prayer

The Seven Eyes of God

The Shaping of the Unbegotten

The Signs of the End (1967)

The Signs of the End (1968)

The Sin Against the Holy Spirit

The Son Revealed

The Source

The Sphere Within

The Spirit of Truth

The Spirit Within

The Spiritual Cause

The State of Vision

The Story of Judas

The Talent

The Tree of Life

The True Knowledge of God

VOLUME XI

The True Vine

The Truth of Christ Is Here

The Ultimate Sense

The Value of Dreams

There Is No Fiction

They Related Their Own Experience

Three Propositions

True Forgiveness

Trust in God

Truth, the Word of God

Walk by Faith

Walk on the Water

What Are You Doing?

What Is Truth? (1968)

What Is Truth? (1970)

Where Are You From?

Where Are You Staying?

Where Is Golgotha?

Who Paul Really Is

Who Is the Real Messiah?

Who Is the Son of Man?

Who Am I? (May 1968)

Who Am I? (July 1968)

Whom Do You Seek?

Whom God Has Afflicted

VOLUME XII

Wonder Working Power

You Are a Cosmic Being

You Can Forgive Sin

You Can Never Outgrow I AM

You Dare to Assume

You Must Experience God (no date)

You Must Experience God (1972)

Your Husband

Your Maker

Your Supreme Dominion

Yours for the Taking

Consciousness is the Only Reality (Lesson 1)

Assumptions Harden into Fact (Lesson 2)

Thinking Fourth-Dimensionally (Lesson 3)

No One to Change but Self (Lesson 4)

Remain Faithful to Your Idea (Lesson 5)

Questions and Answers (1970)

Be What You Wish; Be What You Believe (Radio Talk)

By Imagination We Become (Radio Talk)

Answered Prayer (Radio Talk)

Meditation (Radio Talk)

The Law of Assumption (Radio Talk)

Truth (Radio Talk)

Stone, Water or Wine? (Radio Talk)

Feeling Is the Secret (Radio Talk)

Affirm the Reality of Our Own Greatness (Radio Talk)

Favor

If you enjoyed this series of lectures, may I ask a small favor? Please go back to Amazon and leave an honest review of the "Neville Goddard Lecture Series". Reviews help us spread the word of Neville Goddard to the world more effectively, and sustain our efforts. We appreciate your continued support.

Thank you,
Barry J. Peterson

Neville Goddard Resources:

Neville Goddard: The Complete Reader
Includes all 10 of Neville's spiritual classics in one book
www.NevilleGoddardReader.com

www.TheNevilleGoddardProject.org

Largest Neville Goddard Resource on the Internet
www.AudioEnlightenment.com (Membership Website)

www.AudioEnlightenmentPress.com

Gnostic Audio Selection:

To access the audio book version of "Neville Goddard Lecture Series"
please visit www.GnosticAudio.Com and follow the directions
to access your free streaming audio version of this book.
(This is a streaming audio only; audio book is NOT downloadable)

Interesting Read:

Reading to the Dead: A Transitional Grief Therapy for the Living
www.ReadingToTheDead.com
Author: Barry J. Peterson

CPSIA information can be obtained
at www.ICGtesting.com
Printed in the USA
BVOW04s1452091216
470312BV00001B/26/P